Kenneth P. Goldberg has taught math, math education, and educational statistics since 1969. He teaches courses at New York University on the use of hand-held calculators and on microcomputers, has given numerous lectures and workshops, and has written a basic statistics textbook and a number of articles on math-related topics, five of which appear in the 1982 edition of *Encyclopaedia Britannica*.

A SPECTRUM BOOK

Prentice-Hall, Inc., Englewood Cliffs, New Jersey 07632

KENNETH P. GOLDBERG

PUSHBUTTON MATHEMATICS

CALCULATOR MATH PROBLEMS, EXAMPLES, AND ACTIVITIES

Library of Congress Cataloging in Publication Data

GOLDBERG, KENNETH P.
  Pushbutton mathematics.

  "A Spectrum Book."
  Includes index.
    1. Calculating-machines—Problems, exercises,
  etc.   2. Mathematics—Problems, exercises, etc.
  I. Title.
  QA75.G59   510'.7'8   81-17788
  ISBN 0-13-743310-7   AACR2
  ISBN 0-13-743302-6 (pbk.)

This Spectrum Book can be made available to businesses and organizations
at a special discount when ordered in large quantities. For
information, contact Prentice-Hall, Inc., General Publishing Division,
Special Sales, Englewood Cliffs, N.J. 07632.

ISBN 0-13-743310-7

ISBN 0-13-743302-6 {PBK.}

10 9 8 7 6 5 4 3 2 1

Editorial/production supervision by Louise M. Marcewicz
Cover design by Hal Siegel
Manufacturing buyer: Donna Sullivan

Prentice-Hall International, Inc., *London*
Prentice-Hall of Australia Pty. Limited, *Sydney*
Prentice-Hall Canada, Inc., *Toronto*
Prentice-Hall of India Private Limited, *New Delhi*
Prentice-Hall of Japan, Inc., *Tokyo*
Prentice-Hall of Southeast Asia Pte. Ltd., *Singapore*
Whitehall Books Limited, *Wellington, New Zealand*

7038754

To my wife, Jeanne, for all her patience.

CONTENTS

Preface   *ix*

1   The Calculator in the Classroom—How, Why, and When?   *1*

2   Getting to Know Your Calculator   *5*

3   Elementary Algebra (Algebra One)   *19*

4   Trigonometry   *45*

5   Intermediate/Advanced Algebra (Algebra Two)   *71*

6   Geometry   *95*

7   Business and Consumer Mathematics   *121*

8   Probability and Statistics   *141*

9   Elementary Calculus   *159*

10   Programmable Calculators   *177*

Index   *193*

PREFACE

This book is written for the high school or junior college mathematics teacher—or prospective mathematics teacher—who wants to know more about what calculators are, how they differ from one another, how to select one for personal use or teaching, and how to actually teach with one. This book can be used with any of the so-called "algebraic logic" calculators; that is, any calculator with an "equal" key on it.

The first two chapters emphasize general characteristics of calculators and focus on such topics as ordinary and scientific display capability, special keys that a calculator might have (and one special key the calculator *must* have if it is to be used to teach mathematics), investigating the calculator's behavior when illegal operations are performed, and the different types of error messages the calculator may employ. Finally, I have described the three different types of calculator logic (Reverse Polish Logic, Left-to-Right Algebraic Logic, and Hierarchy Algebraic Logic), the difference between them, and how to determine which your calculator uses.

Chapters 3 through 9 are the book's subject chapters, and cover seven of the most common, most important subject areas in high school and junior college mathematics: Elementary Algebra (Algebra One), Trigonometry, Intermediate Algebra (Algebra Two), Geometry, Business and Consumer Mathematics, Probability and Statistics, and Elementary Calculus. The first half of each of these seven subject chapters is devoted to an in-depth look at how the calculator can be integrated into the mathematics classroom in two or three of that subject's major topics. This includes both use of the calculator as an aid in computation and as a tool in the development and clarification of important concepts. Numerous examples are given and discussed for each of these topics; appropriate calculator keystroke sequences are given and discussed, and the rationale behind the use of the calculator is explained. In the second half of each of the seven subject chapters, titled "Additional Calculator Activities," most of the other important topics of that subject are covered. Provided for each of these additional topics is a calculator activity that corresponds to that topic, the objective of the activity, any special calculator keys that are required, the procedure to be employed when using the activity in the classroom or as a homework assignment (including the corresponding calculator keystroke sequence), and, if appropriate, an example and solution.

Chapter 10 contains a discussion of the rudiments of programmable calculators and of programming. In order to show the method, advantages, and special capabilities of the programmable calculator, Chapter 10 takes several of the topics already covered and discussed in earlier chapters for the non-programmable calculator, and adapts them to the more advanced type. The actual program is given and discussed for each activity selected.

This book can be used by either the teacher who is actually in the classroom, or the prospective teacher who is preparing to go into the classroom. It can be used as a resource book by simply using the numerous calculator activities described for each of the subjects treated. It can also be used as a source of ideas and suggestions from which the teacher, using his or her own imagination, can develop original calculator activities, games, and assignments. Finally, it can be used as a methods course textbook to let the prospective or in-service mathematics teacher become aware of the numerous and varied ways the calculator can be employed to complement and enhance his teaching. If this book has one basic, underlying theme, it is that the calculator is a tool (although an extremely useful and powerful one) to be used by the teacher in a manner that the teacher feels is appropriate. This book is aimed at helping the teacher feel more comfortable and informed when making the decisions as to "when," "if," and "how."

In conclusion, I hope you enjoy this book, and that it helps you and your students to better understand, use, and enjoy your calculators.

1

THE CALCULATOR
IN THE CLASSROOM—
HOW, WHY, AND WHEN?

This guide is about calculators: those hand-held, ten- and fifteen-dollar wonders that first appeared in the mid-1970s and that are now as widely available and as basic to American households as the telephone and the television set. In particular, this is a guide expressly written for mathematics teachers and aimed at answering many of their questions about this new, unavoidable "marvel" of education.

Whether we like them or not, there is no avoiding the facts that calculators are available, that they are fairly inexpensive, that they are in use in the "real world" our students will be entering after they leave school, and that they are a tool we must teach our students to use and to understand. Ignoring calculators in the classroom and letting students go through school without using them—when they are so common and necessary in the world outside the school—is like forbidding secretarial students from using typewriters in the training program. Calculators are becoming more and more of an unavoidable tool in almost every area of our society. If we do not expose our students to them and teach them how to use these machines thoughtfully and well, they will have to gain that experience on their own or be at a distinct disadvantage when competing against others who do have this skill.

But if this were the only reason for using calculators in the math class, then the requirement would be a dull and dreary one indeed. Luckily for the students, as well as for us, such is not the case at all. There need be nothing dull or dreary about using calculators to teach and to do math. In fact, the calculator is a marvelous aid to teaching that can make mathematics much more interesting and alive, and more of a discovery, if it *is* used imaginatively when appropriate and *not* used when inappropriate.

What? Are there times when using a calculator is not appropriate? Yes, that is exactly what I said! The calculator is simply a tool that can be used when the teacher thinks it will help in the teaching and learning process, and that should not be used when it will not help. It is certainly not a cure-all for all the problems in mathematics teaching. And, most important of all, its use can actually be harmful if it is used at the wrong time for the wrong purpose, like a serum that can help cure one medical problem but that can be harmful if used on the wrong problem.

How can the use of a calculator be harmful or counterproductive? For one thing, if teaching the topic or solving the problem by calculator is much more complicated than doing it by hand or just thinking it out, then worrying about how to use the calculator overshadows the mathematics itself. Using the calculator can also be harmful if it is used on a topic for which it is simply not suited. For example, calculators are designed to work with decimals rather than fractions (although a very few can handle fractional computation), so topics involving the use of fractions may not be suited to calculators.

It has been my experience, from many years of teaching a course on calculators and from using them in my own teaching, that *there is no one, correct way to use a calculator in teaching mathematics*! Why is this true? Why shouldn't there be a *correct way* to use calculators that anyone can follow? Because teachers are human beings, and, as such, they each have their own style of teaching that works best for them. Just as some people can be stand-up comedians and others cannot, or just as some people are effective public speakers and others are not, some teachers like to include anecdotes and funny stories in their teaching and others prepare a lesson plan and adhere to it regardless of how well or badly it is working. Teachers have their own individual styles of teaching that they feel comfortable with and that work for them.

In the same way, teachers must learn to make use of the calculator in a way that will complement and enhance their styles. What works for one teacher will not necessarily work for another teacher with a different style, a different class, or a different topic. Also, inasmuch as all students are individuals, the way a calculator is used—or even whether it is used at all for a particular topic—depends on whether the teacher thinks its use will be beneficial. The final decisions as to when and how are always the teacher's. This is why the calculator is merely a tool to be employed when deemed helpful and appropriate by the real educational expert, the teacher.

If there is no one, correct way to use calculators in teaching and doing mathematics, what, then, is the purpose of this book? Its purpose is manifold:

- It gives you ideas about how the calculator *can* be used.
- It shows you examples of topics that the calculator *is* suitable for and why it is suitable.
- It gives you basic information about the types of calculators available, how they differ, and what to look for in a calculator in terms of using it as a teaching and computational aid.

Once you have become familiar with what calculators can and cannot do, as well as comfortable with using them, you will think of them and use them in your teaching the same way you think about and make use of the ditto machine, the overhead projector, and (at least in the past) the slide rule.

In Chapter 2 we will discuss general characteristics of calculators such as the type of logic used, their mode of display, and their specialty keys. The format for Chapters 3 through 9, the subject matter chapters that focus on particular subjects, is as follows: In the first half of each chapter, we will select two or three major topics and illustrate, in depth, how the calculator can be used in them. In the second half, titled "Additional Calculator Activities," we will take most of the other important topics in the subject and briefly show how the calculator might be used with them as well. For ease of use, each additional calculator activity will be accompanied by:

- the name of the mathematical topic it applies to;
- the objective of the activity;
- any special calculator keys the activity requires;
- the procedure to follow in using the activity; and
- an example and solution, if appropriate.

Finally, in Chapter 10 we will discuss programmable calculators and illustrate the fundamentals of programming.

This is probably a good time to emphasize two things: First, there is often more than one way to do a computation or to evaluate an expression by calculator.

Second, the method used will, of course, depend on which specialized keys your calculator has. For example, consider the simple expression:

$$\frac{1}{t - 3}$$

On a calculator with parentheses keys, this expression could be evaluated using the keystroke sequence:

$$\boxed{1} \ \boxed{\div} \ \boxed{(} \ \boxed{t} \ \boxed{-} \ \boxed{3} \ \boxed{)} \ \boxed{=}$$

However, on a calculator with a reciprocal key it could just as simply and correctly be evaluated with the keystroke sequence:

$$\boxed{t} \ \boxed{-} \ \boxed{3} \ \boxed{=} \ \boxed{1/x}$$

For this reason, the calculator keystroke sequences given in this book should be taken as illustrations of how the relevant expressions *could* be evaluated by calculator, but certainly not as the *only* way they could be evaluated.

Well, enough talk about calculators. The best way to learn about calculators is to actually use them and to see how they work. So if you have a calculator, or if you can borrow one from a friend, now is the time to get it and start learning about it.

2

GETTING TO KNOW YOUR CALCULATOR

How calculators differ

You're probably thinking that this is a very strange title to give a chapter. After all, to paraphrase an old saying, a calculator is a calculator is a calculator. They all have keys that let you enter numbers into them. They all let you do calculations such as addition, subtraction, multiplication, and division. And they all have visual displays so you can see the numbers you enter as well as the results of your computations. So they are all alike, right?

Wrong! They are all about as much alike as all people are alike. Sure, all people have arms and legs, and all people have certain common physical and mental abilities. But some people have longer legs than others, and this difference gives them an advantage in, say, running and playing basketball. And some people have longer and more supple fingers than others, and this difference gives them an advantage in such activities as playing the piano or typing. And some people have more mathematical ability than others, a difference that gives them an advantage in activities like learning statistics and filling out income tax forms.

So all calculators are alike only in the simple sense that they all let you enter numbers, that they all let you do computations, and that they all have visual displays. Beyond these simple similarities, however, there are many differences among calculators: in how they work and what you can do with them, in the keys they contain, in the way they display numbers, and in many other things that are less obvious to the casual user but important to the doing and teaching of mathematics.

Now don't get me wrong! You don't have to spend years thinking and learning about calculators before you can go out and buy one. Not at all. What I am saying is that you have to look at a few major things in calculators that any buyer should be aware of, and we will discuss these characteristics in this chapter. Also, other differences among calculators may not be important to the ordinary calculator user, but they may make a difference in using the calculator as a teaching tool or simply in being able to do classroom mathematics. These other, more subtle differences may affect the way the calculator must be used to solve certain problems or even whether the calculator can be used to solve certain problems. For this reason, you should be aware of these differences and how to check a calculator for them.

In this chapter, we will point out and discuss some of the more important of these characteristics and differences, as well as how to check for them. The point, once again, is not to tell you everything to look for, since doing so is impossible. The point is to show you the types of things to be aware of and to get you yourself started in investigating calculators (yours, your friends', the ones on display in stores you visit) for the fun and discovery of it. You may find something that you will be able to use later on in your teaching, and you will certainly start feeling more comfortable with, as well as knowledgeable about, calculators in general.

We will begin by discussing four of the most important characteristics of, and differences among, calculators:

- the type of logic they use,
- whether they are rechargeable,
- how they display the results of computations, and
- whether they have a "change sign" key.

Algebraic Logic
(Left-to-Right or Hierarchy)
Versus Reverse Polish Logic (RPL)

There are many good, reliable brands of calculators. Just a few of the major calculator companies that are quite reliable at this writing are Texas Instruments (usually referred to as "TI"), Casio, Sharp, Rockwell, Radio Shack, Sears, APF, and Hewlett–Packard (usually referred to as "HP"). Of course, there are many others as well, but these are some of the better known ones. The major point of distinction among all these calculators, and the most important in terms of actually using them, is their *logic*. By "logic," we mean the way numbers are entered into the calculator and how computations are performed by the calculator. Progressing from the least acceptable for teaching purposes to the most acceptable, the three basic types of calculator logic that are used by virtually every calculator are:

- Reverse Polish Logic (RPL),
- Left-to-Right Algebraic Logic, and
- Hierarchy Algebraic Logic.

Reverse Polish Logic (RPL).

On a calculator with such logic, there is no simple $=$ key. Instead, it usually has a key that tells the calculator to remember the number you just gave it. On the Hewlett–Packard calculators, this key is given the name ENTER . For example, if you wanted to add 2 + 4 on a Hewlett–Packard RPL calculator, the keystroke sequence would be:

$$2 + 4: \quad \boxed{2} \quad \boxed{\text{ENTER}} \quad \boxed{4} \quad \boxed{+}$$

In other words, you give the calculator the first number to be operated on, 2; then you tell the machine to remember this number by pressing the ENTER key; the second number to be operated on, 4, is then entered; finally, you tell the calculator what to do with these two numbers by pressing the operation key $+$. The result of the computation, 6, then appears in the calculator's display as the answer. Notice that, since the $=$ key is not used, the RPL calculator does not have such a key. On an RPL calculator the key that produces the result is the operation key, not the equal key. Notice also that the keystrokes in the sequence occur in a rather backward, reverse way, since the operation comes at the very end of the sequence.

The only major calculator company that presently uses Reverse Polish Logic is Hewlett–Packard. All the other major manufacturers use the two types of Algebraic Logic. The reason is that Hewlett–Packard appears to be catering to the scientific market (engineers, professional mathematicians, statisticians, economists, and the like). So if you can learn to handle the awkwardness of RPL, it has some advantages over the Algebraic Logics, such as letting you perform some computations and some programming a bit faster. For most people, however, and especially for students who are using calculators as part of their learning of mathematics, the Algebraic Logics are just as fast as RPL. Also, they parallel ordinary mathematical thinking and pencil-and-paper methods much better. So when you want to use the calculator to teach mathematics and to complement the students' standard mode of thinking and problem solving (as we do), and not go against it, stick to the Algebraic Logic calculators and *do not use an RPL calculator*. Calculators with Reverse Polish Logic are therefore not discussed or described in this book. As long as your calculator has a plain and simple $=$ key on it, it is using an algebraic type of logic. So look for the plain and simple $=$ key!

Algebraic Logic

The two types of Algebraic Logic are used by virtually every major calculator manufacturer except Hewlett–Packard, and so we will use and illustrate these types in this book. They are Left-to-Right and Hierarchy Algebraic Logic. The terms "Left-to-Right" and "Hierarchy" are our own; since no one else has named them, we have taken the liberty of doing so. Most calculator manufacturers simply do not differentiate between these two quite different logics, and, since they are different in their operation and their use (as we shall soon see), we must be able to distinguish between them.

With either type, the calculator has an $=$ key, and you enter numbers and perform computations essentially as you would do so with pencil and paper. For example, on an Algebraic Logic calculator, you add 2 + 4 with the keystroke sequence:

$$2 + 4: \quad \boxed{2} \; \boxed{+} \; \boxed{4} \; \boxed{=}$$

The answer, 6, would appear in the calculator's display.

The difference between a Left-to-Right logic calculator and a Hierarchy logic calculator can be seen and appreciated when we try to evaluate an expression like

(2–1) $$1 + 2 \times 3$$

in which the hierarchy of arithmetic operations is involved. If we try to evaluate expression (2–1) simply by going from left to right as the operations occur, then the addition would be incorrectly performed before the multiplication (since it occurs before the multiplication), and we would obtain the incorrect answer

(2–2) $$1 + 2 \times 3 = 3 \times 3 = 9 \quad \text{(Incorrect!)}$$

But this is exactly how the Left-to-Right logic calculator would evaluate the expression using the keystroke sequence

(2–3) $\boxed{1}$ $\boxed{+}$ $\boxed{2}$ $\boxed{\times}$ $\boxed{3}$ $\boxed{=}$

The Left-to-Right logic calculator simply performs the operations as the keystroke sequence gives them from left to right, without taking into consideration that, mathematically, multiplication should take precedence over addition. This is why I have called calculators that operate this way "Left-to-Right" logic calculators.

If you press keystroke sequence (2–3) on a Hierarchy Algebraic Logic calculator, however, it would automatically wait to do the addition until after it had performed the multiplication and would therefore give the correct result of:

(2–4) $1 + 2 \times 3 = 1 + 6 = 7$ (Correct!)

In other words, *the Hierarchy logic calculator is preprogrammed to obey the hierarchy of arithmetic operations while the Left-to-Right logic calculator is not.* The only major calculator manufacturer that explicitly distinguishes between these two types of Algebraic Logic is Texas Instruments, which explicitly advertises their AOS (Algebraic Operating System) logic calculators as obeying the hierarchy of arithmetic operations. (The AOS logic is the same as what we have called Hierarchy logic.) Most other companies simply say that their calculators have "Algebraic" logic and leave it at that. Of course, it is very simple to determine whether a particular calculator uses Hierarchy or Left-to-Right logic. Simply enter keystroke sequence (2–3) into the calculator. If you get the correct answer of 7 in the display for the corresponding expression (2–1), that calculator uses Hierarchy logic; if you get the incorrect answer of 9 in the display, that calculator uses Left-to-Right logic.

Of course, for many algebraic expressions exactly the same keystroke sequence will work equally well on a calculator with either type of Algebraic Logic. For example, consider the expression

$$2 \times 3 + 4.$$

From left to right in this expression, the operation of multiplication comes before the operation of addition. Since this order is in fact the correct hierarchy of operations, both Hierarchy and Left-to-Right logic calculators will give the same correct answer 10 for this expression, using the keystroke sequence

$2 \times 3 + 4$: $\boxed{2}$ $\boxed{\times}$ $\boxed{3}$ $\boxed{+}$ $\boxed{4}$ $\boxed{=}$

Of course there are also many expressions, such as (2–1), for which the two different types of Algebraic Logic require different keystroke sequences to obtain the correct answer. Here's how we will handle this problem: If one keystroke sequence will work equally well for both types of Algebraic Logic, we will simply give that keystroke sequence. If the two types of algebraic logic require different keystroke sequences, we will supply both of them and indicate the respective keystroke sequences to which they correspond.

Of the two types, while a Hierarchy Algebraic Logic calculator is generally preferable because it automatically obeys the hierarchy of arithmetic operations, either type is perfectly acceptable, easy to use, and convenient to teach with. You and your students should simply be aware of the difference and know which type you are using.

Rechargeable and nonrechargeable calculators

The second major point of distinction among calculators is whether they are rechargeable or nonrechargeable. If a calculator is rechargeable, you simply plug it into an electrical outlet overnight, using the recharger that comes with the machine. The next day the battery is recharged, and you are ready to use the calculator again. But when the battery dies in a nonrechargeable calculator, you have to replace it with a new battery just as you would with a radio or a flashlight. With either type of calculator you can usually buy an *adapter* (some calculators come with an adapter at no extra charge) that allows you to plug the machine into an electric outlet and not use up the battery. However, since you cannot always assume an outlet will be handy or available, the type of battery your calculator has can be quite important in terms of the long-run cost of using the machine.

The rechargeable calculator is usually a bit larger and heavier than the nonrechargeable type due to the special battery it carries. Some people consider the extra size and weight a disadvantage since they like nice, light calculators that fit easily into purse or pocket. When hand-held calculators first became available, the rechargeable calculator was somewhat cheaper than the non-rechargeable in the long run (although its initial cost was higher), since the initial cost was offset by the cost of periodically replacing the batteries. But even a rechargeable battery eventually wears out and must be replaced (at a fairly high cost). For this reason, as well as due to the extremely long-lasting wristwatch-type cadmium batteries in the new nonrechargeable calculators, the non-rechargeable calculators today are just as good a buy, dollar for dollar, as the rechargeable ones. So just go and find a good calculator that feels and works comfortably for you, and don't worry about whether it is rechargeable or not. Personally, I have several of each, and they are all equally dependable and economical. It is a good idea, however, to buy an adapter that lets you run the calculator on ordinary electric current if it does not automatically come with one. For long periods of use, the adapter saves wear and tear on the battery and keeps you from having to continually turn the machine on and off to save the battery.

Calculator display

Suppose you have a calculator with a display that has room for 8 digits, plus an extra space for a negative sign when needed. Ordinarily, on such a calculator the largest number that could be displayed or worked with would be 99,999,999 and the smallest would be 0.0000001. (The commas in 99,999,999 and in other large numbers in the text do not always appear in the display, but we include them for your reading convenience. The decimal point *does* appear, of course, but it does not take up a space, it fits automatically between the spaces in the appropriate position.) This restriction on the size of the numbers that can be handled is not a major limitation since, in the majority of problems, the numbers used are within this range. For example, however, suppose you are performing a series of calculations, and the result of these calculations should be 256,000,000,000. On a calculator with ordinary 8-digit display capability, this answer could not be shown since it has 12 digits. As soon as one of the partial results in the series of calculation exceeded the display capability of 99,999,999, the display would either freeze, revert to zero, or do some such thing to indicate that you had exceeded the display limit. You would then have to either turn the calculator off and on again, or press the CLEAR key once or twice, to get the calculator working again. In either case you would not be able to simply and directly perform the entire series of calculations.

But there is really no need for this restriction, and most calculators are able to circumvent it by means of *scientific notation display capability*. You will recall that any positive number can be written as a number between 1 and 10 multiplied by an appropriate power of 10. For example, 729 can be written as 7.29×10^2; 0.00578 can be written as 5.78×10^{-3}; and 5,378.925 can be written as 5.378925×10^3. Similarly, any negative number can be written in such a form just by placing a negative sign first.

Most modern calculators get around the display restriction by automatically switching to scientific notation whenever the result of a calculation is either too large or too small to be displayed in the usual fashion. Calculators that automatically switch also sometimes have a key, usually labeled $\boxed{\text{EE}}$, to allow the user to enter numbers into the calculator by hand in scientific notation. On such a calculator, you would be able to do all the calculations in the series to produce the final answer of 256,000,000,000 in the previous example. That answer would be displayed in the form:

$$2.56 \quad 11$$

or 2.56×10^{11} in scientific notation. The calculator, of course, is unable to display a power, so it simply leaves an open space between the 2.56 and the power 11.

Similarly, suppose your series of calculations should have the result 0.00000000256. On a calculator with automatic conversion to scientific notation, this result would be displayed in the form

$$2.56 \quad -9$$

or 2.56×10^{-9} in scientific notation. Once again, the calculator simply leaves a space between the 2.56 and the power -9 since it has no way to show an exponent. Of course, the easiest way to transform the calculator's scientific notation result is to say to yourself, for example, that

$$2.56 \quad 11$$

means "take the number 2.56 and move the decimal point 11 places to the right," while

$$2.56 \quad -9$$

means "take the number 2.56 and move the decimal point 9 places to the left." But if you want your students to be familiar with scientific notation, make it standard procedure for them to transform the calculator's "scientific notation" result into standard scientific notation form and then finally into ordinary notation.

Several years ago you had to pay a higher price to get a calculator with scientific notation capability. Now virtually all but the most basic calculators come with this feature. Even so, since some calculators do not have such a capability, it is worth making sure that the one you have or are thinking of buying does. If the accompanying instructions do not explicitly tell whether the calculator has this capability, you can check it yourself in a very simple way: Just take the calculator and keep multiplying the number 9 (or any other number greater than 1) by itself over and over. If the calculator has scientific notation, then once the numbers involved get too large for ordinary display, the calculator will automatically switch to scientific notation, which you will see on the display. If the calculator does not have scientific notation, then once the numbers involved get too large for ordinary display, the display will either remain fixed, revert to zero, or do something else that the manufacturer has programmed it to do to inform you that the display limit of the machine has been reached.

Let's demonstrate this checking procedure with two of my own calculators, the Casio Memory–8F, which does not have scientific notation capability, and the Casio fx–1000, which does. On each of these calculators, as I multiply the number 9 by itself over and over again, my display registers 9, then 81, then 729, then 6,561, and so on. On both of these 8-digit display calculators, the largest result that can be displayed in ordinary notation is 43,046,721 (which is 9 to the power 8). When I multiply this result by 9 one more time on the Casio Memory–8F, the machine displays the message E for error. This particular calculator has been programmed by its manufacturer to let me know with such a display that I have exceeded its display capacity. Consequently, I know that this particular calculator does not have automatic conversion to scientific notation. On the Casio fx–1000 calculator, however, when I multiply 43,046,721 by 9 once again, the display shows 3.8742   08 as the result. This result represents the scientific notation number 3.8742×10^8, so we now know that this calculator does have automatic conversion to scientific notation. To transform the display value to ordinary notation, just take the number 3.8742 and move the decimal point 8 places to the right to obtain the answer 387,420,000.

Aside from identifying which calculator automatically converts to scientific notation, you should notice something else. If you take the number 43,046,721 and multiply it by 9 using pencil and paper, the correct result is 387,420,489, not the 387,420,000 we obtain from the Casio fx–1000. This rounding occurs because, when the calculator uses scientific notation, 3 of its 8 available display positions are used up by the 2 digits for the power of 10 and by the space to separate the leading digits from the power. Only 5 spaces remain for the number, and so the calculator gives only the 5 leading digits of the actual answer. In the correct result of 387,420,489, the 5 leading digits are 38742. So these are displayed while the remaining 4 digits, 0489, are omitted. This kind of subtle "rounding-off" is something we must always be aware of, especially if we want to make use of such a calculator to teach about scientific notation.

An extra key your calculator should have: $\boxed{\text{CHS}}$ or $\boxed{+/-}$

In addition to the basic keys that any calculator has, many others are available individually or in a variety of combinations: logarithm and inverse logarithm keys, exponentiation keys, trigonometric and inverse trigonometric keys, and many more. The extra keys you need on your calculator obviously depend on the topics you intend to use it with, and we discuss just which keys we need for each chapter and for every topic (although you can do the problems and topics *in a different way with different keys from the ones we use*).

Your calculator and your students' calculators, however, really should have one particular type of extra key, no matter which topics you will use it on. This key "changes the sign" of the number in display, and it usually appears as either $\boxed{\text{CHS}}$ (CHANGE SIGN) or $\boxed{+/-}$ (PLUS/MINUS) on most calculators. Let's discuss the importance of these keys and why they are so essential.

One of the most subtle, and important, points in basic arithmetic concerns two of the different meanings of the negative sign. On the one hand, the negative sign can denote the operation of subtraction, the inverse operation to addition. On the other hand, the negative sign can be used to denote a negative number, the additive inverse of a positive number. This distinction is not essential to stress when performing simple arithmetic calculations with pencil and paper, and even professional mathematicians think nothing of referring to the number -5 as "minus five" rather than the more correct "negative five." ("Minus" should be used only when describing the operation of subtraction, such as in "seven minus five is two," not when referring to the additive inverse of a positive number.) On the calculator, however, this distinction *is* important. The $\boxed{-}$ key on a calculator is used for the operation of subtraction and not for denoting a negative number. If you try to use it for the latter purpose you may get an incorrect answer depending on the particular calculator you are using. For example, suppose I try to multiply -5 by -3 on my Casio fx–1000 calculator. Using the $\boxed{-}$ key for *all* negatives, the keystroke sequence would be

(2–5) $\qquad\qquad\qquad$ $\boxed{-}$ $\boxed{5}$ $\boxed{\times}$ $\boxed{-}$ $\boxed{3}$ $\boxed{=}$

But the answer with keystroke sequence (2–5) on the Casio fx–1000 is -8, not the correct answer of 15. Why?

After some investigation, I discover that, on this particular calculator, when more than one "operation" key is pressed in a row, the calculator ignores all but the final operation. So, when I pressed $\boxed{\times}$ $\boxed{-}$ in sequence (2–5), since $\boxed{-}$ is an operation key, the calculator ignored the previous multiplication and in effect performed the calculation $\cdots\cdots$?

$$\boxed{-}\ \boxed{5}\ \boxed{-}\ \boxed{3}\ \boxed{=}$$

In other words, it *subtracted* 3 from -5 and gave us the result -8. Sometimes the $\boxed{-}$ key will *work* as if it denoted "negative," but not consistently. And if you want to use a calculator to teach or to do mathematics, then it is imperative that the behavior of the calculator be consistent, or you won't know when it is giving a correct answer and when it is not.

What you need is a separate and specific "negative" key, two of which are in common use. One has the symbol $\boxed{+/-}$ on it and is called the PLUS/MINUS key the other has $\boxed{\text{CHS}}$ on it and is called the CHANGE SIGN key. Whichever of these two keys your calculator has, when you press it, it will change the sign of the number in display from $+$ to $-$ or from $-$ to $+$. The correct keystroke sequence for multiplying -5 by -3 using either of these two appropriate keys would be

$$\boxed{5}\ \boxed{+/-}\ \boxed{\times}\ \boxed{3}\ \boxed{+/-}\ \boxed{=}$$

or

$$\boxed{5}\ \boxed{\text{CHS}}\ \boxed{\times}\ \boxed{3}\ \boxed{\text{CHS}}\ \boxed{=}$$

While one of these two keys is essential if you want to be able to perform arithmetic computations involving negative numbers, many basic calculators do not have either. So make sure you look for one of these keys and inform your students to do the same.

Other differences to look for

These four differences among calculators are the major ones any calculator shopper or user should be aware of. To use the calculator to teach or to do classroom mathematics, however, you should be aware of several additional "minor" variations among calculators as well.

Illegal operations on the calculator

To begin with, let's investigate what happens on your calculator when you try to perform an "illegal" operation. Any calculator worth using will let you know, in some definite and obvious way, whenever you have performed an illegal operation. Yet how they do so varies widely even among one manufacturer's products. For example, let's see what happens when we try to divide 1 by 0 on four different calculators. The displays on both the Casio Memory–8F and the Casio fx–1000 calculators show E for error when you divide 1 by 0. When you do the same on the Texas Instruments TI–57 Programmable Calculator, the display shows 9.9999999 99 and it keeps blinking on–off–on. Finally, the Sharp Elsimate EL–502 display shows 0.0.0.0.0.0.0.0.0.0. If you try to divide 0 by 0, the two Casios and the Sharp give their same error messages, while the TI–57 displays a blinking number 1. After any of these error messages, you must either turn the calculator off and then on again, or press the CLEAR key once or twice, before you can do any more computations.

While these four calculators have different ways of alerting the user to an illegal operation, they are all perfectly adequate for classroom use as long as the person using them remembers the "error message." Of course, the best error message would be for a calculator to display the words "illegal operation," but I know of no calculator that does so. Some calculators do display the entire word ERROR, and this is as clear as you could ask for. But for practical purposes any error message is acceptable as long as it is obvious and consistent, such as the letter E for the two Casios, the blinking display for the TI–57, and the 0.0.0.0.0.0.0.0.0. for the Sharp.

Of course, just because a calculator "knows" that dividing by 0 is illegal and "balks" at doing so, it does not necessarily have to pick up on and alert the user to other illegal operations. For example, both of the Casio calculators have square root keys, which are very useful in a variety of topics (as we will see). As we all know, negative numbers in the real number system do not have square roots. So trying to take the square root of a negative number is an illegal operation, and we would like the calculator to give us an error message when this is attempted. When you enter the number -4 on the Casio fx–1000 (by pressing 4 followed by the $\boxed{+/-}$ key to change the sign to a negative) and then press the square root key $\boxed{\sqrt{}}$, the display shows E to inform you that you have attempted an illegal operation. When you do the same on a Casio Memory–8F, however, you get an answer of -2. In other words, the Casio Memory–8F takes the square root of the numerical value 4 and puts a negative sign in front of it. For anyone who did not know better, this calculator would seem to be saying that the square root of -4 is -2. In such a case, you have to do one of two things: Either do not use this calculator in class and not let your students use it either; or specifically point out this type of error to the class so they are not misled by the result if they get it.

What other illegal operations should you check out on the calculator before you either buy it or use it? You should ideally check any of the illegal operations that might come up in the class in which you will be using the calculator. Simply keep these two points in mind: (1) Any illegal operation that the calculator does catch can help to remind your students of the prohibited operation (as we will see in Chapter 3 on "Elementary Algebra"). (2) Any illegal operation that your calculator (or your students') does not point out to the user is one that you must warn your students about so they will not be misled. A few other obvious illegal operations that generally you should be aware of and check are:

- what your calculator does when you try to take the logarithm of zero or of a negative number (assuming your calculator has a logarithm key);
- what your calculator does when you try to find the factorial of a negative number or even of a nonintegral positive value (assuming your calculator has a factorial key); and
- what your calculator does when you take the arc Sin and/or arc Cos of a value larger than 1 or smaller than -1 (assuming your calculator has keys for arc Sin and arc Cos).

The exponentiation key $\boxed{x^y}$ *or* $\boxed{y^x}$

Another interesting fact about calculators concerns the exponentiation key $\boxed{x^y}$ or $\boxed{y^x}$. Suppose your calculator has the exponentiation key $\boxed{x^y}$, and you want to use this key to evaluate 2^3. The keystroke sequence for this on most calculators with an exponential key would be:

$$\boxed{2} \quad \boxed{x^y} \quad \boxed{3} \quad \boxed{=}$$

That is, you enter the base 2; then you press the $\boxed{x^y}$ key to tell the calculator you want to compute an exponential expression. You enter the power 3, and finally you press the $\boxed{=}$ key to get the answer. The answer, 8, would now appear in the display. If, however, you had wanted to evaluate the expression $(-2)^3$ and had tried to do so with the keystroke sequence

$$\boxed{2} \quad \boxed{+/-} \quad \boxed{x^y} \quad \boxed{3} \quad \boxed{=}$$

your calculator would very likely indicate an error or an illegal operation. Why? Because most (though not all) calculators with an exponential key compute the exponential by internally converting the problem to an equivalent logarithm problem. So by asking the calculator to find

(2–6) $$y = a^b$$

most calculators do so by finding

(2–7) $$\ln y = b \ln a$$

first and then taking the antilogarithm. If the base a is negative (as it is when raising -2 to the power 3), then even though (2–6) is a legal expression and should give a finite answer, (2–7) is not. Hence the calculator signifies an illegal operation. This is, in fact, exactly what happens when you try to evaluate $(-2)^3$ on calculators with an $\boxed{x^y}$ or $\boxed{y^x}$ key, even though $(-2)^3$ does exist and is equal to -8. Of the four that I own, the TI–57 blinks on and off; the TI–30 displays the word ERROR; the Sharp Elsimate EL–502 displays 0.0.0.0.0.0.0.0.0.; and the Casio fx–1000 displays E. Simply be aware that this may happen when you use the exponent key with a negative base, and be sure to warn your students about it as well.

Raising any value to a positive integer power

This discussion of the exponent key and its limitations brings up an interesting fact about calculators. Some calculators tend to have odd traits and odd ways of operating. Manufacturers do not intentionally build these odd traits into the machines; they are simply a byproduct of the way the calculator is wired (so to speak). Some of these unintentional calculator traits can, in fact, be very useful, and so you should try to remember them when they accidentally occur. For example, as we saw, most calculators with an exponent key $\boxed{x^y}$ will not give you the value of the expression when the base is negative. How, then, can you evaluate expressions like $(-2)^8$ or $(-23.45)^6$? Well, you use a handy "extra" feature that many calculators, even very simple ones with only the four basic operation keys, have. Suppose you want to evaluate 3^8. To do so without using an exponent key, you would use the keystroke sequence

$$\boxed{3}\ \boxed{\times}\ \boxed{3}\ \boxed{\times}\ \boxed{3}\ \boxed{\times}\ \boxed{3}\ \boxed{\times}\ \boxed{3}\ \boxed{\times}\ \boxed{3}\ \boxed{\times}\ \boxed{3}\ \boxed{\times}\ \boxed{3}\ \boxed{=}$$

and you would obtain the correct answer of 6,561. This approach isn't really too bad, but consider the time involved and the chance for error if, instead of 3^8, you were trying to evaluate 23.184^8 or even $(-23.184)^8$ this way. Some less cumbersome way would be extremely helpful and such a way does in fact exist. The following short-cut procedure for raising a number to a positive-integral power can be used on many calculators, and it will work with any value as a base: positive, negative, integer, or noninteger. To evaluate the expression a^b you:

- Enter the base value a.
- Press the multiplication key $\boxed{\times}$ once or twice (you will have to try both on your calculator to see which will work on your machine).
- Press the equal key $\boxed{=}$, one less time than the power b.

Let's illustrate this procedure by evaluating 3^8. We would press the base, 3; then we would press the multiplication key $\boxed{\times}$ once or twice depending on which works with our calculator. Then we would press the equal key $\boxed{=}$ 7 times to get the power 8. The keystroke sequence would be

$$\boxed{3}\ \boxed{\times}\ \boxed{\times}\ \boxed{=}\ \boxed{=}\ \boxed{=}\ \boxed{=}\ \boxed{=}\ \boxed{=}\ \boxed{=}$$

or

$$\boxed{3}\ \boxed{\times}\ \boxed{=}\ \boxed{=}\ \boxed{=}\ \boxed{=}\ \boxed{=}\ \boxed{=}\ \boxed{=}$$

While this procedure does not work on all calculators, it does work on many of them and allows you to compute exponential expressions with an integer exponent quickly and easily. Even on a calculator with an exponent key, this procedure would still be useful when the base is negative and the exponent key will not give an answer.

Why is this procedure so much easier and less prone to error than the standard keystroke sequence? It requires you to enter the base a only once at the very beginning—quite a savings when the base is a decimal value, negative, or both. For example, take the expression $(-23.184)^6$. Ordinarily, we would have to enter the base, -23.184, 6 times and use the keystroke sequence:

$$\boxed{23.184}\ \boxed{+/-}\ \boxed{\times}\ \boxed{23.184}\ \boxed{+/-}\ \boxed{\times}\ \boxed{23.184}\ \boxed{+/-}\ \boxed{\times}$$
$$\boxed{23.184}\ \boxed{+/-}\ \boxed{\times}\ \boxed{23.184}\ \boxed{+/-}\ \boxed{\times}\ \boxed{23.184}\ \boxed{+/-}\ \boxed{\times}$$

If our short-cut procedure works on your calculator, the base -23.184 would be entered only once, and the keystroke sequence would be much simpler:

$$\boxed{23.184}\ \boxed{+/-}\ \boxed{\times}\ \boxed{\times}\ \boxed{=}\ \boxed{=}\ \boxed{=}\ \boxed{=}\ \boxed{=}$$

or

Unfortunately, not all calculators have this simple but very useful "incidental" feature. Of my four basic calculators, both the Casio Memory–8F and the Casio fx–1000 have this feature, and they both require that the multiplication key $\boxed{\times}$ be pressed twice. My Sharp Elsimate EL–502 also has it but requires that the multiplication key $\boxed{\times}$ be pressed only once. Yet neither my TI–30 nor my TI–57 has this feature. Why does one calculator have this feature and another one not—especially since the feature is usually only incidental rather than purposely put in? There is no specific reason. So, in general, the only way you can tell whether a calculator has this feature is to try it with a simple example like 2^4 and see if it works.

I hope that what we've talked about in this chapter has given you some idea of what its title means—"Getting To Know Your Calculator." The best and most enjoyable way of learning the many things there are to learn about a calculator is by approaching things as if playing a new game—by trying it and thinking about it and then trying it again. Calculators, although fascinating gadgets, are, in the last analysis, simply devices that do what you want them to do. Learn about your calculator so that you will be better able to use it, teach with it, and enjoy it.

3

ELEMENTARY ALGEBRA
(ALGEBRA ONE)

Algebra has often been referred to as "generalized arithmetic." Since the basic function of the calculator is to perform arithmetic operations, not surprisingly it can be very useful in teaching algebra. While the calculator can, of course, be used simply to evaluate numerical expressions in mixture problems, motion problems, and interest problems, it can also be profitably employed to help the student discover and learn about the rules of algebra. In this chapter we will look at some examples of both such applications.

Algebraic expressions

Evaluating algebraic expressions

The calculator can be used in several ways in the topic of algebraic expressions. The simplest and most direct—and the most useful in the long run— is as an aid in the evaluation of such expressions for specified values of the variable. So let's start with this use.

Let's assume that you have introduced the class to the concept of an algebraic expression. You explain and demonstrate how to evaluate such an expression by hand by substituting a particular value of the variable and performing the arithmetic operations with pencil and paper. You should next make it a point to also show the class, whenever appropriate, how to evaluate the expression on their calculators. For example, suppose one of the expressions you are working with is:

$$2s + 3$$

Show the students that the appropriate calculator keystroke sequence for evaluating this expression for any value of s is

$$2s + 3: \quad \boxed{2} \; \boxed{\times} \; \boxed{s} \; \boxed{+} \; \boxed{3} \; \boxed{=}$$

Also demonstrate the use of this keystroke sequence by repeating one or two of the evaluations already performed with pencil and paper. Show that the results are identical both ways. Similarly, if the expression is:

(3–1)
$$\frac{1}{3t - 6}$$

show the class that the corresponding calculator keystroke sequence on a calculator with reciprocal key $\boxed{1/x}$ is:

$$\frac{1}{3t - 6}: \quad \boxed{3} \; \boxed{\times} \; \boxed{t} \; \boxed{-} \; \boxed{6} \; \boxed{=} \; \boxed{1/x}$$

and illustrate this keystroke sequence with a few values of t. Point out to the students that this is only one of the many possible ways of evaluating expression (3–1) on a calculator, and that how they do it on their own calculator depends on which keys they have. You can then, just to give them a "how-to" idea, write out two or three additional keystroke sequences for expression (3–1) using keys other than the reciprocal key $\boxed{1/x}$. For example, with parentheses keys $\boxed{(}$ and $\boxed{)}$, the appropriate keystroke sequence would be:

$$\frac{1}{3t - 6}: \quad \boxed{1} \; \boxed{\div} \; \boxed{(} \; \boxed{3} \; \boxed{\times} \; \boxed{t} \; \boxed{-} \; \boxed{6} \; \boxed{)} \; \boxed{=}$$

With keys $\boxed{\text{STO}}$ and $\boxed{\text{RCL}}$ for, respectively, storing a displayed value in memory and recalling it, the appropriate keystroke sequence would be:

$$\frac{1}{3t - 6}: \quad \boxed{3} \; \boxed{\times} \; \boxed{t} \; \boxed{-} \; \boxed{6} \; \boxed{=} \; \boxed{\text{STO}} \; \boxed{1} \; \boxed{\div} \; \boxed{\text{RCL}} \; \boxed{=}$$

Once the students have seen a few examples like these, they should get the idea and be able to develop appropriate keystroke sequences for their own calculators.

Of course, not every algebraic expression can be evaluated on every calculator using a simple keystroke sequence. But many can, and for these expressions calculator evaluation can save a great deal of time and effort. Keep in mind that the need to evaluate algebraic expressions for specific values of the variable occurs in a wide range of mathematical topics. For example, it is used in sketching graphs by plotting points, in evaluating perimeters and areas using perimeter and area formulas, in applying the Law of Sines and Law of Cosines, in obtaining approximations of plane areas in calculus using Simpson's rule, and in many other cases. The exposure students get to the calculator evaluation of algebraic expressions at this time, as well as the practice they have in it, will serve as an extremely useful tool throughout their school years and beyond. For this reason you should try, when you cover this topic, to include problems for calculator evaluation in both your classroom discussion and your homework assignments.

A calculator reminder of illegal operations

The calculator evaluation of algebraic expressions also provides, as a side benefit, a reminder for students of two basic rules of arithmetic that often cause trouble in algebra: (1) that division by zero is an illegal operation, and (2) that negative numbers do not have square roots in the set of real numbers. Give the class a simple algebraic fraction for calculator evaluation, and include in the values of the variable to be substituted the value that will make the denominator of the fraction vanish. For example:

Problem: Use your calculator to evaluate the algebraic expression:

$$\frac{1}{4t - 8} \quad \text{for } t = 4, 3, 2$$

The calculator keystroke sequence for evaluating this expression on a calculator with a reciprocal key is:

$$\frac{1}{4t - 8}: \quad \boxed{4} \; \boxed{\times} \; \boxed{t} \; \boxed{-} \; \boxed{8} \; \boxed{=} \; \boxed{1/x}$$

When 4 and 3 are substituted into this expression, the calculator will correctly display the answers 0.125 and 0.25, respectively. Yet when $t = 2$ is substituted, the calculator will display some type of error message (as discussed in Chapter 2). You can now show the class just what this error is by performing this last evaluation by hand on the board:

$$\frac{1}{4t-8} = \frac{1}{4(2)-8} = \frac{1}{8-8} = \frac{1}{0}$$

This is a meaningless expression since division by zero is not allowed in mathematics.

Similarly, to emphasize that negative numbers do not have real square roots, give a problem like the following:

Problem: Use your calculator and the square root key to evaluate the expression:

$$\sqrt{3a-6} \qquad \text{for } a = 5, 3, 1$$

Once again the calculator will give the correct answers for $a = 5$ and $a = 3$, but it will indicate an error when $t = 1$ is substituted. You can now go through this last evaluation by hand on the board:

$$\sqrt{3a-6} = \sqrt{3(1)-6} = \sqrt{3-6} = \sqrt{-3}$$

Remind the class that, when working with the real numbers, negative numbers do not have square roots. To reinforce these two rules, simply intersperse expressions like these into your homework assignments and instruct the students that whenever the calculator indicates an error they must re-do the problem by hand and discover what the error is.

Additional examples

The following several examples of algebraic expressions can be evaluated on a calculator using a simple keystroke sequence. One such keystroke sequence is provided with each example. Included are examples of algebraic fractions that can be used to emphasize that division by zero is illegal, along with examples of algebraic radicals that can be used to emphasize that negative numbers do not have real square roots.

Note: Examples 1, 2, and 4 require the $\boxed{x^2}$ key. If your calculator has only an exponential key $\boxed{x^y}$, you should logically be able to use that with $y = 2$ instead. Unfortunately, most calculators don't seem to let you do so. Using the $\boxed{x^2}$ key amid a series of operations seems to be all right, whereas using the $\boxed{x^y}$ key that way destroys the previous operations. If you do not have an $\boxed{x^2}$ key but if you do have an $\boxed{x^y}$ key, *try* to use the latter, but be prepared for it not to work.

1. *Expression:* $a^2 + 5$
   Special key: $\boxed{x^2}$
   Keystroke sequence: $\boxed{a}$ $\boxed{x^2}$ $\boxed{+}$ $\boxed{5}$ $\boxed{=}$

2. *Expression:* $(a - 3)a^2$
   Special key: $\boxed{x^2}$
   Keystroke sequence: $\boxed{a}$ $\boxed{-}$ $\boxed{3}$ $\boxed{=}$ $\boxed{\times}$ $\boxed{a}$ $\boxed{x^2}$ $\boxed{=}$

3. *Expression:* $b - \dfrac{1}{b}$
   Special key: $\boxed{1/x}$
   Keystroke sequence: $\boxed{b}$ $\boxed{-}$ $\boxed{b}$ $\boxed{1/x}$ $\boxed{=}$

Demonstrates arithmetic rule: The calculator will indicate an error due to division by zero when $b = 0$ is used.

4. *Expression:* $\dfrac{1}{b^2 - 4b + 3}$

   Special keys: $\boxed{1/x}$ $\boxed{x^2}$

   Keystroke sequence:

   Hierarchy:

   $\boxed{b}$ $\boxed{x^2}$ $\boxed{-}$ $\boxed{4}$ $\boxed{\times}$ $\boxed{b}$ $\boxed{+}$ $\boxed{3}$ $\boxed{=}$ $\boxed{1/x}$

   Left-to-right [write $b^2 - 4b + 3$ as $(b - 4)b + 3$]:

   $\boxed{b}$ $\boxed{-}$ $\boxed{4}$ $\boxed{\times}$ $\boxed{b}$ $\boxed{+}$ $\boxed{3}$ $\boxed{=}$ $\boxed{1/x}$

   Demonstrates arithmetic rule: The calculator will indicate an error due to dividing by zero when $b = 1$ and when $b = 3$.

5. *Expression:* $\sqrt{5s - 13}$

   Special key: $\boxed{\sqrt{}}$

   Keystroke sequence: $\boxed{5}$ $\boxed{\times}$ $\boxed{s}$ $\boxed{-}$ $\boxed{13}$ $\boxed{=}$ $\boxed{\sqrt{}}$

   Demonstrates arithmetic rule: The calculator will indicate an error due to taking the square root of a negative number for any value of s less than 2.6.

6. *Expression:* $\sqrt{\dfrac{7}{s} - 1}$

   Special key: $\boxed{\sqrt{}}$

   Keystroke sequence: $\boxed{7}$ $\boxed{\div}$ $\boxed{s}$ $\boxed{-}$ $\boxed{1}$ $\boxed{=}$ $\boxed{\sqrt{}}$

   Demonstrates arithmetic rule: The calculator will indicate an error due to division by zero for $s = 0$; and it will indicate an error due to taking the square root of a negative number for any value of $s > 7$ or $s < 0$.

Functions

The calculator as a function machine

One of the simplest and most effective ways of teaching about functions is with the so-called "function machine" approach. In this approach the student is told to think of a function as represented by a box-like machine with a conveyor belt leading into it on its left side and another conveyor belt leading out from it on its right side. Whenever an element of the domain s is fed into the machine on the left, its corresponding function value $f(s)$ comes out on the right. For example, if the function is $f(s) = 2s + 3$, and the domain value $s = 4$ is fed in, the corresponding function value $f(4) = 11$ will come out (Figure 3–1).

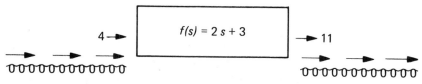

Figure 3-1   *The function machine for* f(s) = 2s + 3

There are several reasons for the effectiveness of the function machine approach. First, instead of an abstract concept, it gives students a concrete and physical embodiment of the function concept that they can visualize whenever functions are discussed or studied. Second, the function machine representation allows students to interpret many of the basic properties and definitions of functions in a very simple, mechanical way. For example, the concept of an inverse function is difficult for some students to grasp. The function machine for the inverse f^{-1}, however, is nothing more than the function machine for f set to run in reverse, and this is easy to visualize. Similarly, the composite of two functions, $g \circ f$, is a difficult concept for some students to grasp and work with. But the function machine for the composite $g \circ f$ is nothing more complicated than the machines for f and g set side-by-side. This arrangement is not at all difficult to visualize (Figure 3–2).

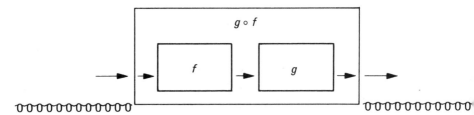

Figure 3-2　*The function machine for the composite function* g ∘ f

What does the function machine idea have to do with the calculator? Everything! In essence, the calculator *is* a function machine come to life. In fact it is many function machines come to life and all rolled into one. It is a function machine that the students can actually get their hands on and operate instead of just imagining how it might operate. Since a function is nothing more than an algebraic expression with a name attached to the resulting value, a function can be thought of as being represented by the calculator with an appropriate keystroke sequence. For example, let's take the simple linear function $f(s) = 2s + 3$. The calculator keystroke sequence for evaluating this function is

$$f(s) = 2s + 3: \quad \boxed{2} \ \boxed{\times} \ \boxed{s} \ \boxed{+} \ \boxed{3} \ \boxed{=}$$

If the student selects any value of s and presses this keystroke sequence with it, the corresponding function value $2s + 3$ will appear in the display. This is just what a function machine is supposed to do. If we can start to think of the calculator as a pseudo-function machine, then we should be able to use it to complement and augment (but not to replace) the function machine approach to the topic of functions. Let's look now at some specific examples of how this can be done.

Graphing functions

The most obvious and useful application of the calculator is in the evaluation of simple functions when obtaining range values for given domain values or for graphing the function. Just point out to the class, when you first give the definition of a function, that rules for functions are nothing more than algebraic expressions of a certain type with names attached for the range values. Consequently, most functions can be evaluated by calculator using an appropriate keystroke sequence, just the way most algebraic expressions can. With this in mind, the calculator can be used to answer questions like the following:

> *Problem:* Given the function $f(s) = 2s + 3$, and the domain $\{1, 2, 3, 4\}$, write out a calculator keystroke sequence for evaluating this function. Use your calculator to find the function value $f(s)$ for each s in the domain, and then graph this function.

It's now fairly straightforward for the student to obtain the pairs of values [s, $f(s)$], which define this function and the corresponding graph (Figure 3–3).

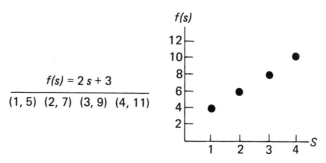

$$f(s) = 2\,s + 3$$

$$(1, 5)\ \ (2, 7)\ \ (3, 9)\ \ (4, 11)$$

Figure 3-3

With the help of the calculator, you can also give this type of problem with functions of second degree, as a stepping stone toward the identification of different types of curves.

> *Problem:* Given the function $g(t) = t^2 - t + 2$, and the domain $\{-2, -1, 0, 1, 2, 3\}$, write out a calculator keystroke sequence for evaluating this function. Use your calculator to find the function value $g(t)$ for each t in the domain, and then graph this function. Based on your graph, do you think the graph of a function involving a second-degree power is linear?

The keystroke sequence for this function is:

$$g(t) = t^2 - t + 2:\quad \boxed{t}\ \boxed{x^2}\ \boxed{-}\ \boxed{t}\ \boxed{+}\ \boxed{2}\ \boxed{=}$$

Once again it is a straightforward matter to obtain all the pairs [t, $g(t)$], graph the function, and discover that the graph is *not* linear (Figure 3–4).

$$g(t) = t^2 - t + 2$$

$$(-2, 8)\ \ (-1, 4)\ \ (0, 2)$$
$$(1, 2)\ \ (2, 4)\ \ (3, 8)$$

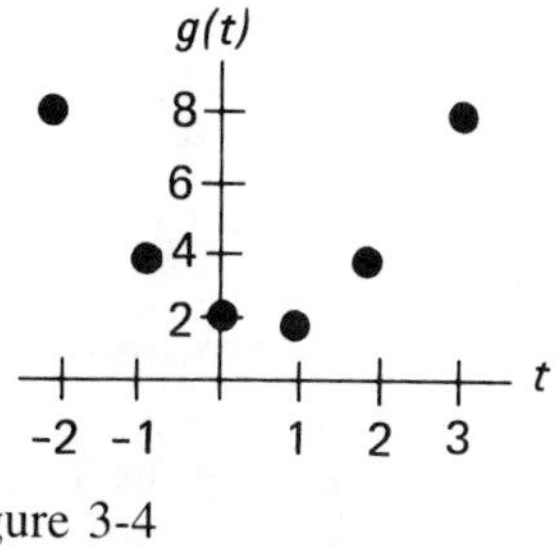

Figure 3-4

The advantage of calculator evaluation of functions over pencil-and-paper evaluation is more than just a simple saving of time and effort, although that saving can be considerable and very much appreciated. The real advantage is that the calculator lets you assign the kinds of problems that involve so much computation that you simply wouldn't assign them without the calculator. For example, suppose your class already knows that functions of second degree have parabola-type graphs and that a function with the entire set of real numbers as domain can be graphed by plotting a suitable number of points. You can then give the following problem, which entails a bit of calculator "search":

> *Problem:* Given the function $f(s) = s^2 - 18s + 76$, with domain the set of all real numbers, use your calculator to locate the turning point of the graph of this function. Also find the minimum value the function takes on, and estimate the zero(s) of the function to the nearest integer.

Without the calculator this problem would be perhaps too difficult, since the turning point occurs at $s = 9$ and not at one of the small values near the origin where most "made-up" problems center. By calculator, however, it's relatively quick and easy. The keystroke sequences for this function are:

Hierarchy: $(s^2 - 18s + 76)$:

$\boxed{s}\ \boxed{x^2}\ \boxed{-}\ \boxed{18}\ \boxed{\times}\ \boxed{s}\ \boxed{+}\ \boxed{76}\ \boxed{=}$

Left-to-Right [write $s^2 - 18s + 76$ as $(s - 18)s + 76$]:

$\boxed{s}\ \boxed{-}\ \boxed{18}\ \boxed{\times}\ \boxed{s}\ \boxed{+}\ \boxed{76}\ \boxed{=}$

It does not take very many guesses and evaluations to locate the turning point and to sketch the graph in a neighborhood of this value by plotting several points. From the table of values and corresponding graph in Figure 3–5, it's clear that the graph turns at $s = 9$ and has a minimum value there of $f(9) = -5$ at this point.

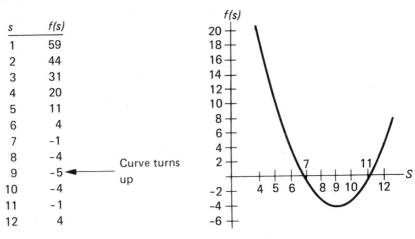

s	f(s)
1	59
2	44
3	31
4	20
5	11
6	4
7	-1
8	-4
9	-5
10	-4
11	-1
12	4

Curve turns up

Figure 3-5

Furthermore, since the function changes from positive to negative between $s = 6$ and $s = 7$, and from negative to positive between $s = 11$ and $s = 12$, the zeros of the function must be between these pairs of values. Using our calculator keystroke sequence, you can now easily obtain $f(6.5) = 1.25$. Since this is a positive value, the first zero of $f(s)$ must be strictly between $s = 6.5$ and $s = 7$ and so, to the nearest integer, is 7. Similarly, since $f(11.5) = 1.25$ is also positive, the second zero of $f(s)$ must be strictly between $s = 11$ and $s = 11.5$ and so, to the nearest integer, is 11. This procedure could be continued to obtain the zeros of $f(s)$ to any desired degree of accuracy. Yet since the problem asked for the zeros only to the nearest integer, we can stop at this point.

Verifying a function's domain and range.

A second and less obvious use of the calculator is in verifying the domain of a given function. For example, a standard problem of this type might be:

Problem: What are the domains of the following functions, if we assume that the domain is the set of all real numbers for which the defining formula yields a finite real number?

(a) $f(s) = s - \dfrac{1}{s}$

(b) $g(t) = \sqrt{\dfrac{5}{t} - 1}$

Recalling the basic rules of arithmetic from the preceding section, the student should have no trouble in showing that the domain of $f(s)$ is $s \neq 0$, and that the domain of $g(t)$ is $0 < t \leqslant 5$.

Yet there is always the possibility of an arithmetic mistake in answering a question like this [especially with a function like $g(t)$ which involves both an algebraic fraction and a radical]. So it's helpful to be able to verify that the set the student has found is in fact the correct domain of the function. To verify the domain by calculator, use it to evaluate the function for a variety of values of the variable, including not only values in the supposed domain, but also values not in the supposed domain. If the domain the student found is correct, then whenever a domain value is substituted, the calculator should give a finite, real value as the corresponding function value; and whenever a value not in the domain is substituted, the calculator should indicate an error. If either does not happen, then the supposed domain is incorrect. The student must then go back and redo the problem to discover the source of this error. In our current problem, for example, the keystroke sequences for the functions $f(s)$ and $g(t)$ are:

$$f(s) = s - \frac{1}{s}: \quad \boxed{s}\ \boxed{-}\ \boxed{s}\ \boxed{1/x}\ \boxed{=}$$

$$g(t) = \sqrt{\frac{5}{t} - 1}: \quad \boxed{5}\ \boxed{\div}\ \boxed{t}\ \boxed{-}\ \boxed{1}\ \boxed{=}\ \boxed{\sqrt{\ }}$$

The student should now use the first keystroke sequence to evaluate $f(s)$ for several values of s including $s = 0$, as well as to verify: (1) that, when $s = 0$ is tried, the calculator indicates an error; but (2) that, when any other value of s is tried, the calculator produces a finite, real function value. Similarly, the student should use the second keystroke sequence to evaluate $g(t)$ for several values of t, as well as to verify: (1) that for values of t in the interval $0 < t \leqslant 5$ the calculator produces a finite, real function value; but (2) that, when any other value of t is tried, the calculator indicates an error. This verification is fairly easy, and, although the solution is still possibly incorrect and our particular choice of values of s or t might fail to disclose the error, it's really very unlikely that such would happen.

Inverse functions and composition of functions.

The calculator can also be used to verify the answers to problems involving inverse functions or composition of functions. Suppose, for example, that the following problem was given:

Problem: Find the inverse of the function $f(s) = 2s + 3$.

Let's assume that the student obtains the correct answer, $f^{-1}(s) = (s - 3)/2$. If this is in fact the correct inverse of the given function $f(s)$, then whenever a and b are values such that $f(a) = b$, it should be true that $f^{-1}(b) = a$ as well. You can verify this by calculator in the following way: Have the students write out a keystroke sequence for both $f(s)$ and $f^{-1}(s)$, as follows:

$$f(s) = 2s + 3: \quad \boxed{2}\ \boxed{\times}\ \boxed{s}\ \boxed{+}\ \boxed{3}\ \boxed{=}$$
$$f^{-1}(s) = (s - 3)/2: \quad \boxed{s}\ \boxed{-}\ \boxed{3}\ \boxed{=}\ \boxed{\div}\ \boxed{2}\ \boxed{=}$$

Now have the students fill in the following verification table according to the accompanying instructions:

Select any 10 values for the first column, labeled a, of the following table. These should include both positive and negative integers, as well as both positive and negative decimals. When the first column is filled in, use your calculator and the keystroke sequences for $f(s)$ and $f^{-1}(s)$ to complete the rest of the table *one row of the table at a time*.

a	$f(a) = b$	b	$f^{-1}(b)$

Are these columns the same?

If the first and last columns of this table are *not* identical, then $f^{-1}(s)$ is most likely *not* the correct inverse of $f(s)$. If the first and last columns of this table *are* identical, then $f^{-1}(s)$ *is* most likely the correct inverse of $f(s)$, since it is virtually impossible for the function $f^{-1}(s)$ not to be the true inverse and yet match the true inverse for these ten arbitrarily selected values of the variable. This type of verification table should be made a standard part of any inverse function problem given in class or as part of a homework assignment.

   Note: The instructions to the student for completing this verification table state that the table is to be filled in *one row of the table at a time.* This is an important instruction for the following reason. Most calculators actually have a few internal, unseen digits in addition to their display digits to help in rounding off answers and in making computational results more accurate. If the student fills in the verification table or similar tables one *column* at a time by writing the displayed values of $f(a) = b$ in columns 2 and 3 and using these written-down values of b to obtain column 4, they are throwing away the extra nondisplayed digits. This loss of intermediate accuracy can quite possibly produce differences between column 4 and column 1 even if $f^{-1}(s)$ is correct. By completing the table one *row* at a time, and by doing all the work on the calculator, both the displayed and nondisplayed digits of the calculator are used. The resulting greater accuracy should make column 4 and column 1 equal virtually all the time when $f^{-1}(s)$ is the correct inverse function.

   This same procedure can be used to verify the answer to any problem involving the composition of two functions, such as:

> *Problem:* Given the functions $f(s) = 2s + 3$ and $g(t) = t^2 + 1$, express the composite function $g \circ f$ given by $g \circ f(s) = g[f(s)]$ in simplified form.

The correct answer to this problem is:

$$\begin{aligned}
g \circ f(s) &= g[f(s)] = g[2s + 3] \\
&= [2s + 3]^2 + 1 \\
&= 4s^2 + 12s + 9 + 1 \\
&= 4s^2 + 12s + 10
\end{aligned}$$

To verify this result, have the students write out a keystroke sequence for each of the functions f, g, and $g \circ f$ as follows:

$f(s) = 2s + 3$: | 2 | × | s | + | 3 | = |

$g(t) = t^2 + 1$: | t | x² | + | 1 | = |

$g \circ f(s) = 4s^2 + 12s + 10$:

Hierarchy:

| 4 | × | s | x² | + | 12 | × | s | + | 10 | = |

Left-to-Right [write $g \circ f(s)$ as $(4s + 12)s + 10$]:

| 4 | × | s | + | 12 | × | s | + | 10 | = |

Now have the students use their calculators with these keystroke sequences to complete the following verification table according to the accompanying instructions:

   Select any 10 values for the first column, labeled a of the following table. These values should include both positive and negative integers, as well as both positive and negative decimals. When the first column is filled in, use your calculator and the keystroke sequences for f, g, and $g \circ f$ to complete the rest of the table *one row of the table at a time*:

a	$f(a) = b$	$g(b)$	$g \circ f(a)$

↑ Are these two columns the same? ↑

If the last two columns are *not* identical, then $g \circ f$ is most likely *not* the correct composite of f and g. If the last two columns *are* identical, then $g \circ f$ *is* most likely the correct composite of f and g, since it is virtually impossible for the function $g \circ f$ not to be the correct composite and yet match the true composite function for all ten arbitrarily selected values of a. (Once again, note that the instructions specify filling in the table one row at a time, so that both the calculator's display digits and internal digits are used in the computations for greater accuracy in the intermediate results.) A verification table like this should also be made a standard part of any composite function problem given in class or as a homework assignment.

Additional examples

The following additional examples illustrate the kinds of function problems that can be solved with the use of a calculator.

1. *Problem:* Use your calculator to find the range of the function:

$$t = h(s) = s + \frac{1}{s}$$

Special key: $\boxed{1/x}$

Keystroke sequence: $\boxed{s}\ \boxed{+}\ \boxed{s}\ \boxed{1/x}\ \boxed{=}$

Solution: The range of this function is $\{t \le -2\} \cup \{t \ge 2\}$.

2. *Problem:* Find the domain of the function $h(s) = \sqrt{s^2 - 5s + 4}$, and then verify your answer using your calculator.

Special keys: $\boxed{x^2}\ \boxed{\sqrt{}}$

Keystroke sequences:

Hierarchy:

$\boxed{s}\ \boxed{x^2}\ \boxed{-}\ \boxed{5}\ \boxed{\times}\ \boxed{s}\ \boxed{+}\ \boxed{4}\ \boxed{=}\ \boxed{\sqrt{}}$

Left-to-Right [write $s^2 - 5s + 4$ as $(s - 5)s + 4$]:

$\boxed{s}\ \boxed{-}\ \boxed{5}\ \boxed{\times}\ \boxed{s}\ \boxed{+}\ \boxed{4}\ \boxed{=}\ \boxed{\sqrt{}}$

Solution: The domain of this function is $\{s \leq 1\} \cup \{s \geq 4\}$.

3. *Problem:* Find the inverse of the function $f(a) = 2a^2 - 5$, and verify your answer using your calculator and a verification table.

Special keys: $\boxed{x^2}\ \boxed{\sqrt{}}$

Keystroke sequences:

$f(a) = 2a^2 - 5$: $\boxed{2}\ \boxed{\times}\ \boxed{a}\ \boxed{x^2}\ \boxed{-}\ \boxed{5}\ \boxed{=}$

$f^{-}(a) = \sqrt{\dfrac{a + 5}{2}}$: $\boxed{a}\ \boxed{+}\ \boxed{5}\ \boxed{=}\ \boxed{\div}\ \boxed{2}\ \boxed{=}\ \boxed{\sqrt{}}$

or

$f^{-1}(a) = -\sqrt{\dfrac{a + 5}{2}}$: $\boxed{a}\ \boxed{+}\ \boxed{5}\ \boxed{=}\ \boxed{\div}\ \boxed{2}\ \boxed{=}\ \boxed{\sqrt{}}\ \boxed{+/-}$

Solution: $2^{-1}(a) = \sqrt{\dfrac{a + 5}{2}}$ or $f^{-1}(a) = -\sqrt{\dfrac{a + 5}{2}}$

4. *Problem:* Given the functions $f(s) = \dfrac{2}{s}$ and $g(t) = \dfrac{4}{t^2}$. Express the composite function $g \circ f$ in simplified form, and verify your answer using your calculator and a verification table.

Special key: $\boxed{x^2}$

Keystroke sequences:

$f(s) = \dfrac{2}{s}$: $\boxed{2}\ \boxed{\div}\ \boxed{s}\ \boxed{=}$

$g(t) = \dfrac{4}{t^2}$: $\boxed{4}\ \boxed{\div}\ \boxed{t}\ \boxed{x^2}\ \boxed{=}$

$g \circ f(s) = s^2$: $\boxed{s}\ \boxed{x^2}$

Solution: $g \circ f(s) = s^2$

Mixture and investment problems

Mixture problems

There are two basic types of mixture problems. In the first, two products at given prices are to be combined to give a mixture with a specified price that is between the original two. The problem is to find the proportion of each that must be used in the mixture. An example of this kind of mixture problem is:

Problem 1: A dealer wants to mix candy worth 65¢ per pound with candy worth 90¢ per pound to produce 40 pounds of candy that can be sold at 75¢ per pound. How many pounds of each type of candy should be used in the mixture?

In the second type of mixture problem, two solutions with given concentrates are to be combined to give a mixture with a specified concentrate that is between the original two. The problem is to find the proportion of each solution that must be used in the mixture. An example of this kind of mixture problem is:

Problem 2: A chemist has one solution that is 18 percent acid and another which is 24 percent acid. How many ounces of each concentrate should be used to produce a mixture of 90 ounces that is 22 percent acid?

Both problem 1 and problem 2 can be solved, and usually are solved, by expressing the problem algebraically and solving the resulting algebraic equation. Both, however, can also be solved by making a simplistic guess of the solution and then using the calculator to correct any error with a simple arithmetic correction factor. This *guess-and-correct procedure* was developed by Dr. Harrison A. Geiselmann of Cornell University.* Let's illustrate this procedure with problems 1 and 2:

Solution to problem 1: Our first guess is to use *equal amounts* (20 pounds each) of the two types of candy. This gives a mixture with price per pound equal to the average of the two given prices, or $(65 + 90)/2 = 77.5¢$ per pound. Notice from Figure 3–6 that more of the 65¢ candy must be used in the mixture

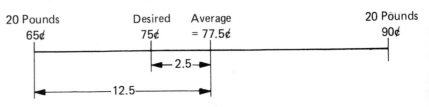

20 Pounds   Desired   Average   20 Pounds
  65¢   75¢   = 77.5¢   90¢

← 2.5 →

—12.5—

Figure 3-6

to correct the first guess, which gives 77.5¢ per pound, to the desired lower price of 75¢ per pound. The correction factor for the additional amount of 65¢ candy that must be used is:

$$\frac{2.5}{12.5} \times 20 \text{ pounds}$$

A calculator evaluation of this expression using the keystroke sequence is:

$$\boxed{2.5} \; \boxed{\div} \; \boxed{12.5} \; \boxed{\times} \; \boxed{20} \; \boxed{=}$$

This sequence gives the correction factor as 4 pounds. The correct solution is therefore

*Described and illustrated in New York State Mathematics Teachers' Journal (Fall 1978).

$$
\begin{array}{rl}
\text{First guess} & \text{20 pounds of 65}\cent\text{ candy} \\
+ \ \underline{\text{Correction factor}} & \underline{\text{4 pounds of 65}\cent\text{ candy}} \\
\text{Total} = & \text{24 pounds of 65}\cent\text{ candy}
\end{array}
$$

and the remaining 16 pounds of 90¢ candy.

Solution to problem 2: Our first guess is to use *equal amounts* (45 ounces each) of the two concentrates. This guess gives a mixture with a concentration equal to the average of the two given concentrations, or (18 percent + 24 percent)/2 = 21 percent. Notice from Figure 3–7 that more of the 24-percent

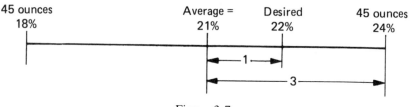

Figure 3-7

solution must be used in the mixture to correct the first guess, which gives 21 percent, to the desired larger concentration of 22 percent. The correction factor for the additional amount of 24 percent solution to be used in the mixture is

$$
\frac{1}{3} \times 45 \text{ ounces}
$$

The calculator evaluation of this expression using the keystroke sequence is:

$$
\boxed{1} \ \boxed{\div} \ \boxed{3} \ \boxed{\times} \ \boxed{45} \ \boxed{=}
$$

which gives the correction factor as 15 ounces. The correct solution is therefore

$$
\begin{array}{rl}
\text{First guess} & \text{45 ounces of 24\% solution} \\
+ \ \underline{\text{Correction factor}} & \underline{\text{15 ounces of 24\% solution}} \\
\text{Total} = & \text{60 ounces of 24\% solution}
\end{array}
$$

and the remaining 30 ounces of the 18-percent solution.

This guess-and-correct calculator procedure can be used to solve any mixture problem of the types illustrated. Yet, since one of the major uses of mixture problems is to give the students practice in the use of algebraic equations, you should *not* use this method *instead* of the algebraic approach. Instead, use it either as a method of checking an algebraic solution or as a change of pace for those students who have mastered the algebraic approach.

Investment problems

The guess-and-correct procedure can also be applied to investment problems of the following type:

Problem 3: Mr. Brown has invested $2,500, part at 4-percent interest a year and the remainder at 7-percent interest a year. At the end of the year he receives $145 in total interest. How much of the $2,500 did he have invested at each rate?

Solution to problem 3: Begin by expressing the year's interest, $145, as a percentage since the guess-and-correct procedure works with percentages and proportions. This percentage would be 145/2,500 = 5.8 percent. Our first guess is that *equal amounts* ($1,250) were invested at each of the two rates of interest. This guess would give an investment with total interest rate equal to the average of the two individual interest rates, or (4 percent + 7 percent)/2 = 5.5 percent. Figure 3–8 makes it clear that more of the money must be invested at the higher

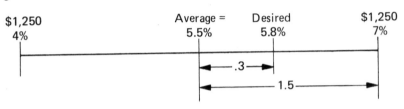

Figure 3-8

7-percent interest rate. The correction factor is given by:

$$\frac{.3}{1.5} \times \$1,250$$

and this can be evaluated by calculator using the keystroke sequence:

$$\boxed{.3} \ \boxed{\div} \ \boxed{1.5} \ \boxed{\times} \ \boxed{1,250} \ \boxed{=}$$

as $250. The correct solution is therefore:

$$
\begin{array}{rl}
\text{First guess} & \$1,250 \text{ at } 7\% \\
+ \text{ Correction factor} & \underline{\$\ \ 250 \text{ at } 7\%} \\
\text{Total} = & \$1,500 \text{ at } 7\%
\end{array}
$$

and the remaining $1,000 at 4 percent.

Additional examples

The following additional examples demonstrate the guess-and-correct method with both mixture and investment problems.

1. *Problem:* Peanuts worth 20¢ per ounce are to be combined with cashews worth 65¢ per ounce to give a mixture of 45 ounces that will be worth 35¢ per ounce. How many ounces of each should be used?

    First guess: Our first guess would be to use equal amounts of the two types of nut (22.5 ounces of each), and the price of such a mixture would be (20¢ + 65¢)/2 = 42.5¢ per ounce (Figure 3–9).

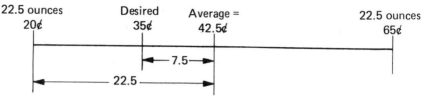

Figure 3-9

Correction factor: The correction factor is (7.5/22.5) × 22.5 more ounces of the 20¢ per ounce nuts, and the calculator evaluation of this expression using the keystroke sequence

$$\boxed{7.5} \; \boxed{\div} \; \boxed{22.5} \; \boxed{\times} \; \boxed{22.5} \; \boxed{=}$$

gives 7.5 ounces.

Solution: A first guess of 22.5 ounces of the 20¢ nuts, plus a correction factor of 7.5 ounces of the 20¢ nuts, gives a final solution of 30 ounces of the 20¢-per-ounce peanuts and the remaining 15 ounces of the 65¢-per-ounce cashews.

2. *Problem:* The "Tast-E Fruit Juice" Company puts out one fruit juice drink that has 30 percent real juice in it and another that has 80 percent real juice in it. How much of each juice drink must be combined to obtain a mixture of 100 gallons that has 50 percent real juice?

First guess: Our first guess would be to use equal amounts (50 gallons) of each juice drink, and this would give a mixture with (30 percent + 80 percent)/2 = 55 percent real juice in it. (Figure 3–10.)

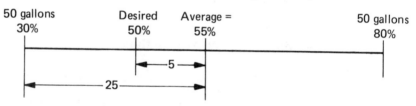

Figure 3-10

Correction factor: The correction factor is (5/25) × 50 more gallons of the 30 percent juice drink. This can be evaluated by calculator using the keystroke sequence

$$\boxed{5} \; \boxed{\div} \; \boxed{25} \; \boxed{\times} \; \boxed{50} \; \boxed{=}$$

as 10 gallons.

Solution: A first guess of 50 gallons of the 30 percent juice drink, plus a correction factor of 10 gallons of the 30 percent juice drink, gives a final solution of 60 gallons of the 30 percent juice drink and the remaining 40 gallons of the 80 percent juice drink.

3. *Problem:* Betsy invested one sum of money at 8-percent interest a year and another sum of money at 12-percent interest a year. At the end of the year she received a total of $210 in interest. If the total amount invested was $2,000, how much was invested at each of the two interest rates?

First guess: Our first guess would be that equal amounts ($1,000 each) were invested at each rate. This would give a total rate of return of (8 percent + 12 percent)/2 = 10 percent. The rate of return she actually received was 210/2000 = 10.5 percent (Figure 3–11).

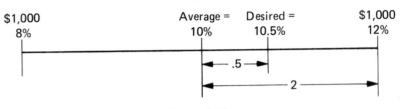

Figure 3-11

Correction factor: The correction factor is (.5/2) × 1,000 more dollars invested at the 12-percent rate of interest. This expression can be evaluated by calculator using the keystroke sequence

$$\boxed{.5} \ \boxed{\div} \ \boxed{2} \ \boxed{\times} \ \boxed{1,000} \ \boxed{=}$$

as $250.

Solution: The first guess of $1,000 invested at the 12-percent interest rate, plus the correction factor of $250 invested at 12 percent, gives a final solution of $1,250 invested at 12 percent and the remaining $750 invested at 8 percent.

Additional calculator activities

1. *Topic:* Open sentences and truth (or solution) sets

Objective: Given an open sentence and a replacement set, use the calculator to find the solution set of the sentence.

Example: Using the replacement set {0, 1, 2, 3}, find the solution set for the open sentence: 3s > 5.

Solution: The appropriate keystroke sequence is:

$$3s: \quad \boxed{3} \ \boxed{\times} \ \boxed{s} \ \boxed{=}$$

With this sequence, the solution set is found to be:

{2, 3}

2. *Topic:* Ordering of signed numbers

Objective: Given two real numbers *a* and *b*, along with the conditions:
(a) *a* is equal to *b* if and only if *a* − *b* is zero.
(b) *a* is greater than *b* if and only if *a* − *b* is positive.

(c) *a* is less than *b* if and only if $a - b$ is negative.
Use the calculator to check which is the larger number and which is the smaller.

Example: For each of the following pairs of signed numbers, determine which is larger by using their positions on the real number line. Then use your calculator to check each answer by calculating the "larger" number minus the "smaller" number and verifying that the result is positive:
(a) 7, 3
(b) −2, 4
(c) −3.5, −5.8
(d) 0, −2

Solution: The appropriate keystroke sequence to use is

$$a - b: \quad \boxed{a} \ \boxed{-} \ \boxed{b} \ \boxed{=}$$

The solutions are:
(a) $7 > 3$
(b) $4 > -2$
(c) $-3.5 > -5.8$
(d) $0 > -2$
These answers check since the "larger" number minus the "smaller" number gives a positive result in each case.

3. *Topic:* Linear equations

Objective: Use the calculator to check the solution to a linear equation.

Example: Find the solution to each of the following linear equations, and then check your answer by substituting it back into the original equation using your calculator.
(a) $2.5t - 1.5 = 6$
(b) $5m - 3m + m = 10.5$

Solution: The solutions are: (a) $t = 3$ and (b) $m = 3.5$. The appropriate keystroke sequences for checking these solutions are:

$2.5t - 1.5:$ $\boxed{2.5} \ \boxed{\times} \ \boxed{t} \ \boxed{-} \ \boxed{1.5} \ \boxed{=}$
$5m - 3m + m$
    Hierarchy:
    $\boxed{5} \ \boxed{\times} \ \boxed{m} \ \boxed{-} \ \boxed{3} \ \boxed{\times} \ \boxed{m} \ \boxed{+} \ \boxed{m} \ \boxed{=}$
    Left-to-Right [write $5m - 3m + m$ as $(5 - 3 + 1)m$]:
    $\boxed{5} \ \boxed{-} \ \boxed{3} \ \boxed{+} \ \boxed{1} \ \boxed{\times} \ \boxed{m} \ \boxed{=}$

4. *Topic:* Linear inequalities

Objective: Use the calculator to verify the solution by substituting into the inequality several values from the supposed solution set and several values not in the supposed solution set.

Example: Solve the following inequalities. Then check your solutions by using your calculator to try several values of the supposed solution sets in their respective inequalities, and several values not in the solution sets in their respective inequalities.

(a) $3s - 7 > 5$

(b) $4 - 1.5s < -0.5$

Solution: The solutions to the two given inequalities are:

(a) $s > 4$

(b) $s > 3$

The appropriate keystroke sequences for checking values in the two inequalities are:

$3s - 7$: $\boxed{3}$ $\boxed{\times}$ $\boxed{s}$ $\boxed{-}$ $\boxed{7}$ $\boxed{=}$

$4 - 1.5s$

    Hierarchy:

    $\boxed{4}$ $\boxed{-}$ $\boxed{1.5}$ $\boxed{\times}$ $\boxed{s}$ $\boxed{=}$

    Left-to-Right:

    $\boxed{1.5}$ $\boxed{\times}$ $\boxed{s}$ $\boxed{+/-}$ $\boxed{+}$ $\boxed{4}$ $\boxed{=}$

5. *Topic:* Quadratic equations

Objective: Use the calculator to determine the number and the nature of the roots of a given quadratic equation by evaluating the discriminant $b^2 - 4ac$.

Special Key: $\boxed{x^2}$

Example: For each of the following quadratic equations, determine the number and the nature of the solutions by evaluating the discriminant with your calculator:

(a) $a^2 + 3a + 2 = 0$

(b) $3a^2 - 6a + 3 = 0$

(c) $4a^2 + 3a + 1 = 0$

Solution: The appropriate keystroke sequences for evaluating the discriminant are:

$b^2 - 4ac$

    Hierarchy:

    $\boxed{b}$ $\boxed{x^2}$ $\boxed{-}$ $\boxed{4}$ $\boxed{\times}$ $\boxed{a}$ $\boxed{\times}$ $\boxed{c}$ $\boxed{=}$

    Left-to-Right:

    $\boxed{4}$ $\boxed{\times}$ $\boxed{a}$ $\boxed{\times}$ $\boxed{c}$ $\boxed{+/-}$ $\boxed{+}$ $\boxed{b}$ $\boxed{x^2}$ $\boxed{=}$

The solutions are:

(a) Two real and distinct solutions since the discriminant is $+1$,

(b) One real solution (a double root) since the discriminant is 0,

(c) No real solutions since the discriminant is -7.

6. *Topic:* Quadratic equations

Objective: Use the calculator to check solutions to quadratic equations.

Special Key: $\boxed{x^2}$

Example: Solve the quadratic equation $a^2 + 3a + 2 = 0$, and then use your calculator to check the solution(s).

Solution: The solutions to this quadratic equation are $a = -1$ and $a = -2$. The appropriate keystroke sequences for checking these values are:

$$a^2 + 3a + 2$$

Hierarchy:

$\boxed{a}\ \boxed{x^2}\ \boxed{+}\ \boxed{3}\ \boxed{\times}\ \boxed{a}\ \boxed{+}\ \boxed{2}\ \boxed{=}$

Left-to-Right [write $a^2 + 3a + 2$ as $(a + 3)a + 2$]:

$\boxed{a}\ \boxed{+}\ \boxed{3}\ \boxed{\times}\ \boxed{a}\ \boxed{+}\ \boxed{2}\ \boxed{=}$

Both solutions check when substituted using these sequences on the calculator.

7. *Topic:* Linear equation $y = mx + b$

Objective: Use the calculator to illustrate to the class that m represents the slope of the corresponding line.

Procedure: Have the students complete the following table according to the accompanying directions, and then use the completed table to answer the questions that follow.

Select any real value for b in the following table, and then use your calculator to fill in the table. When the table is complete, use the second, third, fourth, and fifth columns to sketch the graphs of $y = mx + b$ for $m = 1, 2, 5,$ and -2 respectively. Then answer the questions that follow.

(1) x	(2) $x + b$	(3) $2x + b$	(4) $5x + b$	(5) $-2x + b$
-2				
-1				
0				
1				
2				

Question 1: Are all the graphs linear?

Question 2: Do all the graphs cross the y-axis at the same point (that is, the same height)?

Question 3: In what one, specific way do all four of these graphs differ? Based on these graphs, what characteristic of the graph of the linear equation $y = mx + b$ do you think the number m represents?

8. *Topic:* Linear equation $y = mx + b$

Objective: Use the calculator to illustrate to the class that b represents the y-intercept of the corresponding line.

Procedure: Have the students complete the table according to the accompanying directions, and then use the completed table to answer the questions that follow.

Select any real value for *m* in the following table, and then use your calculator to fill in the table. When the table is complete, use the second, third, fourth, fifth, and sixth columns to sketch the graphs of $y = mx + b$ for $b = -2, -1, 0, 2$, and 5.5 respectively. Then answer the questions that follow.

(1) *x*	(2) *mx* − 2	(3) *mx* − 1	(4) *mx*	(5) *mx* + 2	(6) *mx* + 5.5
− 2					
− 1					
0					
1					
2					

Question 1: Are all the graphs linear?

Question 2: Do all the graphs have the same slope (that is, do they all rise at the same rate in the same direction)?

Question 3: In what one, specific way do all five of these graphs differ? Based on these graphs, what characteristic of the graph of the linear equation $y = mx + b$ do you think the number *b* represents?

9. *Topic:* Properties of exponents

Objective: Use the calculator to illustrate the properties

$$x^a \, b \, x^b = x^{a+b} \quad and \quad x^{a^b} = x^{ab}$$

where *x* is a signed number and *a* and *b* are positive integers.

Special Key: $\boxed{x^y}$

Procedure: Have the students in the class fill in the two tables according to the accompanying directions, and then use the completed tables to answer the questions that follow.

Select any positive integer values of *a* and *b* for the second and third columns of the following tables. Then use your calculator and the $\boxed{x^y}$ key to complete the table *one row of the table at a time*, and answer the questions that follow.

(1) *x*	(2) *a*	(3) *b*	(4) *a* + *b*	(5) x^a	(6) x^b	(7) $x^a \, b \, x^b$	(8) x^{a+b}
1							
2							
3.5							
4.2							
− 2							

(1) x	(2) a	(3) b	(4) $a\,b\,b$	(5) x^a	(6) $(x^a)^b$	(7) $x^{a\,\cdot\,b}$
1						
2						
3.5						
4.2						
−2						

Question 1: Are the values in the last two columns of the first table the same for all the given values of x?

Question 2: Are the values in the last two columns of the second table the same for all the given values of x?

Question 3: Based on your answers to questions 1 and 2, fill in the missing word in each of the following two rules for powers, respectively.

> *Rule 1:* When multiplying powers having the same base, the result will have the same base, and the power of the result will be the _____ of the individual powers.
>
> *Rule 2:* When raising a power to a power, the result will have the same base as the original expression, and the power of the result will be the _____ of the individual powers.

10. *Topic:* Rules with radicals

Objective: Use the calculator to illustrate the radical properties:

$$\sqrt{ab} = \sqrt{a} \cdot \sqrt{b} \qquad \text{for } a \text{ and } b \text{ non-negative real numbers}$$

$$\sqrt{\frac{a}{b}} = \frac{\sqrt{a}}{\sqrt{b}} \qquad \text{for } a \text{ non-negative and } b \text{ positive}$$

Special Key: $\boxed{\sqrt{}}$

Procedure: Have the students complete the tables and then answer the questions that follow.

In the first table, column 1 gives several positive numbers and columns 2 and 3 show ways of factoring each number as a product. In the second table, column 1 gives positive numbers and columns 2 and 3 show

(1) ab	=	(2) a	×	(3) b	(4) $\sqrt{a}$	(5) $\sqrt{b}$	(6) $\sqrt{a} \times \sqrt{b}$	(7) $\sqrt{ab}$
30		15		2				
30		10		3				
30		5		6				
12		6		2				
12		3		4				
18		9		2				
18		6		3				

ways of writing each number as a quotient. Use the $\boxed{\sqrt{}}$ key on your calculator to fill in both tables one row at a time, and then answer the questions that follow.

(1)		(2)		(3)	(4)	(5)	(6)	(7)
$a \div b$	$=$	a	$\div$	b	$\sqrt{a}$	$\sqrt{b}$	$\sqrt{a} \div \sqrt{b}$	$\sqrt{a \div b}$
3		6		2				
5		15		3				
3.5		7		2				
5		6		1.2				

Question 1: Are the values in the last two columns of the first table the same for all values of a and b?

Question 2: Are the values in the last two columns of the second table the same for all values of a and b?

Question 3: Based on your answers to questions 1 and 2, fill in the missing word in each of the following two rules for radicals, respectively.

    Rule 1: When taking the square root of a product, you can get the same result by taking the square root of each factor and _____ the individual square roots.

    Rule 2: When taking the square root of a quotient, you can get the same result by taking the square root of the numerator and denominator and _____ the individual square roots.

    Note: The procedure employed in topic 10 can easily be modified to show the class any or all of the following additional results:

    (a) $\sqrt{a + b} \neq \sqrt{a} + \sqrt{b}$ for all $a \geqslant 0, b \geqslant 0$
    (b) $\sqrt{a - b} \neq \sqrt{a} - \sqrt{b}$ for all $a \geqslant 0, b \geqslant 0$ with $a - b \geqslant 0$
    (c) $\sqrt{a^2 + b^2} \neq a + b$ for all a and b
    (d) $(a + b)^2 \neq a^2 + b^2$ for all a and b

11. *Topic:* Formulas

Objective: Use the calculator to evaluate formulas for given values of the variable(s).

Example: The formulas for the volume V and surface area S of a rectangular solid are given in Figure 3–12. Use these formulas and your calculator to

$V = L \times W \times H$

$S = 2LW + 2HL + 2HW$

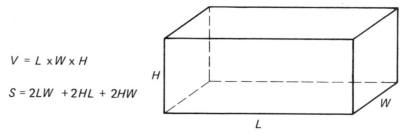

Figure 3-12

find V and S when

(a) $L = 3'$, $W = 2'$, $H = 4'$
(b) $L = 20''$, $W = 6.5''$, $H = 7.2''$

Solution: The appropriate keystroke sequences for evaluating V and S are:

$V = L \times W \times H$: $\boxed{L}$ $\boxed{\times}$ $\boxed{W}$ $\boxed{\times}$ $\boxed{H}$ $\boxed{=}$
$S = 2LW + 2HL + 2HW$

Hierarchy:
$\boxed{2}$ $\boxed{\times}$ $\boxed{L}$ $\boxed{\times}$ $\boxed{W}$ $\boxed{+}$ $\boxed{2}$ $\boxed{\times}$ $\boxed{H}$ $\boxed{\times}$ $\boxed{L}$ $\boxed{+}$ $\boxed{2}$ $\boxed{\times}$ $\boxed{H}$ $\boxed{\times}$ $\boxed{W}$ $\boxed{=}$

Left-to-Right:
$\boxed{2}$ $\boxed{\times}$ $\boxed{L}$ $\boxed{\times}$ $\boxed{W}$ $\boxed{\text{STO}}$ $\boxed{2}$ $\boxed{\times}$ $\boxed{H}$ $\boxed{\times}$ $\boxed{L}$ $\boxed{+}$ $\boxed{\text{RCL}}$ $\boxed{=}$ $\boxed{\text{STO}}$
$\boxed{2}$ $\boxed{\times}$ $\boxed{H}$ $\boxed{\times}$ $\boxed{W}$ $\boxed{+}$ $\boxed{\text{RCL}}$ $\boxed{=}$

Using these keystroke sequences we find: (a) $V = 24$ cubic feet and $S = 52$ square feet
(b) $V = 936$ cubic inches and $S = 641.6$ square inches

12. *Topic:* Formulas

Objective: Use the calculator to verify the answer obtained when a formula, given in terms of one variable, is solved in terms of a different variable.

Procedure: Use the calculator and a verification table to substitute corresponding values into both equations to verify that they are in fact equivalent formulas.

Example: Transform the formula $F = 1.8C + 32$ giving temperature in Fahrenheit units (F) as a function of temperature in Celsius units (C), so that C is expressed as a function of F. Then use your calculator and a verification table to verify the result.

Solution: Algebraic manipulation of the given equation gives:

$$C = \frac{F = 32}{1.8}$$

To verify this result we fill in the following table one row at a time and verify that the first and last columns are the same:

C	$F = 1.8C + 32$	$\dfrac{F - 32}{1.8}$
-40		
-20		
0		
20		
40		

↖ Are these columns the same? ↗

The appropriate keystroke sequences for this problem are:

$1.8C + 32$: $\boxed{1.8}$ $\boxed{\times}$ $\boxed{C}$ $\boxed{+}$ $\boxed{32}$ $\boxed{=}$

$\dfrac{F - 32}{1.8}$: $\boxed{F}$ $\boxed{-}$ $\boxed{32}$ $\boxed{=}$ $\boxed{\div}$ $\boxed{1.8}$ $\boxed{=}$

13. *Topic:* Pythagorean theorem

Objective: Use the Pythagorean theorem and the calculator to determine whether a triangle with given lengths of sides a, b, and c (with c the longest side) is a right triangle.

Procedure: We use the calculator to evaluate $c^2 - a^2 - b^2$. The triangle is a right triangle if and only if the result is zero.

Special Key: $\boxed{x^2}$.

Keystroke Sequence:

$c^2 - a^2 - b^2$: $\boxed{c}$ $\boxed{x^2}$ $\boxed{-}$ $\boxed{a}$ $\boxed{x^2}$ $\boxed{-}$ $\boxed{b}$ $\boxed{x^2}$ $\boxed{=}$

Example: For the triangles with the sides as given, use your calculator to determine which, if either, is a right triangle.
(a) 4, 7, 12
(b) 9, 12, 15

Solution: Using $c = 12$ in part a gives $c^2 - a^2 - b^2 = 79$ so the triangle in part a is *not* a right triangle. Using $c = 15$ in part b gives $c^2 - a^2 - b^2 = 0$, so the triangle in part b *is* a right triangle.

4

TRIGONOMETRY

On a popular television game show, one hundred people are asked certain questions, and the contestants must try to guess the most common responses. My guess is that, if these one hundred people were all math teachers, and if they were asked to name the mathematics topic for which the calculator would be the least helpful as a teaching aid, the most common response would be "trigonometry."

Why do I think so? At first glance the natural limitations of the calculator appear to be just the sort of limitations that would be counterproductive to what we try to teach in trigonometry. For example, take the teaching of the basic properties of the trigonometric functions. Since this topic involves thinking, understanding, but very little calculation, the calculator would not seem to be very helpful because its basic use is in calculation. Or take the teaching of trigonometric identities like $\sin^2 x + \cos^2 x = 1$. Since trigonometric identities involve exact equivalence between two expressions, and since the calculator must always somehow approximate decimals that exceed its finite capacity, you would think that the calculator would be not only useless, but perhaps even misleading in this case.

Well, if your believe such things, you are badly mistaken. The calculator can and should be used as an aid in teaching these, and many other, topics in trigonometry. Before we discuss how to do so, however, let's first take another look at the calculator itself.

Trigonometric function calculators

First of all, not every calculator has trigonometric function capability. To make sure that the calculator you are using does, simply look for keys labeled $\boxed{\text{SIN}}$, $\boxed{\text{COS}}$, and, if possible, $\boxed{\text{TAN}}$. Most trigonometric function calculators do not have special keys for the other three trigonometric functions secant, cosecant, and cotangent, but you can get along without these very nicely just by combining sine, cosine, and tangent with a reciprocal key $\boxed{1/x}$. In fact, if you have to, you can even get along without the tangent key since the functions sine and cosine are the really important ones for developing and doing basic trigonometry. While you may have to pay a few extra dollars to get a calculator with trigonometric capability, the slight extra cost will be well worth it for the long-run use that both you and your students will get from it.

Angular mode: degrees, radians, or gradients?

Three main units are used for angular measurement: degrees, radians, and gradients. The basic relationship among these three units is:

$$180 \text{ degrees} = (3.1415927\ldots) \text{ radians} = 200 \text{ gradients}$$

Any calculator with trigonometric function capability will be constructed to have one of these units as its normal mode of operation, so that, whenever you turn the calculator on, you are automatically in that mode. The most common normal modes are degree and radian.

Let's look at your calculator now to determine its normal mode of operation.

Your calculator may be designed to show you which mode it is in at any time by displaying DEG, RAD, or GRAD somewhere on the display. Even if the calculator does not display the mode it is in, however, you can still determine this at any time using the following method:

- Turn your calculator on and enter the number 30, then press the ⎡SIN⎤ key.
- If the display shows 0.5, then your calculator's normal mode is degrees since sin 30° = 0.5.
- Similarly, if the display shows −0.9880316, then your calculator's normal mode is radians.
- And if the display shows 0.4539905, then your calculator's normal mode is gradients.

Keep in mind that, once you know your calculator's normal mode, anytime you turn the calculator off and then on again you will find yourself in that mode. Most trigonometric calculators, however, will allow you to switch from their normal mode to either or both of the other modes and back again. To do so, they will have either individual keys such as ⎡DEG⎤, ⎡RAD⎤, and ⎡GRAD⎤, or one key for alternately switching to all the different modes, such as ⎡DRG⎤. If you must use a single-mode calculator, the degree mode is probably the most useful; but try to get a trigonometric calculator with at least the degree and radian modes if possible.

Now that we have some idea of what to look for in a trigonometric function calculator, let's look at some ways in which we can make use of such a calculator.

Discovery activities with the calculator

As a wonderful example of a function machine come to life, the calculator offers trigonometry teachers a splendid opportunity to let their students "discover" by themselves the basic properties and rules of the trigonometric functions, instead of simply being given these properties and rules. The easiest approach to such a discovery is to have the students use their calculators to develop their own sine, cosine, and tangent tables for use throughout the year. Just assign the following classroom or homework problem as soon as you have defined the trigonometric functions, using either the wrapping function $P(t)$ definitions or the right triangle definitions.

Problem: Use the ⎡SIN⎤, ⎡COS⎤, and ⎡TAN⎤ keys on your calculator to make a table of values for these three basic trigonometric functions. Do so in degree mode, and let the angles in your table range from 0° to 90° inclusive, using increments of 5° at a time.

You might then assign the following problem intended to let the students discover for themselves the basic properties of the sine function (or any other function you want them to investigate for themselves).

Problem: Use your calculator to extend the sine column of your table to include angles ranging from −360° to +360° inclusive using increments of 5° at a time. Use this expanded table to sketch a graph of the sine curve in this interval, and see if you notice any interesting properties of the function.

The properties we want the students to discover are as follows:

- The sine function has range between -1 and $+1$ inclusive,
- The sine function is periodic with period 360°,
- The sine function is odd.

Of course, if the students are having trouble discovering these properties, there's nothing wrong in helping them out with a few well placed questions or suggestions. For example, to focus attention on the range of the function, you might ask the class in general whether anyone has found a value of θ for which $\sin \theta$ is greater than 100. When it's clear that no one has, you can ask if anyone has found a value of θ for which $\sin \theta$ is greater than 10. You can then ask what *is* the largest value of $\sin \theta$ anyone has found, and the smallest value as well.

Similarly, to focus attention on the oddness of sine, ask the class to compare the values of $\sin 20°$ and $\sin (-20°)$, $\sin 52°$ and $\sin (-52°)$, and $\sin 273.5°$ and $\sin (-273.5°)$. Ask them to tell you if they notice anything interesting about these pairs of values.

Whenever one of these properties is discovered by the class using their calculators, a good idea is to follow up this discovery by verifying the property mathematically using the basic definition of the sine function. This follow-up shows the students that, while the calculator can be used to quickly and easily investigate a given expression or function at a *large* number of values of the variable, the only way to prove a trigonometric result true for *all* values of the variable is to do it mathematically. For example, if you have defined the sine function in terms of the wrapping function $P(t)$ as the ordinate of the corresponding point on the unit circle, then you could verify that the range of the function is between -1 and $+1$ inclusive by pointing out that these are the only heights that points on the unit circle can attain. The other properties can be verified in the same way.

This is a very good opportunity to point out the power of mathematical techniques and methods of proof to show, simply and incontrovertably, the truth of a statement or formula for an infinite number of cases in one step. The mathematical techniques developed over a period of centuries form a tool of immense and widespread use, and students should be made aware of them sometime during their mathematical education. This is a good starting point.

You can also assign problems in which the calculator must be used to investigate the properties of a function composed of sine, cosine, and tangent, such as:

Problem: Use your calculator and an appropriate keystroke sequence to find the domain, range, and evenness or oddness of the function:

$$f(\theta) = \frac{1}{\cos \theta - \sin \theta}$$

for θ between $-90°$ and $+90°$ inclusive.

The appropriate calculator keystroke sequence for this expression is:

$$\frac{1}{\cos\theta - \sin\theta}$$ $\boxed{\theta}$ $\boxed{\cos}$ $\boxed{-}$ $\boxed{\theta}$ $\boxed{\sin}$ $\boxed{=}$ $\boxed{1/x}$

Using this keystroke sequence the student can now develop a table of function values for this function and use them to sketch a graph of $f(\theta)$, as illustrated in Figure 4–1. The table of values and the corresponding graph in this figure make

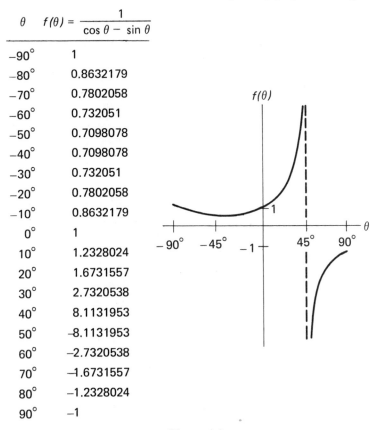

θ	$f(\theta) = \dfrac{1}{\cos\theta - \sin\theta}$
$-90°$	1
$-80°$	0.8632179
$-70°$	0.7802058
$-60°$	0.732051
$-50°$	0.7098078
$-40°$	0.7098078
$-30°$	0.732051
$-20°$	0.7802058
$-10°$	0.8632179
$0°$	1
$10°$	1.2328024
$20°$	1.6731557
$30°$	2.7320538
$40°$	8.1131953
$50°$	–8.1131953
$60°$	–2.7320538
$70°$	–1.6731557
$80°$	–1.2328024
$90°$	–1

Figure 4-1

it clear that this function is neither even nor odd. The interesting part of the function is between $40°$ and $50°$, where the values jump from a large positive value to a large negative value. This range from $40°$ to $50°$ should now be studied more closely by using the keystroke sequence to evaluate the function at several values within this interval of interest. This more detailed investigation will reveal that:

- the values of $f(\theta)$ become positive without bound as θ approaches $45°$ from below,
- the values of $f(\theta)$ decrease without bound as θ approaches $45°$ from above, and
- $f(\theta)$ is undefined at $\theta = 45°$.

The domain of the function in the given interval is therefore all values except 45°. Finally, from the graph and the table, the smallest positive value of the function on this domain occurs at $\theta = -45°$ and is approximately $f(-45°) = \sqrt{2}/2 = 0.70710678$; and the largest negative value of the function on this domain occurs at $\theta = 90°$ and is $f(90°) = -1$. So the range of the function for the given domain is:

$$\text{Range:} \quad \{f(\theta) \geq .70710678\} \cup \{f(\theta) \leq -1\}$$

Note: In this problem, the keystroke given for evaluating $f(\theta)$ was:

(4–1) $\boxed{\theta}$ $\boxed{\text{COS}}$ $\boxed{-}$ $\boxed{\theta}$ $\boxed{\text{SIN}}$ $\boxed{=}$ $\boxed{1/x}$

On most trigonometric function calculators, this keystroke sequence can be used and will work perfectly. The reason is that, on most calculators, pressing such special function keys as $\boxed{\text{SIN}}$, $\boxed{\text{COS}}$, $\boxed{\text{TAN}}$, $\boxed{x^2}$, or $\boxed{\sqrt{}}$ in the middle of a keystroke sequence simply initiates the indicated operation on the displayed value and does not disrupt the preceding operations. But on a few calculators, such as the Sharp Elsimate EL–502, when you press the trigonometric keys $\boxed{\text{SIN}}$, $\boxed{\text{COS}}$, or $\boxed{\text{TAN}}$ in the middle of a keystroke sequence, the preceding operations are lost, and the keystroke sequence cannot be completed. For example, in keystroke sequence (4–1), when the key $\boxed{\text{SIN}}$ is pressed, everything that came before it is lost, and you no longer have the first term cos θ or the operation of subtraction. Beware of calculators with this restriction since it will severely hamper your ability to do trigonometry on it. In fact, most of the keystroke sequences we will use in this chapter will not work on such a calculator. Luckily, very few calculators have this restriction. But, just to be sure yours is not one of them, see if your calculator will correctly evaluate keystroke sequence (4–1) for a simple angle like 30°.

An interesting side benefit of these calculator discovery problems is that they can be used to give a brief preview of material that will be covered more explicitly later in the year. For example, suppose you assign the problem:

> *Problem:* Use your calculator-generated table of the sine and cosine functions to sketch the graphs of the two functions between 0° and 360° inclusive on the same set of coordinate axes. Can you tell from the graphs what the product (sin θ) (cos θ) might look like? Or what its range or period might be? Take a guess, and then use your calculator with an appropriate keystroke sequence to graph this product and answer these questions.

If all you do is look at the two individual graphs you'll find guessing the shape, the range, or the period of the product very difficult. Yet using the keystroke sequence:

(sin θ) (cos θ): $\boxed{\theta}$ $\boxed{\text{SIN}}$ $\boxed{\times}$ $\boxed{\theta}$ $\boxed{\text{COS}}$ $\boxed{=}$

you can easily obtain the table of values and corresponding graph shown in Figure 4–2. This table and graph make it less difficult to see that the function is periodic with period 180° and that the range is between -0.5 and $+0.5$ inclusive. Students might also guess that this curve looks very much like a sine

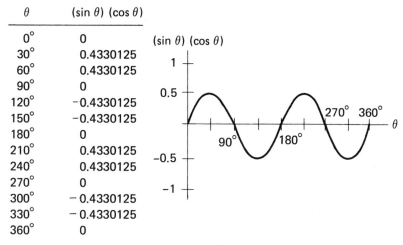

θ	$(\sin \theta)(\cos \theta)$
0°	0
30°	0.4330125
60°	0.4330125
90°	0
120°	−0.4330125
150°	−0.4330125
180°	0
210°	0.4330125
240°	0.4330125
270°	0
300°	−0.4330125
330°	−0.4330125
360°	0

Figure 4-2

curve. You can use this observation to point out to the class that it is in fact a sine curve and that this can be seen from a formula:

$$\sin 2\theta = 2 \sin \theta \cos \theta$$

or, equivalently,

$$\sin \theta \cos \theta = \frac{1}{2} \sin 2\theta$$

which they will be seeing and using again later in the year.

Additional examples

The following additional interesting trigonometric functions can be used as the basis of a classroom or homework calculator discovery activity. Provided with each function is a simple keystroke sequence for evaluating the function and some of the more important properties of the function (range of values, periodicity, and evenness or oddness).

1. *Function:* $y = \sin \theta + \cos \theta$
    Keystroke sequence: $\boxed{\theta}$ $\boxed{\text{SIN}}$ $\boxed{+}$ $\boxed{\theta}$ $\boxed{\text{COS}}$ $\boxed{=}$
    Range: $-\sqrt{2}$ to $+\sqrt{2}$, inclusive
    Periodicity: Period 360° or 2π radians
    Evenness or oddness: Neither even nor odd.

2. *Function:* $y = \sin \theta - \cos \theta$
    Keystroke sequence: $\boxed{\theta}$ $\boxed{\text{SIN}}$ $\boxed{-}$ $\boxed{\theta}$ $\boxed{\text{COS}}$ $\boxed{=}$
    Range: $-\sqrt{2}$ to $+\sqrt{2}$, inclusive
    Periodicity: Period 360° or 2π radians
    Evenness or oddness: Neither even nor odd.

3. *Function:* $y = \dfrac{\cos \theta}{\sin \theta}$ (This is simply the cotangent function.)

51

Keystroke sequence: θ | COS | $\div$ | θ | SIN | $=$
Range: $-\infty$ to $+\infty$
Periodicity: Period 180° or π radians
Evenness or oddness: Odd

4. *Function:* $y = \dfrac{\sin\theta}{\cos\theta}$ (This is just the tangent function.)
   Keystroke sequence: θ | SIN | $\div$ | θ | COS | $=$
   Range: $-\infty$ to $+\infty$
   Periodicity: Period 180° or π radians
   Evenness or oddness: Odd

5. *Function:* $y = \sin(\sin\theta)$ (This is the composite of sine with sine and is to be done in degree mode.)
   Keystroke sequence: θ | SIN | SIN |
   Range: $\sin(-1°)$, approximately -0.0174524, to $\sin(1°)$, approximately 0.0174524, inclusive
   Periodicity: Period 360°
   Evenness or oddness: Odd

6. *Function:* $y = \cos(\cos\theta)$ (This is the composite of cosine with cosine and is to be done in degree mode.)
   Keystroke sequence: θ | COS | COS |
   Range: $\cos(1°)$, approximately 0.9998477, to 1 inclusive
   Periodicity: Period 180°
   Evenness or oddness: Even

7. *Function:* $y = \sin(\cos\theta)$ (This is the composite of cosine with sine and is to be done in degree mode.)
   Keystroke sequence: θ | COS | SIN |
   Range: $\sin(-1°)$, approximately -0.0174524, to $\sin(1°)$, approximately 0.0174524, inclusive
   Periodicity: Period 360°
   Evenness or oddness: Even

8. *Function:* $y = \cos(\sin\theta)$ (This is the composite of sine with cosine and is to be done in degree mode.)
   Keystroke sequence: θ | SIN | COS |
   Range: $\cos(1°)$, approximately 0.9998477, to 1 inclusive
   Periodicity: Period 180°
   Evenness or oddness: Even

Conditional equations and trigonometric identities

Conditional trigonometric equations

There are two ways of using a calculator with the topic of conditional trigonometric equations. The first is to check solutions of such equations obtained algebraically and with the use of a trigonometric table. For example, suppose the class was given the folowing problem:

Problem: Solve the equation $\sin^2 \theta - 1.5 \sin \theta + 0.5 = 0$ for values of θ between $0°$ and $360°$ inclusive.

Solving this trigonometric equation algebraically by factoring the quadratic (possibly after multiplying through by 2 to obtain integer coefficients), we obtain $\sin \theta = 0.5$ or $\sin \theta = 1$. These values give the solutions $\theta = 30°, 90°$, and $150°$ within the specified domain. The calculator can now be used to check these values by using the appropriate keystroke sequences:

$$\sin^2 \theta - 1.5 \sin \theta + 0.5$$

Hierarchy:

| θ | SIN | x^2 | $-$ | 1.5 | $\times$ | θ | SIN | $+$ | .5 | $=$ |

Left-to-Right [write the expression as $(\sin \theta - 1.5)\sin \theta + 0.5$]:

| θ | SIN | $-$ | 1.5 | $\times$ | θ | SIN | $+$ | .5 | $=$ |

If no restriction is put on the domain of the function, there will usually be an infinite number of solutions, and the calculator obviously cannot be used to check them all. But it can be used to check enough of them to make us fairly confident that the answer is correct. For example, suppose the problem that had been given to the class was:

Problem: Solve the equation $\cos^2 \theta - 0.25 = 0$ for all values of θ.

Solving this equation algebraically by factoring (again, after possibly multiplying through by 4 to obtain integer coefficients), we find $\cos \theta = 0.5$ or $\cos \theta = -0.5$, and the corresponding solution set is: $\theta = 60° + k360°$; $120° + k360°$; $240° + k360°$; and $300° + k360°$, where k is an arbitrary integer. We now use our calculator with the keystroke sequence:

$\cos^2 \theta - 0.25$: | θ | COS | x^2 | $-$ | .25 | $=$ |

So we can very quickly check this solution set for two or three values of k and be fairly confident from this partial check that the solution set we found does indeed look correct.

A more profitable use of the calculator is in problems where the answer is not one of the "simple" angles $0°$, $30°$, $45°$, $60°$, or $90°$. In a problem of this type the calculator can be used to give the principal solution using the | ARC | or | INV | key instead of having to look up the answer in a trigonometric table and possibly being forced to interpolate. (For simplicity from this point on, we will use the | ARC | key in all our demonstration keystroke sequences. Yet, the | INV | key—if that's the key your calculator has—works exactly the same way.) This situation would occur, for example, if we alter the first problem of this section slightly to read:

Problem: Solve the equation

$$\sin^2 \theta - 2\sin \theta + 0.5 = 0$$

for values of θ between $0°$ and $360°$ inclusive.

Since this second-degree equation in sin θ cannot be factored easily, we are forced to solve it for sin θ using the quadratic formula to obtain the intermediate result:

$$\sin \theta = 1 \pm \frac{\sqrt{2}}{2}$$

To complete the solution of this problem using a trigonometric table, we would now have to express the two values of sin θ as decimals, look them up in the table, and possibly use interpolation. On the calculator, however, we can find the principal solutions using the keystroke sequences:

$$\theta = \text{arc } \sin(1 + \frac{\sqrt{2}}{2})$$

Hierarchy:

$\boxed{1}\ \boxed{+}\ \boxed{2}\ \boxed{\sqrt{\ }}\ \boxed{\div}\ \boxed{2}\ \boxed{=}\ \boxed{\text{ARC}}\ \boxed{\text{sin}}$

Left-to-Right:

$\boxed{2}\ \boxed{\sqrt{\ }}\ \boxed{\div}\ \boxed{2}\ \boxed{+}\ \boxed{1}\ \boxed{=}\ \boxed{\text{ARC}}\ \boxed{\text{SIN}}$

$$\theta = \text{arc } \sin(1 - \frac{\sqrt{2}}{2})$$

Hierarchy:

$\boxed{1}\ \boxed{-}\ \boxed{2}\ \boxed{\sqrt{\ }}\ \boxed{\div}\ \boxed{2}\ \boxed{=}\ \boxed{\text{ARC}}\ \boxed{\text{SIN}}$

Left-to-Right:

$\boxed{2}\ \boxed{\sqrt{\ }}\ \boxed{\div}\ \boxed{2}\ \boxed{+/-}\ \boxed{+}\ \boxed{1}\ \boxed{=}\ \boxed{\text{ARC}}\ \boxed{\text{SIN}}$

The first keystroke sequence will cause the calculator to display an error message since $1 + \frac{\sqrt{2}}{2}$ is greater than 1 and therefore does not have an arc sine. The second keystroke sequence gives the principal solution θ = 17.0312°, approximately, and from this we can find the other solution 180° − 17.0312° = 162.9688° approximately. These values can now be checked by direct calculator substitution into the original equation.

Trigonometric identities

Despite the limited display capacity of calculators and the rounded-off approximation of decimal values that this limitation entails, calculators will very often display the exact answer to a problem even when they use rounded-off numbers throughout. For this reason, teachers may use the calculator to illustrate and to verify trigonometric identities as long as they try out all identities beforehand to make sure the display shows what it should show. To illustrate this point, let's take the most commonly used first trigonometric identity, $\sin^2 \theta + \cos^2 = 1$. The calculator keystroke sequence for evaluating the left-hand expression in this identity is:

$\sin^2 \theta + \cos^2 \theta$: $\boxed{\theta}\ \boxed{\text{SIN}}\ \boxed{x^2}\ \boxed{+}\ \boxed{\theta}\ \boxed{\text{COS}}\ \boxed{x^2}\ \boxed{=}$

Virtually every calculator in which this keystroke sequence can be entered and used will display a result of exactly 1 when any value of θ is used with this keystroke sequence. You can therefore use this trigonometric identity to introduce the concept of an identity by asking the class to solve the following problem:

> *Problem:* Solve the equation $\sin^2 \theta + \cos^2 \theta = 1$ for θ between 0° and 360° inclusive by using your calculator and an appropriate keystroke sequence to zero in on the solution(s).

While this looks just like the problems the students were working on in the topic of conditional equations, they will get quite a shock upon discovering that every value of θ they use in the calculator keystroke sequence gives a solution. At this point you can explain what a trigonometric identity is and how it differs from a conditional equation. You may be fairly confident that the students will remember both the definition of an identity and this particular basic identity.

As you did for the properties of the trigonometric function, however, you should have the class follow up this calculator verification of the identity by a mathematical proof, to be sure that it holds for *all* values of θ and not just for those you have tried. Once again, this follow-up clearly demonstrates to the class that the calculator is to be used together *with* mathematical theory and techniques, and not *instead* of them. Just as a reminder, the proofs of this identity, using either the right triangle or unit circle definitions of sine and cosine, are as follows:

1. *Right triangle proof:* By definition, given right triangle ABC as in Figure 4–3,

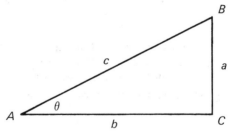

Figure 4-3

$$\sin \theta = \frac{a}{c} \quad \text{and} \quad \cos \theta = \frac{b}{c}$$

But, by the Pythagorean theorem, $a^2 + b^2 = c^2$. Therefore:

$$\sin^2 \theta + \cos^2 \theta = \left(\frac{a}{c}\right)^2 + \left(\frac{b}{c}\right)^2 = \frac{a^2}{c^2} + \frac{b^2}{c^2}$$

$$= \frac{a^2 + b^2}{c^2} = \frac{c^2}{c^2}$$

$$= 1$$

2. *Unit circle proof:* By definition, given the unit circle of Figure 4–4 with wrapping function $P(\theta) = (x, y)$,

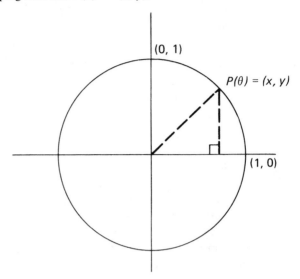

Figure 4-4

$$\sin \theta = y \quad \text{and} \quad \cos \theta = x$$

But since the point (x, y) lies on the unit circle, its coordinates must satisfy the condition $x^2 + y^2 = 1$. Therefore:

$$\sin^2 \theta + \cos^2 \theta = y^2 + x^2 = 1.$$

You can now emphasize the definition of a trigonometric identity by giving the class another identity to "verify" using their calculators. Then once again follow up this verification with a formal mathematical proof of the identity. A good second identity to use might be:

$$\tan^2 \theta + 1 \sec^2 \theta$$

If your calculator has a secant key, then the two expressions that make up this identity can be evaluated using the following calculator keystroke sequences:

$$\tan^2 \theta + 1: \quad \boxed{\theta} \ \boxed{\text{TAN}} \ \boxed{x^2} \ \boxed{+} \ \boxed{1} \ \boxed{=}$$
$$\sec^2 \theta: \quad \boxed{\theta} \ \boxed{\text{SEC}} \ \boxed{x^2}$$

You might prefer, however, to present this identity in the equivalent form:

$$\tan^2 \theta - \sec^2 \theta - 1$$

The advantage of this second form for calculator verification is that the students have to evaluate only the one expression on the left side of the identity (since the right-side expression is constant), instead of the two expressions in the first, more common form of the identity. The keystroke sequence for evaluating the left-hand expression is:

$\tan^2 \theta - \sec^2 \theta$: $\boxed{\theta}$ $\boxed{\text{TAN}}$ $\boxed{x^2}$ $\boxed{-}$ $\boxed{\theta}$ $\boxed{\text{SEC}}$ $\boxed{x^2}$ $\boxed{=}$

Have the students verify the trigonometric identity in this second form, and follow up by using the definitions of the tangent and secant functions to actually prove it mathematically. Then you can go ahead and put the identity into its more familiar form so that it will not look foreign to the students if and when they see it again in a textbook or on an exam.

Additional examples

The following several additional conditional trigonometric equations and several additional trigonometric identities, involving only the sine, cosine, and tangent functions, can be solved or verified by calculator. Provided with each equation are the special keys required, the solution, and the keystroke sequence for checking the solution value(s). Provided with each identity are the special keys required and a calculator keystroke sequence for verifying the identity. (Keep in mind that, before using any of these identities in your classroom, you should try them out on your own calculator for a variety of values of θ to make certain you consistently get the result you want.)

1. *Problem:* Solve the equation $\sin^2 \theta - 0.5 = 0$ for θ between $-90°$ and $+90°$ inclusive.

   Solution: With the quadratic formula, the solution is found to be $\theta = 45°$ and $\theta = -45°$.

   Special Keys: $\boxed{\text{SIN}}$ $\boxed{x^2}$ $\boxed{\text{ARC}}$

   Keystroke sequence for checking solutions:

   $$\sin^2 \theta - 0.5: \quad \boxed{\theta} \; \boxed{\text{SIN}} \; \boxed{x^2} \; \boxed{-} \; \boxed{.5} \; \boxed{=}$$

2. *Problem:* Solve the equation $\sin^2 \theta + \sin \theta - 1 = 0$ for θ between $0°$ and $360°$ inclusive.

   Solution: With the quadratic formula, the solution is found to be $\theta = 38.1727°$ and $\theta = 141.8273°$.

   Special Keys: $\boxed{\text{SIN}}$ $\boxed{x^2}$ $\boxed{\text{ARC}}$

   Keystroke sequence for checking solutions:

   $$\sin^2 \theta + \sin \theta - 1: \quad \boxed{\theta} \; \boxed{\text{SIN}} \; \boxed{x^2} \; \boxed{+} \; \boxed{\theta} \; \boxed{\text{SIN}} \; \boxed{-} \; \boxed{1} \; \boxed{=}$$

3. *Problem:* Verify the identity: $\dfrac{\cos \theta \tan \theta}{\sin \theta} = 1$ for all values of θ for which it is defined.

   Special Keys: $\boxed{\text{SIN}}$ $\boxed{\text{COS}}$ $\boxed{\text{TAN}}$

   Keystroke sequence:

   $$\frac{\cos \theta \tan \theta}{\sin \theta}: \quad \boxed{\theta} \; \boxed{\text{COS}} \; \boxed{\times} \; \boxed{\theta} \; \boxed{\text{TAN}} \; \boxed{\div} \; \boxed{\theta} \; \boxed{\text{SIN}} \; \boxed{=}$$

4. *Problem:* Verify the identity: $\sin \theta \cos \theta \tan \theta + \cos^2 \theta \equiv 1$ for all values of θ for which it is defined.

Special Keys: [SIN] [COS] [TAN] [x^2]

Keystroke sequence:

$\sin \theta \cos \theta \tan \theta + \cos^2 \theta$: [θ] [SIN] [×] [θ] [COS] [×] [θ] [TAN] [+] [θ] [COS] [x^2] [=]

5. *Problem:* Verify the identity: $\sin \theta \cos \theta \tan \theta \cos^2 \theta$ for all values of θ for which it is defined.

Special Keys: [SIN] [COS] [TAN] [x^2]

Keystroke sequences:

$\sin \theta \cos \theta$: [θ] [SIN] [×] [θ] [COS] [=]
$\tan \theta \cos^2 \theta$: [θ] [TAN] [×] [θ] [COS] [x^2] [=]

The calculator versus mathematical theory: a classroom contest

Many problems in trigonometry can be "solved" equally well either by using a calculator to investigate what is happening at specific points or values, or by using more general mathematical formulas and theorems. Since both approaches have certain advantages and disadvantages, it's only reasonable that students should be made aware of, and have practice in, both methods of attack. They should also have some idea of the relative merits of each approach as opposed to the other. One way of making them appreciate those differences is with the *classroom contest*.

In the classroom contest format you give the class a problem that is related to the topics you are covering and that you know beforehand can be investigated and "solved" either with or without a calculator. The class is then divided into two equal (or nearly equal) groups. The first group must try to solve the given problem using their calculators and with as few formulas or theorems as possible. The second group must try to solve the problem using the relevant formulas and theorems, but without using their calculators at all. (Make sure that, as you use this activity, you vary the two groups so that everyone gets a chance to be in both the calculator and the noncalculator groups.) As far as the class is concerned, the purpose of the contest is to see which group can solve the problem faster (or at all). The real purpose of these contests, however, is to give the students practice in both types of problem solving and to allow for a classroom discussion of their respective merits.

Following are two problems in trigonometry that I have used in this contest format in my own classes, along with a discussion of how my students have tried to solve them. Several additional problems that are suitable for classroom contests are given at the end of this section, and you should have no trouble making up many others of your own.

Contest problem 1

One of my students' favorite problems over the past few years has been:

> *Problem 1:* Given the function $y = (\sin \theta)(\cos\theta)$. Find the maximum value y can take on for θ between $0°$ and $360°$ inclusive, and find the value(s) of θ at which this maximum occurs.

The calculator group usually approaches this problem very straightforwardly: They use their trigonometric function calculators to construct a table of (θ, y) values for θ varying between $0°$ and $360°$, and then they employ this table of values to sketch the graph of the function. For example, suppose we decide to use the values $\theta = 0°, 10°, 20°, \ldots, 360°$ for our table. The keystroke sequence for evaluating the expression $(\sin \theta)(\cos \theta)$ is:

$$(\sin \theta)(\cos \theta): \quad \boxed{\theta} \; \boxed{\text{SIN}} \; \boxed{\times} \; \boxed{\theta} \; \boxed{\text{COS}} \; \boxed{=}$$

With a nine-digit display calculator, we would obtain the table of values and associated graph shown in Figure 4–5. The apparent symmetry of the table and graph make it fairly obvious that the maximum value for y occurs halfway between $\theta = 0°$ and $\theta = 90°$ (at $\theta = 45°$), and also halfway between $\theta = 180°$ and $\theta = 270°$ (at $\theta = 225°$). Using our calculator to evaluate the function at either of these values gives the answer to our problem:

$$\text{Maximum } y = 0.5 \text{ at both } \theta = 45° \text{ and } \theta = 225°$$

The simplest and most elegant noncalculator approach that I have seen employs only high school trigonometry and the double angle formula:

(4–2) $$\sin 2\theta = 2 \sin \theta \cos \theta$$

Dividing both sides of formula (4–2) by 2, we find that the given function can be rewritten in the more familiar form

$$y = (\sin \theta)(\cos \theta) = \frac{1}{2} \sin 2\theta$$

Since the sine function takes on a maximum value of 1, this function must have as its maximum value $(\frac{1}{2})(1) = \frac{1}{2} = 0.5$ Furthermore, since the ordinary sine function takes on its maximum value when its angle equals $90°$, this function will take on its maximum value when its angle, 2θ, equals either $90°$ or $360° + 90° = 450°$. (Since we want θ between $0°$ and $360°$, we must look at values of 2θ between $0°$ and $720°$.) But $2\theta = 90°$ or $450°$ reduces to $\theta = 45°$ or $225°$, so the answer to the problem is:

$$\text{Maximum } y = 0.5 \quad \text{at both } \theta = 45° \text{ and } \theta = 225°$$

This is the same answer as the calculator group found.

The first person to find the correct answer (verified by you, of course) wins the contest for his or her group. But don't stop everyone else from working on the problem just because one person has the right answer. They will all learn much more working on the problem themselves and *then* seeing and discussing the various calculator and noncalculator solutions than by just listening to someone

θ	$y = (\sin \theta)(\cos \theta)$	θ	$y = (\sin \theta)(\cos \theta)$
0°	0	190°	0.17101007
10°	0.17101007	200°	0.32139381
20°	0.32139381	210°	0.4330127
30°	0.4330127	220°	0.49240388
40°	0.49240388	230°	0.49240388
50°	0.49240388	240°	0.4330127
60°	0.4330127	250°	0.32139381
70°	0.32139381	260°	0.17101007
80°	0.17101007	270°	0
90°	0	280°	-0.17101007
100°	-0.17101007	290°	-0.32139381
110°	-0.32139381	300°	-0.4330127
120°	-0.4330127	310°	-0.49240388
130°	-0.49240388	320°	-0.49240388
140°	-0.49240388	330°	-0.4330127
150°	-0.4330127	340°	-0.32139381
160°	-0.32139381	350°	-0.17101007
170°	-0.17101007	360°	0
180°	0		

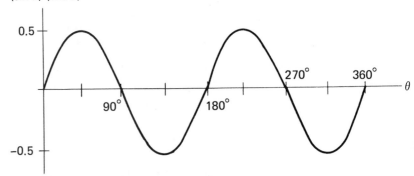

Figure 4-5

else tell them how to do it; so let everyone continue to work on it for a while. After a reasonable amount of time (I've found fifteen or twenty minutes to be about right), ask how many students in each group were able to solve the problem. Then have these students go to the board to show the rest of the class their solutions and to answer any questions about them. If you have the class time available, this is also a good time to discuss more generally the relative merits of the calculator and noncalculator approaches in this type of problem.

For example, if all you are concerned with is the solution to the problem, then the calculator approach is probably more suitable than the noncalculator approach. The calculator approach is simple and straightforward, and it involves very little insight or imagination, while the noncalculator approach requires a bit of ingenuity in selecting just the right formula for changing the given function into an equivalent but more workable form. (So you will usually find that many

60

more people, given a restricted amount of time, are able to solve the problem in the calculator group than in the noncalculator group; the calculator approach just doesn't require as much thinking as the noncalculator approach.)

On the other hand, the noncalculator approach usually provides some extra benefits that the calculator approach lacks. For example, students often wonder why they must learn the additive and double angle trigonometric formulas and what use these formulas could possibly have. Our noncalculator solution gives an immediate and tangible illustration of how these formulas might be used to simplify what at first glance appears to be a complicated expression; then we can see more clearly what it really represents. In addition, it's fascinating for the students to realize that the somewhat unusual function $y = (\sin \theta)(\cos \theta)$ is really nothing more than a horizontal and vertical shrinking of the ordinary sine function to one half its normal amplitude and one half its normal period. Sure, this is just what the double angle formula (4–2) says. But students hardly ever realize this implication of the formula when they just *see* it; they have to *work* with it to really understand what it's telling them. Using the calculator approach, students may certainly recognize the graph as something like a sine function, but they can't be certain of its nature. Besides, their attention is on where the graph reaches its maximum height, not on its shape. The noncalculator approach forces them to realize that it's just a sine curve.

These are just some of the things you might disucss in contrasting the calculator and noncalculator approaches. Sometimes a calculator solution is preferable, and other times a noncalculator solution is appropriate. This contest format gives the students practice in, and exposure to, both.

Contest problem 2

Here's another engaging problem that usually provokes a good discussion:

Problem: Express the function given below in a simpler form:

$$y = \text{arc } \cos(\sin \theta) \qquad 90° \leqslant \theta \leqslant 270°$$

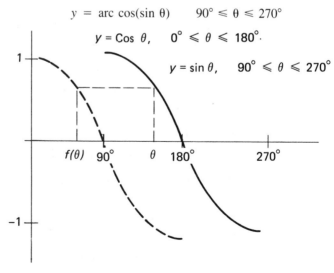

Figure 4-6

The noncalculator approach to this problem requires an understanding of the domain and range of the function $y = \text{arc cos } x$. The simplest way to see what is happening in this problem is to draw the graphs of the functions $y = \sin \theta$ and $y = \cos \theta$ on the same set of coordinate axes (Figure 4–6). Notice from Figure 4–6 that the curve $y = \sin \theta$ for $90° \leqslant \theta \leqslant 270°$ is only a 90° phase shift away from the *principal* cosine function $y = \text{Cos } \theta$, $0° \leqslant \theta \leqslant 180°$. So the simplified form of the given function is

$$y = \text{arc cos}(\sin \theta) = \theta - 90° \qquad 90° \leqslant \theta \leqslant 270°$$

The calculator approach in this problem is simply to evaluate the expression $y = \text{arc cos}(\sin \theta)$ for a variety of values of θ between 90° and 270° inclusive and then to observe that the result is always $y = \theta - 90°$. This result is immediately evident if the student graphs the relationship between θ and y, since this relationship will clearly be linear. The appropriate keystroke sequence for doing so (in degree mode) is:

$$\text{arc cos}(\sin \theta): \quad \boxed{\theta} \ \boxed{\text{SIN}} \ \boxed{\text{ARC}} \ \boxed{\text{COS}}$$

Additional examples

Following are several additional problems that can be solved both by calculator and noncalculator methods and that are therefore suitable as classroom (or homework) contest problems. Provided with each problem are: (1) a simple keystroke sequence for the calculator evaluation of any relevant expressions; (2) a hint as to one noncalculator way of solving the problem; and (3) the solution.

1. *Problem:* Find the maximum value of the function $y = \sin \theta + \cos \theta$ for $0° \leqslant \theta \leqslant 360°$, and where this maximum occurs.

   Relevant keystroke sequence:

   $$\sin \theta + \cos \theta: \quad \boxed{\theta} \ \boxed{\text{SIN}} \ \boxed{+} \ \boxed{\theta} \ \boxed{\text{COS}} \ \boxed{=}$$

   Hint for noncalculator solution: Use the trigonometric formula $\sin(A + B) = \sin A \cos B + \sin B \cos A$ with $A = \theta$ and $B = 45°$.

   Solution: The maximum value is $y = \sqrt{2}$ and occurs at $\theta = 45°$.

2. *Problem:* Find the maximum and minimum values of the function $y = \sin \theta - \cos \theta$ for $0° \leqslant \theta \leqslant 360°$, and where these extrema occur.

   Relevant keystroke sequence:

   $$\sin \theta - \cos \theta: \quad \boxed{\theta} \ \boxed{\text{SIN}} \ \boxed{-} \ \boxed{\theta} \ \boxed{\text{COS}} \ \boxed{=}$$

   Hint for noncalculator solution: Use the trigonometric formula $\sin(A - B) = \sin A \cos B - \sin B \cos A$ with $A = \theta$ and $B = 45°$.

   Solution: The maximum value is $y = \sqrt{2}$ and occurs at $\theta = 135°$; the minimum value is $y = -\sqrt{2}$ and occurs at $\theta = 315°$.

3. *Problem:* Express the following function in a simpler form:

   $$y = \text{arc sin}(\cos \theta) \qquad -180° \leqslant \theta \leqslant 0°$$

Relevant keystroke sequence:

arc sin(cos θ): [θ] [COS] [ARC] [SIN]

Hint for noncalculator solution: Draw the cosine curve and the *principal* sine curve superimposed on the same set of coordinate axes and notice that, for the domain of this problem, the two curves differ by a phase shift of 90°.

Solution: $y = θ + 90°$

4. *Problem:* Find all solutions of $\sin 2θ = \sin θ$, $0° \le θ < 360°$.

Relevant keystroke sequence:

sin 2θ − sin θ: [θ] [×] [2] [=] [SIN] [−] [θ] [SIN] [=]

Hint for noncalculator solution: Use the double angle formula $\sin 2θ = 2 \sin θ \cos θ$, and solve the resulting equation.

Solution: $θ = 0°, 60°, 180°$, and $300°$

5. *Problem:* Find all solutions of $\sin 2θ = \cos θ$, $0° \le θ < 360°$.

Relevant keystroke sequence:

sin 2θ − cos θ: [θ] [×] [2] [=] [SIN] [−] [θ] [COS] [=]

Hint for noncalculator solution: Use the double angle formula $\sin 2θ = 2 \sin θ \cos θ$, and solve the resulting equation.

Solution: $θ = 30°, 90°, 150°$, and $270°$.

6. *Problem:* Find all solutions of $\tan θ = \dfrac{\cos θ}{\sin θ}$, $0° \le θ < 360°$.

Relevant keystroke sequence:

$\dfrac{\cos θ}{\sin θ}$ − tan θ: [θ] [COS] [÷] [θ] [SIN] [−] [θ] [TAN] [=]

Hint for noncalculator solution: Write the equation as $\tan θ = 1/\tan θ$, multiply through by $\tan θ$, and solve.

Solution: $θ = 45°, 135°, 225°$, and $315°$.

Additional calculator activities

1. *Topic:* The circular functions and the wrapping function $P(t)$

Objective: To verify that

$$\cos t = x \qquad \sin t = y \quad \text{and} \quad \tan t = y/x$$

where t is an angle in radian measure and $P(t) = (x, y)$ is the wrapping function defined on the unit circle.

Special Keys: [RAD] [π] [SIN] [COS] [TAN]

Procedure: Have the students fill in the following table according to the accompanying directions, and then use the completed table to answer the questions that follow. Make sure that any radicals in the *x* and *y* columns of the table are converted to decimal form, since the results obtained from the calculator will be in decimal form.

Fill in the following table. The coordinates of *P(t)* are to be found by locating the point *P(t)* on the unit circle, and they should be expressed in decimal form. The values of cos *t*, sin *t*, and tan *t* are to be obtained from your calculator using the ⎡COS⎤, ⎡SIN⎤, and ⎡TAN⎤ keys, respectively.

t	*P(t)*	*x*	*y*	*y/x*	cos *t*	sin *t*	tan *t*
$\frac{1}{2}\pi$							
π							
$\frac{3}{4}\pi$							
$\frac{1}{3}\pi$							
$\frac{2}{3}\pi$							

Question 1: Is the cos *t* column of values the same as any other column in the table? What is cos *t* equal to, according to your first answer?
Question 2: Is the sin *t* column of values the same as any other column in the table? What is sin *t* equal to?
Question 3: Is the tan *t* column of values the same as any other column in the table? What is tan *t* equal to?

2. *Topic:* The relationship between radian and degree measure

Objective: Use the calculator to check answers when angles are converted from radian measure to degree measure, or from degree measure to radian measure.

Special Keys: ⎡RAD⎤ ⎡DEG⎤ ⎡ARC⎤ or ⎡INV⎤ ⎡SIN⎤

Procedure: Given an angle in either radian or degree measure, have the students convert this value to its equivalent angle in the other measure using the conversion formula:

$$\frac{d}{180} = \frac{t}{\pi}$$

(π can be approximated as 3.142.) Have the students then check this result on their calculators using the following keystroke sequences:

Radians to degrees: ⎡*t*⎤ ⎡SIN⎤ ⎡DEG⎤ ⎡ARC⎤ ⎡SIN⎤
Degrees to radians: ⎡*d*⎤ ⎡SIN⎤ ⎡RAD⎤ ⎡ARC⎤ ⎡SIN⎤

Note: The calculator keystroke sequences given here simply take the given angle, find the sine of the angle, switch to the other mode of angular measure, and use the Arc sine function to return to angular measure. Since the Arc sine function only has range [−90°, 90°] in degrees or [−π/2, π/2] in radians, only values from these intervals should be used in this activity.

3. *Topic:* Trigonometric functions of sums and differences

Objective: Use the calculator to demonstrate that the trigonometric functions sine, cosine, and tangent are *not* additive. That is, that in general:

$$\sin (A + B) \neq \sin A + \sin B$$
$$\sin (A - B) \neq \sin A - \sin B$$
$$\cos(A + B) \neq \cos A + \cos B$$
$$\cos(A - B) \neq \cos A - \cos B$$
$$\tan (A + B) \neq \tan A + \tan B$$
$$\tan (A - B) \neq \tan A - \tan B$$

Special Keys: [SIN] [COS] [TAN]

Procedure: (The procedure for the sine function will be described here. The cosine and tangent functions can be treated similarly, or the result for the sine function may be convincing enough for the class, and you can just say to them that the cosine and tangent functions are not additive either.) Have the students fill in the following tables according to the accompanying directions, and then have them use the completed tables to answer the questions that follow:

Fill in the following tables using the [SIN] key on your calculator. You may select any values of A and B that you want for the first two columns of each table. Then answer the questions following each table:

A	B	A + B	sin A	sin B	sin A + sin B	sin(A + B)

Question 1: Are the last two columns of this table the same?
Question 2: What does your answer to question 1 tell you about the expressions sin (A + B) and sin A + sin B? Are they in general equal to each other or not?

A	B	A − B	sin A	sin B	sin A − sin B	sin(A − B)

Question 3: Are the last two columns of this table the same?

Question 4: What does your answer to question 3 tell you about the expressions sin(A − B) and sin A − sin B? Are they in general equal to each other or not?

Note: Similar tables and questions can be used to demonstrate to the class that

$$\sin 2A \neq 2 \sin A \qquad \cos 2A \neq 2 \cos A \qquad \tan 2A \neq 2 \tan A$$

and

$$\sin \left(\tfrac{1}{2}A\right) \neq \tfrac{1}{2} \sin A \qquad \cos \left(\tfrac{1}{2}A\right) \neq \tfrac{1}{2} \cos A \qquad \tan \left(\tfrac{1}{2}A\right) \neq \tfrac{1}{2} \tan A$$

Furthermore, if you feel that the use of such tables for any of these purposes is too time-consuming or cumbersome for your class and your students, simply disregard the tables and instead have the class just do two or three examples with their calculators and point out that the results are always different. This alternative will not have the full impact of a complete and easy-to-read table, but it is much more informal and should have the same desired effect.

4. *Topic:* Trigonometric functions of sums and differences

Objective: Use the calculator to verify the correct formulas for the sums and differences of the trigonometric functions.

Special Keys: [SIN] [COS] [TAN]

Procedure: Have the students fill in the following table by selecting any values of A and B for the first two columns, and then using the [SIN], [COS], and [TAN] keys on their calculators for the remaining columns.

A	B	sin A	sin B	cos A	cos B	tan A	tan B

Once the table is complete, the students are to use the values in the table and the trigonometric function formulas for sums and differences of angles to find:

$$\sin (A + B) \qquad \sin (A - B)$$
$$\cos (A + B) \qquad \cos (A - B)$$
$$\tan (A + B) \qquad \tan (A - B)$$

for each pair of values of A and B in the table. Finally, they are to use the values of A + B and A − B, and the [SIN], [COS], and [TAN] keys on their calculators to check these results. (A similar procedure can be used to verify the correct formulas for double angles and half angles.)

5. *Topic:* The equation $y = A \sin(ax + b)$.

Objective: Use the calculator to demonstrate that $|A|$ represents the amplitude of the function $y = A \sin(ax + b)$, a represents a horizontal stretching or shrinking of the function, and b represents a phase shift. Let's illustrate the procedure for $|A|$ here, since the procedures for a and b are similar.

Special Keys: ⃞DEG ⃞SIN

Procedure: Have the students complete the table and answer the questions that follow.

Select any values of a and b you like (with a positive), and then use your calculator to fill in the table below. When the table is complete, use it to answer the questions that follow.

x	$ax + b$	$\sin(ax + b)$	$2 \sin(ax + b)$	$5 \sin(ax + b)$	$-3 \sin(ax + b)$
0°					
30°					
60°					
90°					
120°					
150°					
180°					
210°					
240°					
270°					
300°					
330°					
360°					

Question 1: Use columns 3, 4, 5, and 6 of this table to sketch the graphs of $y = A \sin(ax + b)$ for $A = 1, 2, 5$, and -3 respectively ($0° \leqslant x \leqslant 360°$). Are all four of the graphs identical? If not, in what specific property do they differ?

Question 2: Based on your answer to question 1, what property of the function $y = A \sin(ax + b)$ do you think $|A|$ represents?

As mentioned in the Objective of this topic, both the table and the accompanying questions can easily be modified to demonstrate the effects of changing the values of a and b in this equation as well. Or you could simply follow up this complete demonstration of what $|A|$ represents by simply telling the students what a and b represent and demonstrating with one or two examples.

6. *Topic:* Inverse trigonometric functions arc sine, arc cosine, and arc tangent

Objective: Use the calculator to help the student discover the domain and the range of the three basic inverse trigonometric functions.

Special Keys: [DEG] [ARC]   or   [INV] [SIN] [COS] [TAN]

Procedure: Have the students use their calculators in degree mode to complete the following table, and then answer the questions that follow:

x	arc sin x	arc cos x	arc tan x
25			
10			
5.3			
2.7			
1			
0.75			
0.50			
0.25			
0			
− 0.25			
− 0.50			
− 0.75			
− 1			
− 4			
− 15			

Question 1: For which values of x were you able to obtain a corresponding value of arc sin x?

Question 2: From the x and arc sin x columns of the table, what do you think are the domain and range of the function $y = $ arc sin x?

Question 3: For which values of x were you able to obtain a corresponding value of arc cos x?

Question 4: From the x and arc cos x columns of the table, what do you think are the domain and range of the function $y = $ arc cos x?

Question 5: For which values of x were you able to obtain a corresponding value of arc tan x?

Question 6: From the x and arc tan x columns of the table, what do you think are the domain and range of the function $y = $ arc tan x?

7. *Topic:* Law of sines and the law of cosines

Objective: Use the calculator in problems involving the law of sines and the law of cosines instead of using tables of trigonometric functions.

Special Keys: [ARC] or [INV] [SIN] [COS]

Example: Given the triangle illustrated in Figure 4–7, use your calculator

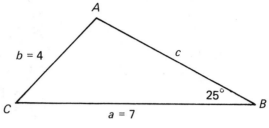

Figure 4-7

with the law of sines and/or the law of cosines to find the length of side *c*.

Solution: Using the law of sines with given sides *a* and *b* and their respective angles *A* and *B*, we have

$$\frac{\sin A}{7} = \frac{\sin 25°}{4}$$

or

$$\sin A = \frac{7 \sin 25°}{4}$$

This can be evaluated by calculator to give sin *A* = 0.7395815. Using this value with the keys [ARC] [SIN] gives the result *A* = 47.6958°, approximately. So, since we now know angles *A* and *B*:

$$C = 180° - A - B = 180° - 25° - 47.6958° =$$
$$107.3042° \quad \text{approximately}$$

Finally, using the law of cosines with the calculator to do the arithmetic, we obtain:

$$c^2 = a^2 + b^2 - 2ab \cos C$$
$$= 49 + 16 - 2(7)(4)\cos(107.3042°)$$
$$= 65 + 16.65692$$
$$= 81.65692$$

so

$$c = 9.0364218 \quad \text{approximately.}$$

8. *Topic:* Law of cosines

Objective: Use the calculator with the law of cosines to determine whether a triangle with given side lengths is a right triangle, an acute triangle, or an obtuse triangle.
Special Key: [x^2]

Procedure: Calculate $c^2 - a^2 - b^2$ where c is the longest of the three sides of the triangle. The triangle will be:

(a) right if this difference is zero;
(b) acute if this difference is negative; and
(c) obtuse if this difference is positive.

Example: For the triangles with side lengths as given below, determine whether the triangles are right, acute, or obtuse:

$$\text{(a) } a = 5, b = 12, c = 13$$
$$\text{(b) } a = 5, b = 6, c = 7$$

Solution: Using the keystroke sequence:

$$c^2 - a^2 - b^2: \quad \boxed{c}\ \boxed{x^2}\ \boxed{-}\ \boxed{a}\ \boxed{x^2}\ \boxed{-}\ \boxed{b}\ \boxed{x^2}\ \boxed{=}$$

we find that the triangle in part a is a right triangle since $c^2 - a^2 - b^2 = 0$; and the triangle in part b is an acute triangle since $c^2 - a^2 - b^2 = -12$.

9. *Topic:* Area formulas for the triangle and parallelogram

Objective: Use the calculator with the area formulas:

$$\text{Area of triangle} = \frac{1}{2}ab \sin C$$

and

$$\text{Area of parallelogram} = ab \sin C$$

Special Key: $\boxed{\text{SIN}}$

Procedure: Assign problems in which these area formulas must be used and then evaluate them with the calculator instead of using tables of the sine function.

5

INTERMEDIATE/
ADVANCED
ALGEBRA
(ALGEBRA TWO)

In Chapter 3 we looked at the ways in which the calculator can be used in elementary algebra (algebra one) to solve problems, to check answers, and to lead to discoveries of algebraic properties and rules. In this chapter we continue this exploration into more advanced algebraic topics and techniques.

Synthetic division and the evaluation of polynomials

Calculator evaluation of polynomials

The evaluation of a polynomial function for particular values of the variable occurs in many different topics of algebra, as well as in such succeeding subjects as precalculus and calculus. For example, it is used to plot points:

- for the sketching of polynomial functions;
- in approximating the roots of a polynomial equation geometrically;
- in the geometric solution of systems of equations involving one or more polynomial equations;
- in the approximation of plane areas using inscribed or circumscribed rectangles or using Simpson's rule; and
- in obtaining successively better and better approximations to the roots of polynomial equations using the Newton–Raphson iterative procedure.

The evaluation of polynomial functions, essentially an arithmetic task, would seem perfectly suited to calculator implementation. For example, suppose we wanted to evaluate the polynomial function:

$$P(a) = 2a^3 + 3a^2 + 4a + 5$$

for $a = 2$. It would not be very difficult, especially on a calculator with exponential key $\boxed{x^y}$, to evaluate this function and discover that $P(2) = 41$.

What is interesting and unexpected is that this polynomial function, and in fact any polynomial function of any degree, can be evaluated quite simply on calculators that have only the basic four operations of addition, subtraction, multiplication, and division and nothing more. This fact is especially important to be aware of since, as we pointed out in Chapter 2, the $\boxed{x^y}$ key on most calculators will work only with a positive base x. We do not want to always have to restrict our work with polynomial functions to positive values of the independent variable.

To put the given polynomial into a form that is suitable for calculator evaluation using only the basic four operation keys, simply follow these steps:

- *Step 1:* Start with the original polynomial:

$$2a^3 + 3a^2 + 4a + 5$$

- *Step 2:* Group those terms involving a, and factor a from them:

$$(2a^2 + 3a + 4)a + 5$$

- *Step 3:* Repeat this process for the expression in parentheses:

$$[(2a + 3)a + 4]a + 5$$

- *Step 4:* Finally, repeat the process within the innermost parentheses to obtain:

$$\{[(2)a + 3]a + 4\}a + 5$$

- *Step 5:* Stop when the innermost expression is a constant.

The resulting final form for $P(a)$ is the form that can be used for calculator evaluation. Starting with the innermost parentheses, the keystroke sequence would be:

$\{[(2)a + 3]a + 4\}a + 5$: $\boxed{2}\ \underbrace{\boxed{\times}\ \boxed{a}\ \boxed{+}\ \boxed{3}\ \boxed{=}}_{(*)}\ \underbrace{\boxed{\times}\ \boxed{a}\ \boxed{+}\ \boxed{4}\ \boxed{=}}_{(*)}$

$\underbrace{\boxed{\times}\ \boxed{a}\ \boxed{+}\ \boxed{5}\ \boxed{=}}_{(*)}$

The answer, 41, would now be in the calculator's display.

Notice the repetitive pattern in this keystroke sequence. Once the first (most innermost) constant value is entered (in this case the number 2), we simply keep repeating over and over, as many times as necessary.

$$\boxed{\times}\ \boxed{a}\ \boxed{+}\ \boxed{\text{CONSTANT}}\ \boxed{=}$$

This repetitive keystroke subsequence is indicated in the preceding keystroke sequence by an asterisk (*). What is important here is that *any* polynomial function, of *any* degree, can be put into this form and evaluated by calculator in this way for *any* value of the independent variable a.

As another example of this procedure, suppose the given polynomial is

$$P(a) = 5a^5 + 4a^4 - 3a^3 + 2a^2 - a + 6$$

$P(a)$ is put into calculator evaluation form in the following sequence of steps:

$$\begin{aligned}
P(a) &= 5a^5 + 4a^4 - 3a^3 + 2a^2 - a + 6 \\
&= (5a^4 + 4a^3 - 3a^2 + 2a - 1)a + 6 \\
&= [(5a^3 + 4a^2 - 3a + 2)a - 1]a + 6 \\
&= \{[(5a^2 + 4a - 3)a + 2]a - 1\}a + 6 \\
&= (\{[(5a + 4)a - 3]a + 2\}a - 1)a + 6 \\
&= [(\{[(5)a + 4]a - 3\}a + 2)a - 1]a + 6
\end{aligned}$$

Using this final form, with the innermost term just a constant (the number 5 in this example), the calculator keystroke sequence for evaluating $P(a)$ would be:

$[(\{[(5)a + 4]a - 3\}a + 2)a - 1]a + 6$: $\boxed{5}\ \underbrace{\boxed{\times}\ \boxed{a}\ \boxed{+}\ \boxed{4}\ \boxed{=}}_{(*)}$

$\underbrace{\boxed{\times}\ \boxed{a}\ \boxed{-}\ \boxed{3}\ \boxed{=}}_{(*)}\ \underbrace{\boxed{\times}\ \boxed{a}\ \boxed{+}\ \boxed{2}\ \boxed{=}}_{(*)}$

$\underbrace{\boxed{\times}\ \boxed{a}\ \boxed{-}\ \boxed{1}\ \boxed{=}}_{(*)}\ \underbrace{\boxed{\times}\ \boxed{a}\ \boxed{+}\ \boxed{6}\ \boxed{=}}_{(*)}$

Once again, the repetitive parts of this keystroke sequence are indicated by the asterisk (*).

A few points need to be made concerning this procedure. First, the process for putting a given polynomial into calculator evaluation form looks much harder than it actually is. All you have to do, once you know what the form looks like, is to pick out the coefficients of the polynomial one at a time from left to right, together with their corresponding signs, and put them into the appropriate positions. This step is illustrated for both the polynomials we have used:

$$P(a) = \quad 2a^3 \quad + 3a^2 + 4a \; + 5$$
$$= \{[(2)a \quad + 3]a + 4\}a + 5$$

$$P(a) = \quad 5a^5 + 4a^4 - 3a^3 + 2a^2 - 1a \; + 6$$
$$[(\{[(5)a \; + 4]a - 3\}a + 2)a - 1]a + 6$$

After just a few practice problems, this transformation procedure becomes almost automatic and quite fast.

The second point that needs to be made concerns missing terms in the polynomial $P(a)$ [that is, terms having coefficient zero that are ordinarily left out of the written form of $P(a)$]. Missing terms in $P(a)$ should be inserted with a coefficient of zero before transforming the polynomial into its calculator evaluation form. For example, suppose we are given the polynomial function:

$$P(a) = 3a^3 - 5a + 1$$

We would first insert the missing "a^2" term and write the polynomial as:

$$P(a) = 3a^3 + 0a^2 - 5a + 1$$

We can now put $P(a)$ into proper calculator evaluation form as shown below:

$$P(a) = \quad 3a^3 \quad + 0a^2 - 5a + 1$$
$$= \{[(3)a \quad + 0]a - 5\}a + 1$$

Finally, the last point to be mentioned is that even this fairly simple calculator evaluation procedure becomes a bit cumbersome and tedious when the value of a to be used is either a long decimal value, a negative value, or both—because it has to be entered each time it is needed in the subsequence (*). To avoid this repetition, simply begin the evaluation keystroke sequence by entering the value of a to be used into the calculator's memory and recalling it from memory into the display whenever it is needed. To do so, use your:

- memory key (which I will denote by $\boxed{\text{STO}}$, but which may be called by other names such as $\boxed{\text{M+}}$ or $\boxed{\text{Min}}$ in other calculators), and
- your memory recall key (which I will denote by $\boxed{\text{RCL}}$, but which may be called by other names such as $\boxed{\text{MR}}$ or $\boxed{\text{RM}}$ in other calculators. For example, to evaluate the polynomial $P(a) = 2a^3 + 3a^2 + 4a + 5$ for $a = -2.0476$, follow this procedure:

$$\{[(2)a + 3]a + 4\}a + 5: \quad \boxed{2.0476} \; \boxed{+/-} \; \boxed{\text{STO}} \; \boxed{2}$$

$$\underbrace{\boxed{\times} \; \boxed{\text{RCL}} \; \boxed{+} \; \boxed{3} \; \boxed{=}}_{(*)} \underbrace{\boxed{\times} \; \boxed{\text{RCL}} \; \boxed{+} \; \boxed{4} \; \boxed{=}}_{(*)} \underbrace{\boxed{\times} \; \boxed{\text{RCL}} \; \boxed{+} \; \boxed{5} \; \boxed{=}}_{(*)}$$

The answer, -7.7822075, would now be seen in the calculator's display. Notice that in this form of the keystroke sequence the cumbersome value $a = -2.0476$ had to be entered by hand only once, at the very beginning when it was put into memory using the $\boxed{\text{STO}}$ key. This procedure is very helpful whenever the value of a is either a long decimal value, a negative value, or both. Encourage your students to do it this way as early as possible.

Calculator synthetic division

As a side benefit of this very same procedure, it can be used to perform synthetic division. That is, it can be used to give the coefficients of the quotient polynomial $Q(a)$, and the value of the remainder R, when the polynomial $P(a)$ is divided by a linear factor $(a - a_1)$. To see how this is done, suppose we want to perform the division:

$$\frac{P(a)}{a - a_1} = \frac{8a^4 + 4a^3 - 28a^2 + 12a - 9}{a - 3}$$

Putting the numerator polynomial $P(a)$ into calculator evaluation form, we obtain:

$$P(a) = (\{[(8)a + 4]a - 28\}a + 12)a - 9$$

with the corresponding keystroke sequence:

$(\{[(8)a + 4]a - 28\}a + 12)a - 9$: $\boxed{8}$ $\boxed{\times}$ $\boxed{a}$ $\boxed{+}$ $\boxed{4}$ $\boxed{=}$
$\boxed{\times}$ $\boxed{a}$ $\boxed{-}$ $\boxed{28}$ $\boxed{=}$ $\boxed{\times}$ $\boxed{a}$ $\boxed{+}$ $\boxed{12}$ $\boxed{=}$ $\boxed{\times}$ $\boxed{a}$ $\boxed{-}$ $\boxed{9}$ $\boxed{=}$

Using this keystroke sequence to evaluate $P(a)$ at $a = a_1 = 3$:

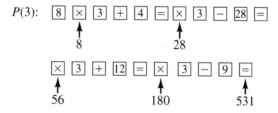

The numbers that appear in the display each time you press the multiplication key $\boxed{\times}$ in this keystroke sequence (indicated as 8, 28, 56, and 180) are just the coefficients of the quotient polynomial $Q(a)$. The final result that appears in the display when you press the $\boxed{=}$ key at the end of the keystroke sequence (indicated as 531) is just the remainder R. So we now know that:

$$\frac{8a^4 + 4a^3 - 28a^2 + 12a - 9}{a - 3} = 8a^3 + 28a^2 + 56a + 180$$
$$\text{with a remainder of 531}$$

This result can also be given in the more familiar form

$$8a^4 + 4a^3 - 28a^2 + 12a - 9 = (8a^3 + 28a^2 + 56a + 180)(a - 3) + 531$$

For practice, let's divide this same polynomial by $(a - 1.5)$:

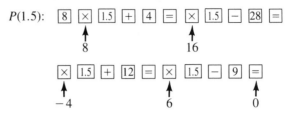

$$P(1.5): \boxed{8} \boxed{\times} \boxed{1.5} \boxed{+} \boxed{4} \boxed{=} \boxed{\times} \boxed{1.5} \boxed{-} \boxed{28} \boxed{=}$$

The values that appear in the display when we press the multiplication key $\boxed{\times}$ are 8, 16, -4, and 6. So the quotient polynomial is $Q(a) = 8a^3 + 16a^2 - 4a + 6$. The value that appears in the display when we press the $\boxed{=}$ key at the end of the keystroke sequence is 0. So the remainder is $R = 0$. Altogether, this gives us the result:

$$\frac{8a^4 + 4a^3 - 28a^2 + 12a - 9}{a - 1.5} = 8a^3 + 16a^2 - 4a + 6$$

or equivalently:

$$8a^4 + 4a^3 - 28a^2 + 12a - 9 = (8a^3 + 16a^2 - 4a + 6)(a - 1.5)$$

Since the remainder term is zero in this division, we know that $a = 1.5$ is a root of $P(a)$, and the result of the division has given us a partial factorization of $P(a)$ with $(a - 1.5)$ as one of the factors. In general, whenever we have a root a_i of a polynomial $P(a)$, this calculator division procedure can be used to obtain a partial factorization of $P(a)$. We can then use the same procedure to locate a root of $Q(a)$ and factor $Q(a)$, which gives at the same time a further factorization of $P(a)$. Assuming all the roots of $P(a)$ are real, this process can be continued one root at a time until a complete factorization of $P(a)$ is obtained.

Additional examples

The following additional polynomial evaluation and synthetic division problems can be performed on a calculator using the procedures described in this section. Provided with each problem is the calculator evaluation form of the polynomial, as well as the solution to the problem. Notice that in problems involving the evaluation of a polynomial at a value that is either a long decimal, negative, or both, the keystroke sequence given makes use of the memory keys $\boxed{\text{STO}}$ and $\boxed{\text{RCL}}$ to avoid having to enter the value of the variable several times by hand.

1. *Problem:* Evaluate $P(a) = 3a^2 - 2a + 4$ for $a = 5$

Calculator evaluation form of $P(a)$: $[(3)a - 2]a + 4$

Keystroke sequence: $\boxed{3} \boxed{\times} \boxed{a} \boxed{-} \boxed{2} \boxed{=} \boxed{\times} \boxed{a} \boxed{+} \boxed{4} \boxed{=}$

Solution: $P(5) = 69$

2. *Problem:* Evaluate $P(a) = 2a^4 + 4a^3 - 2a - 2$ for $a = 1.875$

Calculator evaluation form of $P(a)$: Adding the missing term $0a^2$ into $P(a)$, we find:

$$(\{[(2)a + 4]a + 0\}a - 2)a - 2$$

Keystroke sequence: Using the memory keys since a is a long decimal:

$\boxed{a}\ \boxed{\text{STO}}\ \boxed{2}\ \boxed{\times}\ \boxed{\text{RCL}}\ \boxed{+}\ \boxed{4}\ \boxed{=}\ \boxed{\times}\ \boxed{\text{RCL}}\ \boxed{+}\ \boxed{0}\ \boxed{=}$
$\boxed{\times}\ \boxed{\text{RCL}}\ \boxed{-}\ \boxed{2}\ \boxed{=}\ \boxed{\times}\ \boxed{\text{RCL}}\ \boxed{-}\ \boxed{2}\ \boxed{=}$

Solution: $P(1.875) = 45.336425$

3. *Problem:* Evaluate $P(a) = a^3 + a^2 + a + 1$ for $a = 2$

Calculator evaluation form of $P(a)$: $\{[(1)a + 1]a + 1\}a + 1$

Keystroke sequence: $\boxed{1}\ \boxed{\times}\ \boxed{a}\ \boxed{+}\ \boxed{1}\ \boxed{=}\ \boxed{\times}\ \boxed{a}\ \boxed{+}$
$\boxed{1}\ \boxed{=}\ \boxed{\times}\ \boxed{a}\ \boxed{+}\ \boxed{1}\ \boxed{=}$

Solution: $P(2) = 15$

4. *Problem:* Find the quotient $Q(a)$ and the remainder R when $P(a) = 3a^3 - 2a^2 + a - 1$ is divided by $(a - 2)$.

Calculator evaluation form of $P(a)$: $\{[(3)a - 2]a + 1\}a - 1$

Keystroke sequence: $\boxed{3}\ \boxed{\times}\ \boxed{a}\ \boxed{-}\ \boxed{2}\ \boxed{=}\ \boxed{\times}\ \boxed{a}\ \boxed{+}\ \boxed{1}\ \boxed{=}$
$\boxed{\times}\ \boxed{a}\ \boxed{-}\ \boxed{1}\ \boxed{=}$

Solution: $Q(a) = 3a^2 + 4a + 9 \qquad R = 17$

5. *Problem:* Find the quotient $Q(a)$ and the remainder R when $P(a) = 2a^4 + a^2 - 4$ is divided by $(a - 4.5)$.

Calculator evaluation form of $P(a)$: Adding the missing terms $0a^3$ and $0a$ into $P(a)$, we find:

$$(\{[(2)a + 0]a + 1\}a + 0)a - 4$$

Keystroke sequence: $\boxed{2}\ \boxed{\times}\ \boxed{a}\ \boxed{+}\ \boxed{0}\ \boxed{=}\ \boxed{\times}\ \boxed{a}\ \boxed{+}\ \boxed{1}\ \boxed{=}\ \boxed{\times}\ \boxed{a}\ \boxed{+}$
$\boxed{0}\ \boxed{=}\ \boxed{\times}\ \boxed{a}\ \boxed{-}\ \boxed{4}\ \boxed{=}$

Solution: $Q(a) = 2a^3 + 9a^2 + 41.5a + 186.75 \qquad R = 836.375$

6. *Problem:* Given that $a = 3$ is a root of the polynomial $P(a) = a^3 - 2a^2 - 2a - 3$, factor $P(a)$ into a product with $(a - 3)$ as one of the factors.

Calculator evaluation form of $P(a)$: $\{[(1)a - 2]a - 2\}a - 3$

Keystroke sequence: $\boxed{1}\ \boxed{\times}\ \boxed{a}\ \boxed{-}\ \boxed{2}\ \boxed{=}\ \boxed{\times}\ \boxed{a}\ \boxed{-}\ \boxed{2}\ \boxed{=}$
$\boxed{\times}\ \boxed{a}\ \boxed{-}\ \boxed{3}\ \boxed{=}$

Solution: $Q(a) = a^2 + a + 1$ and $R = 0$ so $a^3 - 2a^2 - 2a - 3 = (a^2 + a + 1)(a - 3)$.

Work problems
and filling and emptying problems

Work problems

In the basic type of work problem that we want to consider here, each of two or more people is known to be able to complete a certain job in a specified amount of time (not necessarily the same amount of time for each person). We are asked to determine the amount of time it would require for all the people working together to do the job. For example:

> *Problem 1:* Jim and Alice have been working on a joint term paper, and the paper is now ready to be typed. If Jim can type the entire term paper himself in 45 minutes, and Alice can type the entire term paper herself in 90 minutes, how many minutes will it take the two of them working together to type the term paper? (Assume, of course, that they will each type different parts of the term paper.)

The standard way to solve a problem of this type is to change the given information—how many minutes it takes each person alone to do the entire job—into the equivalent but more useful information of how much of the job each person can do in one minute working alone. This equivalent is just the reciprocal of the given information. In this problem, we would have:

> Since Jim can do the entire job in 45 minutes, he can do 1/45 of the job in each minute; and since Alice can do the entire job in 90 minutes, she can do 1/90 of the job in each minute. Working together, Jim and Alice can do $(1/45) + (1/90) = 3/90 = 1/30$ of the job in each minute. So it should take them 30 minutes working together to do the entire job.

Essentially, we are solving the equation:

$$(5\text{–}1) \qquad\qquad \frac{1}{45} + \frac{1}{90} = \frac{1}{t}$$

for the unknown t.

This type of problem is perfect for a calculator with a reciprocal key $\boxed{1/x}$. On such a calculator, we can go through an equation like (5–1) from left to right, just as if it contained only additions, subtractions, multiplications, and divisions, emerging with the value of t without ever having to write anything down on paper. Notice that if a and b are given nonzero values and t is the unknown, then we can find t from the equation:

$$\frac{1}{a} + \frac{1}{b} = \frac{1}{t}$$

with the keystroke sequence

$$(5\text{–}2) \qquad\qquad \boxed{a}\ \boxed{1/x}\ \boxed{+}\ \boxed{b}\ \boxed{1/x}\ \boxed{=}\ \boxed{1/x}$$

At the end of this keystroke sequence the value of t would be in the calculator's display. For example, using keystroke sequence (5–2) with $a = 45$ and $b = 90$ to solve equation (5–1), we would have

$$\boxed{45}\ \boxed{1/x}\ \boxed{+}\ \boxed{90}\ \boxed{1/x}\ \boxed{=}\ \boxed{1/x}$$

and obtain the answer 30 for *t* in the display.

There really isn't even any need to write down equation (5–1). As long as the given problem is recognizably of this type, simply use keystroke sequence (5–2) with the individual work times given in the problem. To illustrate, let's look at another work problem of this type:

> *Problem 2:* Before Jim and Alice begin typing their term paper, they are joined by Jim's mother, Mrs. Smith. If Mrs. Smith can type the entire term paper by herself in 60 minutes, how long will it take all three of them working together to type the paper?

The three individual times for completing the job are now 45 minutes (Jim), 90 minutes (Alice), and 60 minutes (Mrs. Smith). So the amount of time *t* it will take them to do the job together is:

which gives a result of 20 minutes. This is just the calculator solution of the implicit reciprocal equation

$$\frac{1}{45} + \frac{1}{90} + \frac{1}{60} = \frac{1}{t}$$

As you can see from problem 2, this calculator evaluation procedure works equally well when more than two people are involved, as long as we are given the individual times for each of them. The procedure can also be used to find the individual time for one person when the total time and all the other individual times are given. This method can be illustrated:

> *Problem 3:* Ms. Bennett is a seventh-grade math teacher. At the beginning of her first class each day two of her best students, Fred and Debbie, have to erase all the writing on the board from the previous day's work. Debbie can erase the entire board by herself in 3 minutes. Together, Fred and Debbie can erase the entire board in 2 minutes. How long does it take Fred to do the entire job by himself?

Instead of the individual times, we are given the combined time. We must "take away" from this time the one individual time of Debbie to get the unknown individual time of Fred as a remainder. If *t* is the unknown amount of time it takes Fred to do the job by himself, then the equation we need to solve for *t* is:

$$\frac{1}{2} - \frac{1}{3} = \frac{1}{t}$$

The calculator keystroke sequence for finding *t* from this equation is:

$$\boxed{2}\ \boxed{1/x}\ \boxed{-}\ \boxed{3}\ \boxed{1/x}\ \boxed{=}\ \boxed{1/x}$$

This gives a result of 6 minutes for Fred working alone to do the entire job. An extension of this problem would be:

> *Problem 4:* Al, Ben, and Carl work in their campus' bookstore, and one of their jobs is to unload the large boxes of textbooks that arrive each day. Al

can unload a box of books by himself in 7 minutes, Ben can unload a box of books by himself in 28 minutes, and together all three of them can unload a box of books in 4 minutes. How long does it take Carl to unload a box of books by himself?

Once again we solve this problem by using our calculator with its reciprocal key. To obtain the one unknown individual time for Carl, start with the combined time of 4 minutes, and "take away" from it the given individual times. The keystroke sequence for this is:

$$\boxed{4}\ \boxed{1/x}\ \boxed{-}\ \boxed{7}\ \boxed{1/x}\ \boxed{-}\ \boxed{28}\ \boxed{1/x}\ \boxed{=}\ \boxed{1/x}$$

and we obtain an answer of 14 minutes for Carl to unload a box of books by himself.

Filling and emptying problems

This same calculator reciprocal procedure can be used to solve a similar type of problem—that of filling and emptying. An example of such a problem is:

Problem 5: One "fill" pipe leads into a certain swimming pool, and one "empty" pipe leads out of it. If the "fill" pipe can fill the pool in 60 minutes when working alone, and the "empty" pipe can empty the pool in 120 minutes when working alone, how long will it take to fill the pool when both pipes are working together?

To do this problem the usual way, we would say that, if the "fill" pipe needs 60 minutes to fill the pool, then it must be able to fill 1/60 of the pool in 1 minute. Correspondingly, if the "empty" pipe needs 120 minutes to empty the pool, then it must empty 1/120 of the pool in 1 minute. The two pipes working together can fill $1/60 - 1/120 = 1/120$ of the pool in 1 minute. So the two pipes working together would take 120 minutes to do the job. This approach is equivalent to solving the equation for t:

$$\frac{1}{60} - \frac{1}{120} = \frac{1}{t}$$

By calculator, we simply use the reciprocal key to solve for t by starting with the fill pipe and "taking away" the emptying pipe:

$$\boxed{60}\ \boxed{1/x}\ \boxed{-}\ \boxed{120}\ \boxed{1/x}\ \boxed{=}\ \boxed{1/x}$$

The value shown in display, 120, is the solution for t.

This same procedure can be used for any number of "fill" pipes and any number of "empty" pipes, in any guise, as long as we start with all the fill pipes and then use the reciprocal key to "take away" all the empty pipes one at a time. It can also be done in the reverse fashion, as the following example shows:

Problem 6: It has been raining and, since there is a hole in the roof of the schoolhouse, a rather large puddle has formed on the floor. Joannie and Johnny are trying to mop up the puddle using sponges but, even as they are doing so, more rain is dropping into the puddle from the hole in the roof. If Joannie could clean up the puddle in 3 minutes (assuming no more water fell), and if Johnny could clean up the puddle in 4 minutes (assuming no more water fell), and if the leak would take 12 minutes to replace the entire puddle at its constant rate, how long will Joannie and Johnny take to sponge up the puddle with the leak leaking? If we think of emptying or refilling the puddle as the "job" that needs to be done, all we have to do is to combine the work of Joannie and Johnny, and then take away the work of the leak. The equation we are solving, with t as the unknown amount of time to entirely clean up the puddle, is:

$$\frac{1}{3} + \frac{1}{4} - \frac{1}{12} = \frac{1}{t}$$

The calculator sequence for finding t is:

$$\boxed{3}\ \boxed{1/x}\ \boxed{+}\ \boxed{4}\ \boxed{1/x}\ \boxed{-}\ \boxed{12}\ \boxed{1/x}\ \boxed{=}\ \boxed{1/x}$$

and t is found to be 2 minutes for the puddle to be cleaned up.

Additional examples

The following additional work and filling/emptying problems entail the use of this reciprocal procedure. Given with each problem are the equation that would be used to solve the problem by hand, the calculator keystroke sequence for solving the problem, and the solution. Until the students are extremely proficient in using the calculator procedure, they should be encouraged always to write down the algebraic equation first, and then transform the equation into its equivalent keystroke sequence.

1. *Problem:* John and Henry are painters. John can paint the Tompkins' house alone in 12 hours while Henry can paint the Tompkins' house alone in 36 hours. How long will it take them working together to paint the Tompkins' house?

    Equation: $\dfrac{1}{12} + \dfrac{1}{36} = \dfrac{1}{t}$

    Keystroke sequence: $\boxed{12}\ \boxed{1/x}\ \boxed{+}\ \boxed{36}\ \boxed{1/x}\ \boxed{=}\ \boxed{1/x}$

    Solution: $t = 9$ hours working together

2. *Problem:* Mr. and Mrs. Phillips have a certain amount of unpaid bills. At his present salary Mr. Phillips could pay off the bills by himself in 4 months. At her present salary Mrs. Phillips could pay them off by herself in 4 months. How long will it take the Phillips to pay off their bills if they pay them off together at their present salaries?

    Equation: $\dfrac{1}{4} + \dfrac{1}{4} = \dfrac{1}{t}$

    Keystroke sequence: $\boxed{4}\ \boxed{1/x}\ \boxed{+}\ \boxed{4}\ \boxed{1/x}\ \boxed{=}\ \boxed{1/x}$

    Solution: $t = 2$ months paying off the bills together.

3. *Problem:* Becky, Barbara, and Brenda have opened up a consulting firm and have had a certain number of business cards printed with all three names on

them. At the present rates of usage Becky could use up all the cards herself in 14 weeks, Barbara could use up all the cards herself in 28 weeks, and Brenda could use up all the cards herself in 56 weeks. How long before all the business cards are used up if all three of the partners are using them?

Equation: $\dfrac{1}{14} + \dfrac{1}{28} + \dfrac{1}{56} = \dfrac{1}{t}$

Keystroke sequence: [14] [1/x] [+] [28] [1/x] [+] [56] [1/x] [=] [1/x]

Solution: $t = 8$ weeks before the cards are used up if all three partners use them.

4. *Problem:* Ted is just opening a savings account, and he has set a certain savings goal. At the rate he is planning to deposit money, he could reach this goal in 21 weeks if he never withdrew anything. Yet he will have to withdraw money from his account at a rate that could empty a full account (an account at his goal), assuming no more money was deposited, in 28 weeks. How long will it take him to reach his goal if he both deposits and withdraws money at the rates described?

    Equation: $\dfrac{1}{21} - \dfrac{1}{28} = \dfrac{1}{t}$

    Keystroke sequence: [21] [1/x] [−] [28] [1/x] [=] [1/x]

    Solution: $t = 84$ weeks to reach his goal.

5. *Problem:* One of the major ski areas in Stowe, Vermont has a snow making machine that can create enough snow to cover a square mile in 7 hours. On a 45° day, however, the sun can melt a square mile of snow in 28 hours. If two of these machines are being used to make snow on a 45° day, how long will it take, considering both the snow being created and the snow being melted, to obtain a square mile of snow?

    Equation: $\dfrac{1}{7} + \dfrac{1}{7} - \dfrac{1}{28} = \dfrac{1}{t}$

    Keystroke sequence: [7] [1/x] [+] [7] [1/x] [−] [28] [1/x] [=] [1/x]

    Solution: $t = 4$ hours to make one square mile of snow.

Expressions with zero and negative integer exponents

One of the banes of a student's mathematical education is the learning of rules and definitions that appear to have no clear and understandable rationale behind them. For example, take the topic of exponential notation. When exponential notation is first introduced, the exponents are usually restricted to the set of positive integers, and a verbal definition is given to help the students understand what this notation means and how to evaluate algebraic expressions using it. We might, for example, write the expression 3^5 on the board and tell the class that this means we are to "take the base number 3 and multiply it by itself 5 times."

We then write:

$$3^5 = 3 \times 3 \times 3 \times 3 \times 3 = 243$$

We then emphasize to the class that, whenever they are given such an expression and want to evaluate it, they should repeat the verbal catch phrase to themselves as a reminder of what the notation means. In other words, if they are given the expression $(2.5)^3$ and told to evaluate it, they should say to themselves: "This means take the base number 2.5 and multiply it by itself 3 times to get: $(2.5)^3 = 2.5 \times 2.5 \times 2.5 = 15.625$."

The difficulty arises when we try to extend this exponential notation to the case in which the exponent can be either zero or a negative integer. Suddenly, the old verbal catch phrase no longer works. When this extension occurs, the teacher explains that it would be meaningless to say that 4^0 means "take the base number 4 and multiply it by itself 0 times." Equally meaningless would be saying that 3^{-5} means, "Take the base number 3 and multiply it by itself -5 times."

So a new definition or rule must be given for evaluating expressions with zero or negative integer exponents, and the students are asked to just accept this new rule because, "This is how it is defined." A better and more understandable way to present this extension of exponential notation is to let the students discover it themselves as a necessary definition to preserve numerical patterns. They can do so, with the aid of a calculator having an exponential key $\boxed{x^y}$ or $\boxed{y^x}$. After you have spent some time on the meaning of positive integer exponents, and when your students are proficient in evaluating them, put the following list on the board:

Exponents with Base 2
$$2^5 = ?$$
$$2^4 = ?$$
$$2^3 = ?$$
$$2^2 = ?$$
$$2^1 = ?$$

Have the students copy this list, evaluate each expression using only the multiplication key on their calculators, and fill in the correct answers. When the list is complete, ask the class if they see any numerical pattern in the list. With a little help from you (if necessary), they should be able to discover two patterns: (1) On the left-side of the equal sign, as you go down the list, you get from one exponent to the next by subtracting 1. (2) On the right-side of the equal sign, as you go down the list, you get from one value to the next by dividing by the base, 2. You can emphasize this pattern right on the list as follows:

Exponents with Base 2

	$2^5 = 32$	
$5 - 1 = 4$		$\div 2$
	$2^4 = 16$	
$4 - 1 = 3$		$\div 2$
	$2^3 = 8$	
$3 - 1 = 2$		$\div 2$
	$2^2 = 4$	
$2 - 1 = 1$		$\div 2$
	$2^1 = 2$	

Now continue the pattern on the left side of the list by adding the expressions 2^0, 2^{-1}, 2^{-2}, and 2^{-3} to your list on the board. Then ask the class what these expressions must be equal to if the pattern they have discovered is to be preserved. It should be clear that, for the pattern to be preserved, we must continue to get from one value to the next on the right-side of the equal sign by dividing by the base, 2. This line of thought leads to the values shown in the following extended table:

Exponents with Base 2

$$2^5 \ = \ 32$$
$$2^4 \ = \ 16$$
$$2^3 \ = \ 8$$
$$2^2 \ = \ 4$$
$$2^1 \ = \ 2$$

$$2^0 \ = \ 2 \div 2 = 1$$
$$2^{-1} = 1 \div 2 = 0.5$$
$$2^{-2} = 0.5 \div 2 = 0.25$$
$$2^{-3} = 0.25 \div 2 = 0.125$$

Now have the students check these additional values they have "discovered" by using the exponential key $\boxed{x^y}$ on their calculators. The keystroke sequence that most of these calculators use is:

$$a^b: \quad \boxed{a} \ \boxed{x^y} \ \boxed{b} \ \boxed{=}$$

They should be pleasantly surprised to find that the calculator corroborates their answers.

To reinforce this idea of defining these new expressions—with zero or negative integer exponents—so as to preserve the numerical patterns, put the following two additional lists of exponential expressions on the board:

Exponents with Base 4		*Exponents with Base 5*	
4^5 =	1,024	5^5 =	3,125
4^4 =	256	5^4 =	625
4^3 =	64	5^3 =	125
4^2 =	16	5^2 =	25
4^1 =	4	5^1 =	5
4^0 =	?	5^0 =	?
4^{-1} =	?	5^{-1} =	?
4^{-2} =	?	5^{-2} =	?
4^{-3} =	?	5^{-3} =	?

Using the previous list with base 2 as a guide, ask the students to try and find the pattern in each list. Tell them to use the pattern and only the multiplication key on their calculators to complete the lists by filling in the correct missing values below the rules in these tables. Then they should check these new values using the exponential key $\boxed{x^y}$ on their calculators.

When these lists are completed and checked, the students will have discovered what these particular zero and negative integer exponential expressions have to be to preserve the numerical patterns. You can then introduce the mathematical definitions that generalize this pattern-preserving procedure:

$$a^0 = 1 \quad \text{for any nonzero base } a$$

and

$$a^{-n} = \frac{1}{a^n} \quad \textit{for any nonzero base } a, \text{ and any positive integer exponent } n$$

In this approach, by the time the definitions of a zero and a negative integer exponent are presented as such, the students have already discovered them for themselves. They are no longer definitions out of thin air that must be memorized simply because "This is the way it's done." We have a much better chance of our students not only remembering the definitions, but of knowing what they mean as well.

Additional calculator activities

1. *Topic:* Absolute value

   Objective: Use the calculator to check the solution(s) to problems involving absolute value equations and absolute value inequalities.

   Procedure: Once the solution set is found, use the calculator to check the solution values in the following way. If there are only a finite number of solution values, as would be the case in an absolute value equation, simply use the calculator to substitute these values into the original equation and verify that they work. If the solution set has an infinite number of values in it, as would ordinarily be the case in an absolute value inequality problem, use the calculator to substitute several values of the supposed solution set in the inequality, and verify that they satisfy the inequality. Then use the calculator to substitute several values not in the supposed solution set in the inequality, and verify that they do not satisfy the inequality. You should explain to the class that, on a calculator, taking the absolute value of a number is accomplished by leaving the number alone if it is non-negative; and pressing the $\boxed{\text{CHS}}$ or $\boxed{+/-}$ key if the number has a negative sign. An alternate way of taking the absolute value of any number is to square the number and then take the positive square root of the square using the sequence of keys $\boxed{x^2}$ $\boxed{\sqrt{}}$.

   Example: Solve the following equation and inequality, then check the solution sets using your calculator:

   (a) $|a - 7| = 3$
   (b) $|a - 7| < 3$

Solution: The algebraic solutions are: (2) $a = 4, 10$; (b) $4 < a < 10$. The keystroke sequence for this problem is

$$|a - 7|: \quad \boxed{a} \ \boxed{-} \ \boxed{7} \ \boxed{=} \quad \text{(with } \boxed{+/-} \text{ if the result has a negative sign)}$$

With this calculator keystroke sequence, the solutions to problem part a check. To check problem part b, we would use the preceding keystroke sequence with several values in the solution set, and they would work. We would also use the same keystroke sequence with several values *not* in the solution set, and they would *not* work. This result would mean the solutions set is most likely correct in part b.

2. *Topic:* Absolute value

   Objective: Use the calculator either to check the answers to problems in which the absolute values of various numbers must be found, or to let the students discover what absolute value means.

   Special keys: $\boxed{x^2}$ $\boxed{\sqrt{}}$

   Procedure: Given any value a, its absolute value can be obtained by calculator using the keystroke sequence

   $$|a|: \quad \boxed{a} \ \boxed{x^2} \ \boxed{\sqrt{}}$$

   Simply give the students class and homework problems for which they must find the absolute values of several numbers. Then have them check their results using this keystroke sequence. An alternate procedure is to give the class this keystroke sequence as a way of obtaining what will be called "the absolute value of a." Then have them use the keystroke sequence on several numbers and see if they can "discover" from these examples what "taking the absolute value of a number" means in simple English.

3. *Topic:* Simplifying radical expressions

   Objective: Use the calculator to check the answer when a radical expression is given and must be simplified.

   Special key: $\boxed{\sqrt{}}$, and possibly $\boxed{x^y}$ depending on the problem.

   Procedure: Use the calculator with the square root key $\boxed{\sqrt{}}$, or the exponentiation key $\boxed{x^y}$ if the radicals involved are third or higher roots, to convert both the original expression and the supposed simplification to decimal form. The simplification is correct if the two decimals agree, and incorrect if they do not agree. (Keep in mind that, even if the two expressions are theoretically the same, the decimals may differ by a minute amount due to calculator round-off. So if the two decimals differ only in the last decimal place, the expressions are probably equivalent.)

   Example: Simplify the following radical expression by rationalizing the denominator, and then check your simplification using your calculator:

   $$\frac{2}{1 - \sqrt{3}}$$

Solution:

$$\frac{2}{1 - \sqrt{3}} = \frac{2}{1 - \sqrt{3}} \times \frac{1 + \sqrt{3}}{1 + \sqrt{3}}$$

$$= \frac{2 + 2\sqrt{3}}{1 - 3} = \frac{2 + 2\sqrt{3}}{-2}$$

$$= -1 - \sqrt{3}$$

To check this answer, convert both the original expression and this final expression to decimal form. The keystroke sequences for doing so are:

$$\frac{2}{1 - \sqrt{3}}: \quad \boxed{1} \boxed{-} \boxed{3} \boxed{\sqrt{}} \boxed{=} \boxed{1/x} \boxed{\times} \boxed{2} \boxed{=}$$

$$-1 - \sqrt{3}: \quad \boxed{1} \boxed{+/-} \boxed{-} \boxed{3} \boxed{\sqrt{}} \boxed{=}$$

Since both keystroke sequences give the same decimal result, -2.7320508 on my 8-digit calculator, the radical expression we obtained as a simplification is correct.

4. *Topic:* Arithmetic operations with radical expressions

Objective: Use the calculator to check the answer to arithmetic problems involving two or more radical expressions.

Special keys: $\boxed{\sqrt{}}$, and possibly $\boxed{x^y}$ depending on the problem

Procedure: Use the calculator to convert both the original radical expression(s) and the resulting radical expression to decimal form. Then do the indicated arithmetic operations on the decimal values using the calculator, and compare the decimal answer with the decimal equivalent of the resultant radical expression. If at all possible, try to do everything completely on the calculator, so as not to lose any of the calculator's internal digits in the intermediate steps. One way of doing so is by storing the decimal equivalent of the first expression in memory using the $\boxed{\text{STO}}$ key, and then recalling it when needed for the arithmetic computations with the $\boxed{\text{RCL}}$ key.

Example: Perform the indicated arithmetic operation, and then check your result with your calculator:

$$(2 + \sqrt{3})(3 + \sqrt{2})$$

Solution: The desired product, in radical form, is:

$$(2 + \sqrt{3})(3 + \sqrt{2}) = 6 + 2\sqrt{2} + 3\sqrt{3} + \sqrt{6}$$

To check this result we will convert the original two expressions into decimal form and multiply these decimals. We will do so on the calculator, without writing anything down, so that the result is as accurate as we can get it without any intermediate loss of accuracy. Use $\boxed{\text{STO}}$ and $\boxed{\text{RCL}}$ keys (or any equivalent keys on other calculators) as follows:

$(2 + \sqrt{3})(3 + \sqrt{2})$: [2] [+] [3] [√] [=] [STO] [3] [+] [2] [√]
[=] [×] [RCL] [=]

The decimal result obtained for this product on my 8-digit calculator is 16.474069. We now convert the supposed radical result into decimal form on the calculator using the keystroke sequences:

$$6 + 2\sqrt{2} + 3\sqrt{3} + \sqrt{6}:$$

Hierarchy:
[6] [+] [2] [×] [2] [√] [+] [3] [×] [3] [√] [+] [6] [√] [=]

Left-to-Right:
[6] [STO] [2] [×] [2] [√] [=] [+] [RCL] [=] [STO] [3] [×] [3] [√]
[=] [+] [RCL] [=] [+] [6] [√] [=]

Since this also gives the decimal 16.474069 on my 8-digit calculator, the radical expression we obtained for the product must be correct.

5. *Topic:* Radical or irrational equations

Objective: Use the calculator to check solutions to radical or irrational equations and to locate extraneous solutions.

Special key: [√]

Example: Solve the following radical equations, and check your solutions with your calculator:
(a) $\sqrt{a - 3} = 5.5$
(b) $\sqrt{a + 5} = -4$

Solution: Solving the two equations by squaring and solving for the unknown a, we obtain:
(a) $a = 33.25$
(b) $a = 11$
We now substitute these values back into the respective original equations using the keystroke sequences:

$$\sqrt{a - 3}: \quad [a] [-] [3] [=] [√]$$
$$\sqrt{a + 5}: \quad [a] [+] [5] [=] [√]$$

The solution we found to equation (a) checks, so it is correct. The solution we found to equation (b) does not check, so it does not have a solution.

6. *Topic:* Systems of equations with one or more quadratic equations

Objective: Use the calculator to check the solution(s) to such systems of equations.
Special key: [x^2]

Example: Solve the following system of equations. Then check your solution(s) using your calculator:

$$2t^2 - s = 3$$
$$7t - s = 6$$

Solution: Solving this system algebraically by using the linear equation to substitute into the quadratic and solving the resulting quadratic equation in t, we obtain the two solutions: $s = 15$, $t = 3$; $s = -2.5$, $t = 0.5$. These solutions are checked by calculator substitution back into the original two equations using the keystroke sequences:

$$2t^2 - s: \quad \boxed{2} \boxed{\times} \boxed{t} \boxed{x^2} \boxed{-} \boxed{s} \boxed{=}$$
$$7t - s: \quad \boxed{7} \boxed{\times} \boxed{t} \boxed{-} \boxed{s} \boxed{=}$$

Both solutions check when substituted in the two equations using these keystroke sequences. So they are both solutions of the original system.

7. *Topic:* Systems of inequalities with one or more quadratics

Objective: Use the calculator to verify the solution set for such a system.

Special key: $\boxed{x^2}$

Procedure: Use an appropriate set of calculator keystroke sequences (one for each expression in the system) to substitute several values from the supposed solution set and several values not from the supposed solution set into the inequalities making up the system. If the supposed solution set is correct, you should find that: (1) the system *is* satisfied for each of the values from the supposed solution set, and (2) for the values not from the supposed solution set *at least one* of the inequalities is *not* satisfied for each of these values.

8. *Topic:* Parabolic equation $t = as^2 + bs + c$

Objective: Use the calculator to illustrate that:
(a) the sign of the coefficient a determines whether the parabola opens upward or downward, and that the absolute value of a determines the width of the parabola;
(b) changing the value of the coefficient b results in a horizontal shift of the parabola; and
(c) changing the value of the coefficient c results in a vertical shift of the parabola.

Special key: $\boxed{x^2}$

Procedure: (The procedure for showing what the coefficient a represents will be described here. The procedures for showing what the coefficients b and c represent are similar, requiring only slight modifications of the table and accompanying questions.) Have the students fill in the following table according to the accompanying directions, and then use the completed table to answer the questions that follow:

> In the first column of the table, labeled s, are 8 different values of the independent variable s. For each value of s, use your calculator to find the corresponding values of the quadratics for the other columns and fill in the values you obtain. When the table is complete, use it to answer the questions that follow:

(1) s	(2) $s^2 + 1$	(3) $2s^2 + 1$	(4) $4s^2 + 1$	(5) $-s^2 + 1$	(6) $-4s^2 + 1$
−4					
−3					
−2					
−1					
0					
1					
2					
3					

Question 1: Use the second, third, and fourth columns of your table to sketch the graphs of the parabolas $t = as^2 + 1$ for $a = 1, 2$, and 4, respectively, on the same set of axes.

Question 2: In what specific characteristic are the three graphs drawn in answer to question 1 different from each other?

Question 3: Based on your answers to questions 1 and 2, what characteristic do you think the value of a represents in the equation $t = as^2 + bs + c$?

Question 4: Use the fifth and sixth columns of your table to sketch the graphs of the parabolas $t = as^2 + 1$ for $a = -1$ and $a = -4$, respectively.

Question 5: Compare the two graphs: one of $t = as^2 + 1$ for $a = 1$ and $a = -1$, and the other for $a = 4$ and $a = -4$. What effect do you think the sign of the coefficient a has on the shape and direction of the general parabola with equation $t = as^2 + bs + c$?

9. *Topic:* Scientific notation

Objective: Use the calculator to check the solutions to problems in which numbers in standard form are converted to scientific notation form, and numbers in scientific notation form are converted to standard form.

Special keys: Keys for converting to and from scientific notation form, such as keys EE for ENTER EXPONENT and INV, which are used on many Texas Instruments calculators.

Procedure: Assign problems in which numbers in standard form are converted to scientific notation, along with problems in which numbers in scientific notation are converted to standard form. Then have the students do the same problems on their calculators to check their answers. For example, on most Texas Instruments calculators the number a would be converted to scientific notation form with the keystroke sequence:

$$\boxed{a} \quad \boxed{\text{EE}} \quad \boxed{=}$$

and the number $a \times 10^b$ in scientific notation could be entered into the calculator and converted to standard form with the keystroke sequence:

$$\boxed{a} \quad \boxed{\text{EE}} \quad \boxed{b} \quad \boxed{\text{INV}} \quad \boxed{\text{EE}} \quad \boxed{=}$$

10. *Topic:* Geometric series

Objective: Use the calculator to check the sum of a finite geometric series.

Example: Use the formula for the sum of a finite geometric series to calculate the following sum, and then check your answer with the calculator:

$$3 - \frac{3}{2} + \frac{3}{4} - \frac{3}{8} + \frac{3}{16}$$

Solution: Noticing that the first term in this series is $a_1 = 3$ and that the common ratio is $-\frac{1}{2}$, we can use the formula:

$$S_n = \frac{a_1 - a_1 r^n}{1 - r}, \qquad r \neq 1$$

to obtain the sum $S_5 = \frac{33}{16}$. To check this result by calculator, first rewrite the series by factoring out the common numerator 3 and by multiplying through by this value at the end of the expression to obtain:

$$3 - \frac{3}{2} + \frac{3}{4} - \frac{3}{8} + \frac{3}{16} = (1 - \frac{1}{2} + \frac{1}{4} - \frac{1}{8} + \frac{1}{16})(3)$$

In this form we can evaluate the geometric series using the simple keystroke sequence:

$$\boxed{1}\ \boxed{-}\ \boxed{2}\ \boxed{1/x}\ \boxed{+}\ \boxed{4}\ \boxed{1/x}\ \boxed{-}\ \boxed{8}\ \boxed{1/x}\ \boxed{+}\ \boxed{16}\ \boxed{1/x}\ \boxed{=}\ \boxed{\times}\ \boxed{3}\ \boxed{=}$$

The result we obtain, 2.0625, is the decimal equivalent of $\frac{33}{16}$, so the answer we obtained earlier using the formula is correct.

11. *Topic:* Polar representation of complex numbers

Objective: Use a calculator instead of trigonometric tables to convert complex numbers to and from polar notation.

Special keys: $\boxed{\text{ARC}}$ or $\boxed{\text{INV}}\ \boxed{\text{SIN}}\ \boxed{\text{COS}}\ \boxed{x^2}\ \boxed{\sqrt{\ }}$

Procedure: Given the relationship

$$a + bi = r(\cos\theta + i\sin\theta)$$

If the complex number is given in polar notation form, we find the values of a and b from the following formulas and corresponding keystroke sequences:

$$a = r\cos\theta: \quad \boxed{r}\ \boxed{\times}\ \boxed{\theta}\ \boxed{\text{COS}}\ \boxed{=}$$
$$b = r\sin\theta: \quad \boxed{r}\ \boxed{\times}\ \boxed{\theta}\ \boxed{\text{SIN}}\ \boxed{=}$$

If the complex number is given in rectangular coordinate form, we find the values of r and θ from the following formulas and corresponding keystroke sequences:

$$r = \sqrt{a^2 + b^2}: \quad \boxed{a}\ \boxed{x^2}\ \boxed{+}\ \boxed{b}\ \boxed{x^2}\ \boxed{=}\ \boxed{\sqrt{\ }}$$

$$\theta = \arc \sin \left(\frac{b}{r}\right): \quad \boxed{b} \; \boxed{\div} \; \boxed{r} \; \boxed{=} \; \boxed{\text{ARC}} \; \boxed{\text{SIN}}$$

12. *Topic:* Rules with logarithms

Objective: Use the calculator either to emphasize, or to let the students discover, the law of products and the law of quotients for logarithms:

$$\log(a \times b) = \log a + \log b \qquad \text{for } a \text{ and } b \text{ positive}$$
$$\log(a \div b) = \log a - \log b \qquad \text{for } a \text{ and } b \text{ positive}$$

Special key: Common log $\boxed{\text{LOG}}$, or natural log $\boxed{\text{LN}}$. The common log is the logarithm to the base 10, while the natural log is the logarithm to the base e. These rules apply to both types of logarithms, as well as to all other bases.

Procedure: Have the students fill out the following two tables according to the accompanying directions, and then use the completed tables to answer the questions that follow.

In the two tables that follow, fill in the first two columns using any positive values of a and b, respectively, that you like. Then use these values and your calculator to fill in the rest of the tables. Do this one row of the tables at a time, and try to do all the work on your calculator so that you do not lose accuracy in intermediate steps. The keystroke sequences for column 4 of each table are, respectively:

$$\log a + \log b: \quad \boxed{a} \; \boxed{\text{LOG}} \; \boxed{+} \; \boxed{b} \; \boxed{\text{LOG}} \; \boxed{=}$$
$$\log a - \log b: \quad \boxed{a} \; \boxed{\text{LOG}} \; \boxed{-} \; \boxed{b} \; \boxed{\text{LOG}} \; \boxed{=}$$

(1) a	(2) b	(3) ab	(4) $\log a + \log b$	(5) $\log ab$

(1) a	(2) b	(3) $a \div b$	(4) $\log a - \log b$	(5) $\log(a \div b)$

Question 1: Are the last two columns of the first table the same? Use this observation to fill in the missing arithmetic operation in the following law of logarithms for products:

$$\log(ab) = \log a \underline{\quad ? \quad} \log b$$

Question 2: Are the last two columns of the second table the same? Use this observation to fill in the missing arithmetic operation in the following law of logarithms for quotients:

$$\log(a \div b) = \log a \underline{\quad ? \quad} \log b$$

13. *Topic:* Properties of the logarithm function

Objective: Use the calculator to let the students discover the properties of the logarithm function for themselves.

Special key: Common log $\boxed{\text{LOG}}$ or natural log $\boxed{\text{LN}}$

Procedure: This is similar to the discovery activity given in Chapter 4 in the section "Discovery activities with the calculator." Simply point out the calculator key $\boxed{\text{LOG}}$ or $\boxed{\text{LN}}$ after you have introduced the respective function in class, and assign to the class the problem of using this key to discover whatever they can about this function. If you assign this as a homework problem, the students will have an adequate amount of time to work on it. Among the properties you want them to discover are that:

- the domain of this function is the set of positive numbers;
- the range of this function is the set of all real numbers;
- the function is monotone increasing; and
- the function increases very slowly; slower, in fact, than any positive power of the independent variable.

Give any hints you think will lead the students to investigate in the right direction, but leave it vague enough so that they must actually use their imaginations rather than just follow orders.

6

GEOMETRY

Geometry is, of course, a predominantly visual rather than numerical subject. Yet for the many topics in geometry that are wholly or partially numerical, the calculator is eminently suitable both for teaching purposes and for problem solving. Some of the most obvious numerical topics in geometry are:

- coordinate geometry, which involves the concepts of length and distance;
- area of two-dimensional figures;
- both surface area and volume of three-dimensional figures; and
- the relationships between the number of sides of two-dimensional polygons and the interior and exterior angles of such figures.

In addition, the calculator is still suitable for many other geometric topics that are less obviously numerical. For example, numerous geometric patterns involving points, lines, or regions can be presented and discussed at various points in the geometry syllabus. These geometric patterns often have corresponding numerical representations in terms of formulas or equations, and the calculator can be used to study the patterns through their numerical counterparts. In this chapter we will look at a variety of ways the calculator can be employed throughout the study of geometry.

The "evaluation" of pi: pi = 3.141592...

If any number can be thought of as a "geometric" number, it is pi. Pi is defined as the ratio of a circle's circumference to its diameter (pi $= C/D$), and as far back as the time of Euclid it was known that this ratio will be the same for all circles. It was not until approximately 240 BC, however, that the value of this ratio was first estimated by Archimedes. In the years between Archimedes' first estimation of pi and the present, many interesting facts about pi have been discovered. For example, we now know that pi is an irrational number, and so it cannot be represented exactly by either a fraction, a terminating decimal, or a repeating decimal. We also know that pi is an example of what is called a "transcendental" number, which means that pi is not the root of any polynomial with rational coefficients. We also know many more digits in the decimal expansion of pi than Archimedes did. Archimedes estimated pi to be between 223/71 and 22/7, which essentially gave him the first three digits 3.14 of the decimal expansion of pi. In 1949, the ENIAC computer at the Army Ballistic Research Laboratories in Aberdeen, Maryland, was used to find the first 2,035 places in the decimal expansion of pi; but this took approximately 70 hours of computer time.

The number pi can be used as the basis of a very interesting classroom activity in which the students themselves duplicate Archimedes' attempt to estimate the value of pi with the added advantage of having the calculator available to simplify what by hand was, and still would be, some very cumbersome numerical computations. Not only does this activity show the power of the calculator, but, more importantly, it demonstrates for the students the power of geometry and the incredible ingenuity and inventiveness of the ancient Greeks like Archimedes who developed and used it.

"Discovering" pi

While math teachers are quite familiar with the fact that the ratio of the circumference of a circle to its diameter is the same for all circles, this can be quite startling when a student first encounters it. For this reason it is a good idea to begin this "pi activity" by helping the students to discover this fact with the use of their calculators. To do so, simply ask your students, on the day before this activity is to be used, to bring with them some circular objects the following day. These can be circular plates, cups, or glasses with circular tops, large circular chocolate chip cookies, or any other circular object.

On the day of the activity, ask the students to take the circular object they have brought and measure, as accurately as they can, both the circumference of the object and its diameter. The diameter is fairly easy to measure with an ordinary ruler since it is a straight length. To measure the circumference you might have available many pieces of string. The student can place the string around the outer edge of the object, mark off where the measurement begins on the string and where it ends, and then pull the string straight and measure this length with a ruler. An alternative is to use one of the "distance pens" that are sold through many catalogues and in many stores for measuring the distance from one point to another on a map. The "pen" has a little roller on its "writing" end and as you move the "pen" along the route on the map or around the edge of the circular object, a gauge tells you the distance you have gone in inches. Now put a chart on the board like the one shown in Table 6–1 and fill in the first two columns by going from student to student and asking them to call out the circumferences and the diameters of their objects.

Table 6–1. Estimating pi

(1) Circumference	(2) Diameter	(3) $\dfrac{\text{Circumference}}{\text{Diameter}}$

When the students have given you their measurements, and they are all entered pairwise in the first two columns of the table, have the students use their calculators to fill in the third column by dividing each circumference by its respective diameter. Since the measurements of C and D will not have been exact, the ratio C/D will not be exactly the same for each row of the chart. But they should be amazingly (and startlingly, to those students who did not expect it) similar. You can now point out to the class that not only are all the ratios C/D similar, but that also they would actually have been identical if the students had been able to measure the circumferences and the diameters exactly. You can then give a little history of the discovery of this fact (available in most history of mathematics books) and inform them that this common value is given the name "pi."

Estimating pi using perimeters of polygons

A natural question for you to ask the class at this juncture is how you might go about estimating this interesting but elusive number pi. Of course, one way is to take any circular object, measure its circumference and diameter, and divide to obtain the ratio. Yet since any such measurements will be only approximations, the value of the ratio would also be an approximation, and the important thing is that we would have no idea how accurate or inaccurate this estimate is. What we want is a procedure that will give approximations of pi that we know are close to the correct value. You can now announce to the class that you will obtain such an approximation the same way the very first estimation of pi was made over 2,000 years ago by Archimedes, but that you will do so with one advantage Archimedes did not have: the availability of a hand-held calculator.

Tell the class that Archimedes approximated a circle by inscribing a regular polygon with a large number of sides and then estimating the circumference of the circle divided by its diameter (pi) by using the perimeter of the inscribed polygon divided by the circle's diameter. In other words, if D is the diameter of the circle, C is the circumference of the circle, and P is the perimeter of the polygon, he reasoned that:

$$\text{pi} = C/D \approx P/D$$

Furthermore, P/D gives a better and better approximation of pi as inscribed polygons with more and more sides are used (Figure 6–1).

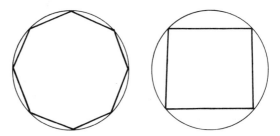

Figure 6-1

To duplicate Archimedes' feat, we begin with a unit circle within which is inscribed a 6-sided polygon (Figure 6–2). Observe, as Archimedes did, that by drawing line segments from the center of the circle to the 6 vertices of the inscribed polygon, the polygon is divided into 6 equilateral triangles with all sides equal to the radius of the circle, 1 (Figure 6–3). So each side of the polygon must be of length 1 and the perimeter of this polygon must be 6. Using this perimeter as an approximation of the circumference of the circle, we obtain our first estimate of pi as:

$$\text{pi} = C/D \approx 6/2 = 3$$

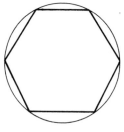

Figure 6-2

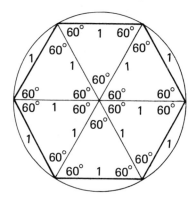

Figure 6-3

Representing the length of each side of this 6-sided regular polygon by the symbol L_6 and the perimeter by the symbol P_6, we can illustrate this first step in tabular form (Table 6–2).

Table 6–2. Estimates of pi

Number of Sides N	Length of Each Side L_N	Perimeter of Polygon $P_N = NL_N$	Estimate pi $\approx P_N/2$
6	1	$6 \times 1 = 6$	$6/2 = 3$

Now came Archimedes' most ingenious observation. Suppose, Archimedes reasoned, that we have inscribed a regular polygon of N sides within the unit circle and have somehow managed to find the length of side L_N for this polygon (as we have just done when $N = 6$). Let us now inscribe a regular polygon with twice as many sides ($2N$ sides) in the circle and see if we can develop a formula for obtaining L_{2N}, the length of side for this new polygon, in terms of the value L_N that we already know. In Figure 6–4, we have focused

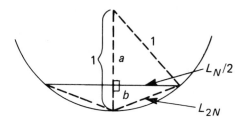

Figure 6-4

attention on one of the triangles and sides of the N-sided polygon. Using the Pythagorean theorem on the right triangle with sides of length a, $L_N/2$, and a hypotenuse of 1, we, obtain:

$$a^2 + (L_N/2)^2 = 1^2$$

which can be solved for a to give:

99

$$a = \sqrt{1 - \frac{L_N^2}{4}}$$

Since the line segments a and b together give a radius of this unit circle, we know further that:

$$b = -a = 1 - \sqrt{1 - L_N^2/4}$$

Finally, from the right triangle with sides of length b, $L_N/2$, and hypotenuse L_{2N}, a second application of the Pythagorean theorem gives:

$$L_{2N}^2 = b^2 + (L_N/2)^2$$

Substituting the expression involving L_N for b, and then simplifying, we convert the theorem to:

(6–1) $$L_{2N} = \sqrt{2 - \sqrt{4 - L_N^2}}$$

Formula (6–1) is just what Archimedes needed. With it, he was able to use the fact that $L_6 = 1$ and its corresponding approximation of pi to obtain $L_{2(6)} = L_{12}$ and its corresponding better approximation of pi. From that he obtained $L_{2(12)} = L_{24}$ and its even better corresponding approximation of pi, and so on. At first glance, of course, formula (6–1) is rather formidable and intimidating since it contains a radical of a radical. Perhaps this is why Archimedes went no further than a polygon of 96 sides ($N = 6, 12, 24, 48, 96$) and obtained in his estimate only the first three correct digits of pi, 3.14. Whatever the reason for his stopping at $N = 96$, this approximation of pi, with only the first three correct digits, was the value that was used for nearly 400 years. Yet with the aid of the hand-held calculator and the square root key, you have no reason to be intimidated by formula (6–1). Neither should your students have any difficulty in reproducing Archimedes' estimate of pi and in improving on it.

Here is how you can do so. Once you and the class have developed formula (6–1), as outlined, hand out copies of the partially filled-in table 6–3. Starting with the known value $L_6 = 1$ given in the table, have the students use their calculators to find L_{12}, L_{24}, L_{48}, and L_{96} and enter these values in the second column of the table. Then, using these values and their calculators, they are to fill in the rest of the table one row at a time until they finally obtain "Archimedes' estimate" of pi. The calculator keystroke sequence for obtaining L_{2N} from L_N using formula (6–1) on a calculator with square root key is:

$$L_{2N} = \sqrt{2 - \sqrt{4 - L_N^2}}:\quad \boxed{L_N}\ \boxed{x^2}\ \boxed{+/-}\ \boxed{+}\ \boxed{4}\ \boxed{=}\ \boxed{\sqrt{}}\ \boxed{+/-}\ \boxed{+}\ \boxed{2}\ \boxed{=}\ \boxed{\sqrt{}}$$

Table 6–3. Estimates of pi

N	L_N	$P_N = N \times L_N$	pi $\approx P_N/2$
6	1	6	3
12			
24			
48			
96			*

*Archimedes' estimate of pi

Actually, Archimedes estimated pi by using an inscribed polygon of 96 sides and a circumscribed polygon of 96 sides to obtain a lower bound and an upper bound for pi, respectively. But this procedure, using only inscribed polygons, gives the flavor of his method, and this is what is important in this activity.

When Table 6–3 is complete, ask the class to fill in Table 6–4, which tells how many correct digits of the decimal expansion of pi are obtained for each value of N in Table 6–3. They can use the fact that the correct first seven digits of pi are known to be pi = 3.141592....

Table 6–4. Correct number of digits using Archimedes' estimates of pi

N	Estimate of Pi	Number of Correct Digits
6	3	1
12		
24		
48		
96		

You can now ask such questions as:

- How many correct digits of pi did Archimedes' estimate give?
- How large a value of N do you think Archimedes would have had to use, based on this table, to get an estimate of pi with one more correct digit than his actual estimate had?
- From the table, is it or is it not true that doubling the number of sides of the inscribed polygon doubles the number of correct digits in the estimate of pi?

Answering these questions should indicate to the class how slowly this method produces better and better estimates in terms of increasing the value of N. Finally, you might ask them to go ahead and improve on Archimedes' result by continuing Table 6–3 until they obtain one more correct digit than he had. After they have done so, and it should take no more than a few minutes, point out to them how really incredible this apparently simple last step is. While it took them just a few minutes of calculator computation to first duplicate Archimedes' estimate and then to improve on it, it took the Greeks—who had no calculators and who relied almost completely on geometric rather than algebraic techniques—nearly 400 years to do as much. This exercise gives some indication of just how far mathematics and mathematical techniques have developed, even in basic geometry and algebra, from Archimedes' time to ours.

Estimating pi using areas of polygons

Another interesting follow-up activity is to estimate pi using areas of inscribed regular polygons rather than perimeters. We know:

- that the circumference of the unit circle is $2 \times$ pi;
- that the area of the unit circle is $pi \times (1)^2$ = pi; and

• that we can approximate the circumference of the unit circle by the perimeter P_N of an inscribed regular polygon with N sides and use this value to estimate pi.

Hence we can also approximate the area of the unit circle by the area A_N of an inscribed polygon with N sides and use this approximate area to estimate pi. This is exactly what we will now do.

In Figure 6–5 is one of the N isosceles triangles that comprise the regular N-sided polygon inscribed in the unit circle. Recalling from our previous

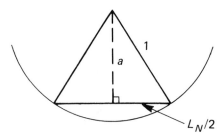

Figure 6-5

computations with this figure that

$$a = \sqrt{1 - L_N^2/4} = (\tfrac{1}{2}) \sqrt{4 - L_N^2}$$

it is clear that the area of this small triangle is

$$\text{Area of triangle} = \tfrac{1}{2} \text{ Base} \times \text{height} = (\tfrac{1}{4})L_N\sqrt{4 - L_N^2}$$

Since the N-sided inscribed regular polygon consists of N of these triangles, the area A_N of this polygon must be given by the formula:

(6–2) $$A_N = (\tfrac{1}{4})(N)L_N\sqrt{4 - L_N^2}$$

The keystroke sequence for obtaining A_N from L_N on a calculator with square key and square root key using formula (6–2) is:

$A_N = (\tfrac{1}{4})(N)L_N\sqrt{4 - L_N^2}$: $\boxed{L_N}\ \boxed{x^2}\ \boxed{+/-}\ \boxed{+}\ \boxed{4}\ \boxed{=}$
$\boxed{\sqrt{}}\ \boxed{\times}\ \boxed{L_N}\ \boxed{\times}\ \boxed{N}\ \boxed{\div}\ \boxed{4}\ \boxed{=}$

Now hand out copies of the following two tables to the students (Tables 6–5 and 6–6).

*Table 6–5. Estimates of pi
using areas*

N	L_N	$pi \approx A_N$
6	1	
12		
24		
48		
96		

Table 6–6. Number of correct digits when estimating pi using areas

N	pi $\approx A_N$	Number of Correct Digits
6		
12		
24		
48		
96		

Instruct the class to fill in the values for the second column of Table 6–5, L_N, from Table 6–3 completed earlier. They are then to use these values, together with their calculators and the keystroke sequence for formula (6–2), to complete Table 6–5. Finally, using these area approximations, they are to complete Table 6–6. They should be interested to note that, for each value of N, Archimedes' "perimeter" method of estimating pi gives a better estimate than this "area" method. As a homework problem, you might ask the students to use their calculators to continue these final two tables to $N = 192, 384$, and so on, to discover how large a value of N would be needed using area approximations to get as good an estimate of pi as Archimedes did using perimeter approximations with $N = 96$.

Additional examples

In the following additional examples, the calculator can be used to obtain better and better estimates of pi. One way of using these additional expressions is to ask the students, as a homework assignment, to try each method with their calculators and rate each one as "better than," "just as good as," or "not as good as" Archimedes' method of estimating pi depending on how long it takes to obtain as good an estimate as Archimedes had. You might also withhold the keystroke sequences and let the students develop them themselves if you want to give extra practice in writing keystroke sequences.

1. *Expression:* $\dfrac{pi}{4} = 1 - \dfrac{1}{3} + \dfrac{1}{5} - \dfrac{1}{7} \dots$

   Special key: $\boxed{1/x}$

   Discussion: This is an infinite series expansion of pi/4. If we stop at successively later and later terms in the series, the resulting partial sums will give better and better approximations of pi/4. Multiplying these partial sums by 4, we obtain successively better and better estimates of pi. Furthermore, if the term you stop at is positive, the estimate will be greater than pi; while if the term you stop at is negative, the estimate will be less than pi. This way you actually have both a set of upper bound estimates for pi and a set of lower bound estimates for pi. The first four such estimates pi_1, pi_2, pi_3, and pi_4 follow:

103

Keystroke sequences:

$pi_1 = (1)4$: $\boxed{1}\ \boxed{\times}\ \boxed{4}\ \boxed{=}$ (4 on any calculator)

$pi_2 = \left(1 - \dfrac{1}{3}\right)4$: $\boxed{1}\ \boxed{-}\ \boxed{3}\ \boxed{1/x}\ \boxed{=}\ \boxed{\times}\ \boxed{4}\ \boxed{=}$ (2.6666666 on an 8-digit display calculator)

$pi_3 = \left(1 - \dfrac{1}{3} + \dfrac{1}{5}\right)4$: $\boxed{1}\ \boxed{-}\ \boxed{3}\ \boxed{1/x}\ \boxed{+}\ \boxed{5}\ \boxed{1/x}\ \boxed{=}\ \boxed{\times}\ \boxed{4}\ \boxed{=}$ (3.4666666 on an 8-digit display calculator)

$pi_4 = \left(1 - \dfrac{1}{3} + \dfrac{1}{5} - \dfrac{1}{7}\right)4$: $\boxed{1}\ \boxed{-}\ \boxed{3}\ \boxed{1/x}\ \boxed{+}\ \boxed{5}\ \boxed{1/x}\ \boxed{-}\ \boxed{7}\ \boxed{1/x}\ \boxed{=}\ \boxed{+}$ $\boxed{4}\ \boxed{=}$ (2.8952380 on an 8-digit display calculator)

2. *Expression:* $\dfrac{pi}{2} = \dfrac{2 \cdot 2 \cdot 4 \cdot 4 \cdot 6 \cdot 6 \cdot 8 \cdot 8 \cdot \ldots}{1 \cdot 3 \cdot 3 \cdot 5 \cdot 5 \cdot 7 \cdot 7 \cdot 9 \cdot \ldots}$

Discussion: This is an infinite product expansion of pi/2. If we stop at successively later and later common positions in the numerator and denominator, the resulting finite products will give better and better approximations of pi/2. By multiplying these values by 2 we get corresponding approximations of pi. Furthermore, since the digits in the denominator are alternately smaller than and larger than the corresponding digits in the numerator, the estimates will be alternately larger and then smaller than pi. Given below are the first four such estimates pi_1, pi_2, pi_3, and pi_4.

Keystroke sequences:

$pi_1 = \left(\dfrac{2}{1}\right)2$: $\boxed{2}\ \boxed{\times}\ \boxed{2}\ \boxed{=}$ (4 on any calculator)

$pi_2 = \left(\dfrac{2\,b\,2}{1\,b\,3}\right)2$: $\boxed{2}\ \boxed{\times}\ \boxed{2}\ \boxed{\div}\ \boxed{3}\ \boxed{\times}\ \boxed{2}\ \boxed{=}$ (2.6666666 on an 8-digit display calculator)

$pi_3 = \left(\dfrac{2\,b\,2\,b\,4}{1\,b\,3\,b\,3}\right)2$: $\boxed{2}\ \boxed{\times}\ \boxed{2}\ \boxed{\times}\ \boxed{4}\ \boxed{\div}\ \boxed{3}\ \boxed{\div}\ \boxed{3}\ \boxed{\times}\ \boxed{2}\ \boxed{=}$ (3.5555555 on an 8-digit display calculator)

$pi_4 = \left(\dfrac{2\,b\,2\,b\,4\,b\,4}{1\,b\,3\,b\,3\,b\,5}\right)2$: $\boxed{2}\ \boxed{\times}\ \boxed{2}\ \boxed{\times}\ \boxed{4}\ \boxed{\times}\ \boxed{4}\ \boxed{\div}\ \boxed{3}\ \boxed{\div}\ \boxed{3}\ \boxed{\div}\ \boxed{5}$ $\boxed{\times}\ \boxed{2}\ \boxed{=}$ (2.8444444 on an 8-digit display calculator)

3. *Expression:* $\dfrac{4}{pi} = 1 + \cfrac{1^2}{2 + \cfrac{3^2}{2 + \cfrac{5^2}{2 + \ldots}}}$

Special keys: $\boxed{1/x}\ \boxed{x^2}$

Discussion: As in the previous two examples, we cut off this infinite continued fraction expression at any denominator 2, and evaluate the resulting finite continued fraction by starting at its last denominator and working backward to the first term 1. Thus we obtain better and better approximations of 4/pi. If we then invert each of these approximations and multiply by 4, we obtain successively better and better estimates of pi. As before, these estimates will be successively greater than, and smaller than, the actual value of pi. The first three such estimates pi_1, pi_2, and pi_3 follow:

Keystroke sequences:

$$pi_1 = \left(\frac{1}{1}\right)4:$$

$\boxed{4}$ (4 on any calculator)

$$pi_2 = \left(\frac{1}{1 + \frac{1^2}{2}}\right)4:$$

$\boxed{2}$ $\boxed{1/x}$ $\boxed{+}$ $\boxed{1}$ $\boxed{=}$ $\boxed{1/x}$ $\boxed{\times}$ $\boxed{4}$ $\boxed{=}$ (2.6666666 on an 8-digit display calculator)

$$pi_3 \left[\left(\frac{1}{1 + \frac{1^2}{2} + \frac{3^2}{2}}\right)\right]4:$$

$\boxed{2}$ $\boxed{1/x}$ $\boxed{\times}$ $\boxed{3}$ $\boxed{x^2}$ $\boxed{+}$ $\boxed{2}$ $\boxed{=}$ $\boxed{1/x}$ $\boxed{+}$ $\boxed{1}$ $\boxed{=}$ $\boxed{1/x}$ $\boxed{\times}$ $\boxed{4}$ $\boxed{=}$ (3.4666666 on an 8-digit display calculator)

Point and line number patterns in geometry

One of the skills a student should develop in geometry, a primarily visual subject, is the ability to recognize and generalize geometric patterns. Most of these geometric patterns, however, also have numerical representations; and with these numerical pattern equivalents the calculator can be used to identify, generalize, and verify.

Calculator investigation of a geometric line pattern

Let's begin with a simple example involving the diagonals of polygons. Pictured in Figure 6–6 are a 3-sided polygon and a 4-sided polygon with the diagonals of each indicated by dotted lines. Notice that the 3-sided polygon has no diagonals

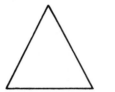 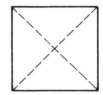

Figure 6-6

while the 4-sided polygon has 2 diagonals. If we let N represent the number of sides and D_N the corresponding number of diagonals, we can express the information contained in Figure 6–6 as in Table 6–7.

Table 6–7. Relationship between number of sides of a polygon, N, and the number of diagonals, D_N	N	D_N
	3	0
	4	2

It's clear that if you ask your students to extend Table 6–7 to polygons having $N = 5$, 6, or more sides, they could do so by drawing the respective polygons, filling in the diagonals with dotted lines, and simply counting. But this is a time-consuming method and admits a good chance of error for large values of N; such figures get quite complicated, and one or more diagonals could easily either be left out and not counted at all, or counted more than once. A better, and more mathematically sophisticated way of proceeding, is to discover a pattern in the relationsip between N and D_N and represent this pattern (if one exists) algebraically.

One way of discovering such a pattern in this situation, that you can either let your students discover with a bit of help or simply point out to them, is obtained as follows. Take the 4-sided polygon shown in Figure 6–6 and, without drawing in any new line segments, simply add a fifth vertex to the picture. This change is illustrated in Figure 6–7 with the original vertices labeled A, B, C, D, and the new vertex labeled E. Now, comparing Figure 6–7 with Figure 6–8, in

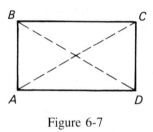

Figure 6-7

which all the sides and diagonals of this 5-sided polygon have been drawn in, we can make the following observations:

- All the diagonals of the 4-sided polygon are still diagonals in the 5-sided

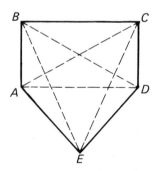

Figure 6-8

polygon, so D_5 is at least equal to D_4.

- The line segment in the 4-sided polygon, which connected the two vertices nearest our new vertex E (that is, the line segment AD in Figure 6–7), was a side of the 4-sided polygon but becomes a diagonal in the 5-sided polygon (compare Figures 6–7 and 6–8). We have therefore obtained a new diagonal, and so D_5 is at least equal to $D_4 + 1$.

- The line segments connecting new point E to all but the nearest two vertices of the 4-sided polygon give new diagonals (BE and CE), while the line segments connecting new point E to the nearest two vertices become sides of the new polygon (BE and DE). This gives, finally, $D_5 = D_4 + 1 + 2 = 2 + 1 + 2 = 5$; and this is just the number of diagonals we count in Figure 6–8.

Why did we bother going to all this trouble to find D_5 when we could just have counted diagonals in Figure 6–8, your students might now ask? The answer is that this same procedure can be easily generalized to let us go from *any* known D_N to the following D_{N+1}. Simply notice that the first two preceding observations will remain true for any value of N, not just $N = 4$. Notice also that in an N-sided polygon in which we are adding a new $N + 1^{st}$ vertex, the third observation easily generalizes to the observation that $N - 2$ of the original N vertices can be connected to this new vertex to give new diagonals. So the general relationship we are looking for is:

$$D_{N+1} = D_N + 1 + (N - 2)$$

or equivalently:

$$D_{N+1} = D_N + N - 1 \qquad (6\text{–}3)$$

Using formula (6–3) and the fact that we have just discovered that $D_5 = 5$, for example, we could now say that:

$$D_6 = D_5 + 5 - 1 = 5 + 5 - 1 = 9$$

In other words, a 6-sided polygon will have 9 diagonals. This is illustrated in Figure 6–9. With formula (6–3) at their disposal, ask your students to write out a

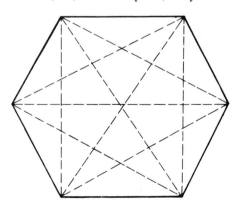

Figure 6-9

keystroke sequence for finding D_{N+1} from N and D_N using formula (6–3) and then use their calculators to complete Table 6–8. The keystroke sequence to be used is:

$$D_{N+1} = D_N + N - 1: \quad \boxed{D_N} \; \boxed{+} \; \boxed{N} \; \boxed{-} \; \boxed{1} \; \boxed{=}$$

Table 6–8. Relationship between number of sides of a polygon, N, and the number of diagonals, D_N

N	D_N
3	0
4	2
5	5
6	9
7	
8	
9	
10	
11	
12	
13	
14	
15	

When the students have all filled in their tables, tell them that formula (6–3) is what is called a *recursive formula*, that is, one in which you must know the previous value D_N in order to get the next value D_{N+1}. Unfortunately, recursive formulas have one major drawback: Just ask your students how they would use formula (6–3) if they were asked to find D_{100}. To do so with formula (6–3), they would have to find every D_i from where Table 6–8 leaves off at D_{15} up to D_{99}, one at a time, and then use D_{99} in formula (6–3) to obtain D_{100}. This is an awful lot of extra work if all you wanted was D_{100} and not all the D_is that precede it.

So what we would now like to do is find a general, nonrecursive formula for D_N that is equivalent to formula (6–3) but that can be used to obtain any particular D_N directly. You can now either ask the students to try and guess a formula for D_N in terms of N using the values in their table (and some hints from you), or you can just give them the formula:

$$D_N = \frac{N^2 - 3N}{2} \tag{6–4}$$

Finally, ask them to verify that this formula is in fact correct by writing out a keystroke sequence for it and then using this keystroke sequence on their calculators for $N = 3$ through $N = 15$ to check that it does give the same values they obtained for Table 6–8 using formula (6–3). The keystroke sequence they would use would be:

$$D_N = \frac{N^2 - 3N}{2}:$$

Hierarchy: $\boxed{N}$ $\boxed{x^2}$ $\boxed{-}$ $\boxed{3}$ $\boxed{\times}$ $\boxed{N}$ $\boxed{=}$ $\boxed{\div}$ $\boxed{2}$ $\boxed{=}$

Left-to-Right: $\boxed{3}$ $\boxed{\times}$ $\boxed{N}$ $\boxed{=}$ $\boxed{+/-}$ $\boxed{+}$ $\boxed{N}$ $\boxed{x^2}$ $\boxed{\div}$ $\boxed{2}$ $\boxed{=}$

Calculator investigation of a geometric point pattern

A second simple but interesting geometric pattern that the calculator can be used with involves what are called "triangular" numbers. Illustrated in Figure 6–10 are sets of points arranged so as to produce triangles of increasing size. Notice

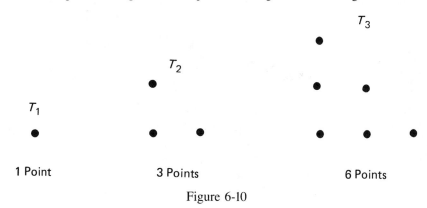

1 Point   3 Points   6 Points

Figure 6-10

that the smallest triangle consists of 1 point, the next smallest consists of 3 points, and the next 6 points. These numbers of points (1, 3, and 6) are called the first three *triangular numbers*. If we let N represent the number of points on each side of the triangle and T_N represent the total number of points making up the triangle, then the observations made from Figure 6–10 can be exhibited in Table 6–9.

Table 6–9. Triangular numbers

N	T_N
1	1
2	3
3	6

With the previous example as a guide, you would now ask your students to develop a recursive formula for T_{N+1} in terms of T_N. One way of doing so, which you might suggest to them, is as follows. Notice from Figure 6–10 that to get from the geometric figure of T_1 to the geometric figure of T_2, all you actually do is add a column of 2 points to the left of T_1. To get from the geometric figure of T_2 to the geometric figure of T_3, all you do is add a column of 3 points to the left of T_2. In other words, $T_2 = T_1 + 2$ and $T_3 = T_2 + 3$. In general, it's not hard to see that to get from figure T_N to figure T_{N+1}, all you do is add a column of $N + 1$ points to the left of T_N, so that $T_{N+1} = T_N + N + 1$. This is the recursive formula we are looking for:

$$T_{N+1} = T_N + N + 1 \qquad (6–5)$$

Now ask the class to write out a keystroke sequence for formula (6–5) and use it to extend Table 6–9 of triangular numbers up to $N = 10$ or so. The keystroke sequence for doing so is:

$$T_{N+1} = T_N + N + 1: \quad \boxed{T_N} \boxed{+} \boxed{N} \boxed{+} \boxed{1} \boxed{=}$$

Finally, have the class use their extended tables to guess, or simply give them, a nonrecursive formula for T_N that is equivalent to recursive formula (6–5). One such formula is:

$$T_N = \frac{N^2 + N}{2}$$

with the corresponding keystroke sequence:

$$T_N = \frac{N^2 + N}{2}: \quad \boxed{N} \boxed{x^2} \boxed{+} \boxed{N} \boxed{=} \boxed{\div} \boxed{2} \boxed{=}$$

They can now verify this nonrecursive formula for T_N by using it with their calculators to redo the values in Table 6–9 and check that they do in fact obtain the same values they found from the recursive formula (6–5).

It might be worth pointing out to the class, after all of this has been completed, that the nonrecursive formula they have just found and verified is equivalent to:

$$1 + 2 + 3 + \ldots + N = \frac{N^2 + N}{2} = \frac{N(N + 1)}{2}$$

since this is a very useful formula to know in a variety of mathematical topics.

Additional examples

Two additional examples of geometric number patterns follow. Each can be either used in the same fashion as the two discussed in this section in the classroom, or

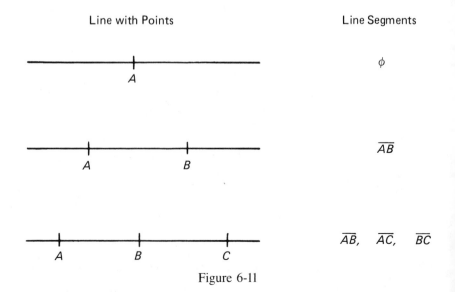

Figure 6-11

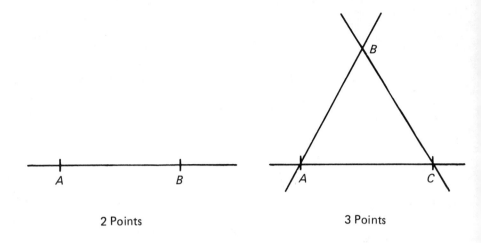

2 Points   3 Points

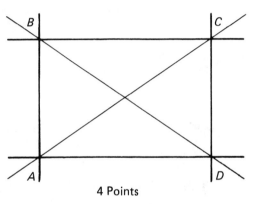

4 Points

Figure 6-12

given as homework problems. Provided with each example is the preliminary table, the recursive formula, and its keystroke sequence, along with the equivalent nonrecursive formula and its keystroke sequence.

1. *Geometric problem:* Given a line with $N = 1$, $N = 2$, or $N = 3$ distinct points in it (Figure 6–11). As shown, the number of distinct line segments, S_N, that could be named would be 0, 1, and 3, respectively, and these observations are:

N	S_N
1	0
2	1
3	3

The problem is to find a formula for the number of distinct line segments S_N corresponding to N distinct points on the line.

Recursive formula and keystroke sequence:
$$S_{N+1} = S_N + N: \quad \boxed{S_N} \; \boxed{+} \; \boxed{N} \; \boxed{=}$$

Nonrecursive formula and keystroke sequence:

$$S_N = \frac{N^2 - N}{2}: \quad \boxed{N}\ \boxed{x^2}\ \boxed{-}\ \boxed{N}\ \boxed{=}\ \boxed{\div}\ \boxed{2}\ \boxed{=}$$

2. *Geometric problem:* Given 2, 3, or 4 points respectively with no three points on the same line. These numbers of points will determine 1, 3, and 6 lines respectively (Figure 6–12). This observation is exhibited in the following table with the number of points represented by N and the corresponding number of lines represented by L_N:

N	L_N
2	1
3	3
4	6

The problem is to find a formula for the number of distinct lines L_N that are determined by N distinct points, no three of which are on the same line.

Recursive formula and keystroke sequence:

$$L_{N+1} = L_N + N: \quad \boxed{L_N}\ \boxed{+}\ \boxed{N}\ \boxed{=}$$

Nonrecursive formula and keystroke sequence:

$$L_N = \frac{N^2 - N}{2}: \quad \boxed{N}\ \boxed{x^2}\ \boxed{-}\ \boxed{N}\ \boxed{=}\ \boxed{\div}\ \boxed{2}\ \boxed{=}$$

Additional calculator activities

1. *Topic:* Complementary and supplementary angles

   Objective: Use the calculator to reinforce the definitions of complement and supplement, as well as their properties.

   Procedure: Have the students fill in the first column of the following table labeled a, with angles between $0°$ and $180°$. They should be instructed to use both integer and noninteger values of a. The only restriction, as indicated in the table, is that the first five values must be acute angles, the sixth value must be a right angle, and the last four values must be obtuse angles. When the first column is filled in, the students are to use their calculators to complete the rest of the table and then answer the questions that follow.

   $$\text{Complement of } a = 90 - a: \quad \boxed{90}\ \boxed{-}\ \boxed{a}\ \boxed{=}$$
   $$\text{Supplement of } a = 180 - a: \quad \boxed{180}\ \boxed{-}\ \boxed{a}\ \boxed{=}$$

   Question 1: Use the first two columns of your table to complete the following statements about supplementary angles.
   (a) The supplement of an acute angle is always a(n) _____ angle.
   (b) The supplement of a right angle is always a(n) _____ angle.

	(1) a	(2) Supplement of a	(3) Complement of a
Acute angles			
Right angle			
Obtuse angles			

(c) The supplement of an obtuse angle is always a(n) _____ angle.

Question 2: Use the first six rows of your table to complete the following statement about the relationship between the supplement and complement of an angle.

"Given any acute or right angle *a*, the difference between its supplementary angle and its complementary angle (that is, its supplement − complement) will always be _____ degrees."

Now prove this statement, as you have completed it, by using the definitions of supplementary angle and complementary angle and a little simple algebra.

2. *Topic:* Classifying triangles according to their angles

Objective: Given a triangle and two of its angles in degrees, use the calculator to find the missing angle and classify the triangle as acute, right, or obtuse.

Keystroke sequence: If *A* and *B* are given angles, and *C* is the missing third angle, then *C* can be obtained from *A* and *B* using the keystroke sequence:

$$C = 180 - A - B: \quad \boxed{180} \; \boxed{-} \; \boxed{A} \; \boxed{-} \; \boxed{B} \; \boxed{=}$$

Example: In Figure 6–13, two angles of the triangle are given. Use these given angles to find the missing third angle and classify the triangle as either acute, right, or obtuse.

Solution: Letting the two given angles be represented as $A = 35.3°$ and $B = 48.8°$, the third angle *C* is found to be:

$$C = 180 - A - B: \quad \boxed{180} \; \boxed{-} \; \boxed{35.3} \; \boxed{-} \; \boxed{48.8} \; \boxed{=} \; (= 95.9)$$

Since the missing angle is $C = 95.9°$, the triangle is obtuse.

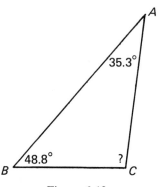

Figure 6-13

3. *Topic:* Relationships among the lengths of the sides of a triangle

   Objective: Given three positive values a, b, and c, use the calculator to determine whether these three values could be the sides of a triangle.

   Procedure: The numbers a, b, and c will be the sides of a nontrivial triangle if and only if the sum of any two sides is greater than the third side. If the sum of any two sides is equal to the third side, then the triangle is a trivial triangle (that is, a line segment). If the sum of any two of the sides is less than the third side, there is no such triangle at all.

   Example: Use your calculator to determine whether the numbers 3.5, 4.8, and 9 can serve as the lengths of the sides of a nontrivial triangle.

   Solution: Letting $a = 3.5$, $b = 4.8$, and $c = 9$, we use the calculator keystroke sequence:

   $$a + b - c: \quad \boxed{3.5} \; \boxed{+} \; \boxed{4.8} \; \boxed{-} \; \boxed{9} \; \boxed{=}$$

   We find that $a + b - c = -0.7$. Since this value is negative, these three numbers cannot be the lengths of the sides of any triangle.

4. *Topic:* Similar triangles

   Objective: Use the calculator to reinforce the definition of similar triangles in terms of angles.

   Procedure: Given two triangles with one missing angle in each. Use the calculator to find the missing angles and determine whether the two triangles are similar.

   Example: Use your calculator to find the missing angles in the triangles of Figure 6–14 and determine whether or not the two triangles are similar.

   Solution: The two missing angles are found using the keystroke sequences:

Triangle *ABC*: $\boxed{180} \; \boxed{-} \; \boxed{72} \; \boxed{-} \; \boxed{67} \; \boxed{=}$	$(C = 41°)$
Triangle *DEF*: $\boxed{180} \; \boxed{-} \; \boxed{72} \; \boxed{-} \; \boxed{67} \; \boxed{=}$	$(E = 67°)$

   Since both triangles have angles of 72°, 67°, and 41°, the triangles are similar.

114

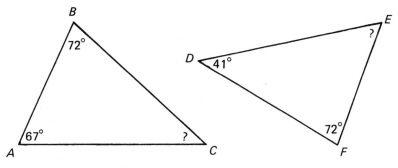

Figure 6-14

5. *Topic:* Similar triangles

Objective: Use the calculator to reinforce the definition of similar triangles in terms of side lengths.

Procedure: Given two triangles and all their side lengths. Use the calculator to compute the ratios of the two triangles' largest sides to each other, middle length sides to each other, and shortest sides to each other (always putting the larger value in the numerator). The triangles will be similar if and only if all three ratios are the same.

Example: Determine, with the aid of your calculator, whether the triangles illustrated in Figure 6–15 are similar.

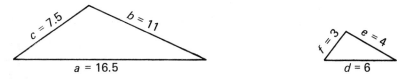

Figure 6-15

Solution: The longest sides are a and d, and their ratio is:

$$\frac{a}{d}: \quad \boxed{16.5} \; \boxed{\div} \; \boxed{6} \; \boxed{=} \quad (\text{Ratio} = 2.75)$$

The middle sides are b and e, and their ratio is:

$$\frac{b}{e}: \quad \boxed{11} \; \boxed{\div} \; \boxed{4} \; \boxed{=} \quad (\text{Ratio} = 2.75)$$

The shortest sides are c and f, and their ratio is:

$$\frac{c}{f}: \quad \boxed{7.5} \; \boxed{\div} \; \boxed{3} \; \boxed{=} \quad (\text{Ratio} = 2.5)$$

Since all three ratios are not the same, these two triangles are not similar.

6. *Topic:* Polygon angle principles for any polygon

Objective: Use the calculator to reinforce, and to give practice in using, the formula(s) relating N, the number of sides of a polygon, and the sum of the interior angles of that polygon S:

115

(a) $S = (N - 2)180°$

(b) $N = \dfrac{S + 360°}{180°}$

Procedure: Have the students write out keystroke sequences for formulas (a) and (b). Then, using these sequences with their calculators, they are to solve problems in which either N is given and S must be found, or S is given and N must be found. The appropriate keystroke sequences are:

(a) $S = (N - 2)180$: $\boxed{N}$ $\boxed{-}$ $\boxed{2}$ $\boxed{=}$ $\boxed{\times}$ $\boxed{180}$ $\boxed{=}$

(b) $N = \dfrac{S + 360}{180}$: $\boxed{S}$ $\boxed{+}$ $\boxed{360}$ $\boxed{=}$ $\boxed{\div}$ $\boxed{180}$ $\boxed{=}$

Example: Mr. Forbes is an architect, and he has just designed a new house for one of his clients. The only problem is that he has forgotten how many sides this house is to have (it is to be a "modern" house and might have more than four sides). Mr. Forbes does remember that the house will be in the shape of a polygon and the sum of its interior angles, S, is 900°. Help Mr. Forbes determine the number of sides of the house, N.

Solution: Using keystroke sequence (b) with $S = 900°$:

$$N = \frac{900 + 360}{180}:\quad \boxed{900}\ \boxed{+}\ \boxed{360}\ \boxed{=}\ \boxed{\div}\ \boxed{180}\ \boxed{=} \quad (N = 7)$$

The number of sides of this polygonal house is therefore 7.

7. *Topic:* Polygon angle principles for regular polygons

Objective: Use the calculator to reinforce, and to give practice in using, the formulas relating the number of sides of a regular polygon N and the values of a corresponding interior angle i and exterior angle e. Use the calculator also to let the students discover the relationship between i and e. The formulas we are talking about are:

(a) $i = \dfrac{180°(N - 2)}{N}$

(b) $e = \dfrac{360°}{N}$

(c) $i + e = 180°$

Procedure: Have the students use their calculators, with the appropriate keystroke sequences for formulas (a) and (b), to fill in the values of the following table one row at a time. When they have done so, ask them to use the values in the last column to state the relationship between i and e for any regular polygon. The keystroke sequences they will need are:

(a) $i = \dfrac{180(N - 2)}{N}$: $\boxed{N}$ $\boxed{-}$ $\boxed{2}$ $\boxed{=}$ $\boxed{\times}$ $\boxed{180}$ $\boxed{\div}$ $\boxed{N}$ $\boxed{=}$

(b) $e = \dfrac{360}{N}$: $\boxed{360}$ $\boxed{\div}$ $\boxed{N}$ $\boxed{=}$

N	i	e	i + e
3			
4			
5			
6			
10			
45			

8. *Topic:* Area of a trapezoid

Objective: Use the calculator to evaluate the area of a trapezoid when the bases and the altitude are given. The formula and corresponding keystroke sequence are:

$$A = \frac{1}{2}h(b + b'): \quad \boxed{b} \; \boxed{+} \; \boxed{b'} \; \boxed{=} \; \boxed{\times} \; \boxed{h} \; \boxed{\div} \; \boxed{2} \; \boxed{=}$$

Example: Use your calculator to find the area of the trapezoid in Figure 6–16.

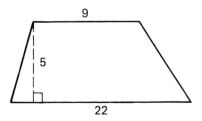

Figure 6-16

Solution: Applying the values $b = 22$, $b' = 9$, and $h = 5$ (from Figure 6–16) to our keystroke sequence:

$$A = \frac{1}{2}(5)(22 + 9): \quad \boxed{22} \; \boxed{+} \; \boxed{9} \; \boxed{=} \; \boxed{\times} \; \boxed{5} \; \boxed{\div} \; \boxed{2} \; \boxed{=} \quad (A = 77.5)$$

so the trapezpoid's area is $A = 77.5$.

9. *Topic:* Area of a circle

Objective: Use the calculator to solve problems involving area of circles.

Special key: $\boxed{x^2}$

Keystroke sequence:

$$A = \text{pi} \; \boxed{\times} \; r^2 \approx 3.14r^2: \quad \boxed{r} \; \boxed{x^2} \; \boxed{\times} \; \boxed{3.14} \; \boxed{=}$$

Example: Joe stops at a pizza parlor on his way home to pick up a pizza or two for his family's dinner. The pizza parlor sells two different-sized pizzas: a medium pizza 20 inches in diameter that costs $3; and a large pizza 40 inches in diameter that costs $6. The two pizzas, their sizes, and their prices are shown in Figure 6–17.

(a) Assuming Joe's family likes the entire pizza, crust and all, use your calculator and the area formula to find out whether Joe does better buying one large pizza for $6 or two medium pizzas for a total of $6.

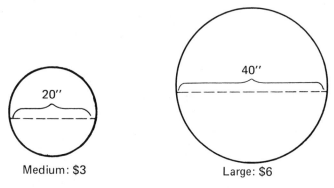

Medium: $3   Large: $6

Figure 6-17

(b) How many medium-sized pizzas would Joe have to buy to get the same amount of pizza (same area) as he gets with one large pizza?

(c) Suppose the crust on either the medium or the large pizza is .5 inches wide (Figure 6–18). And suppose Joe's family eats *only* the crust, and

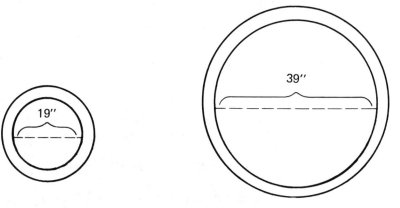

Figure 6-18

nothing else on the pizza. In this case, does he do better (get more crust) with one large pizza or with two medium pizzas?

Solution:

(a) Using the approximation 3.14 for pi in the keystroke sequence for area of a circle, we find that the area of the large pizza is 1,256 square inches while the area of the medium pizza is 314 square inches. So Joe gets more pizza (area) in one large pizza than in two medium pizzas.

(b) Joe would need four medium pizzas at an area of 314 square inches each to equal one large pizza at 1,256 square inches.

(c) The crust area on either pizza is the outside area minus the inside area in Figure 6–18. For the large pizza this works out as 62.015 square inches, while for the medium pizza this works out as 30.615 square inches. So in terms of crust area, one large pizza gives slightly more than two medium pizzas.

10. *Topic:* Coordinate geometry

Objective: Given the coordinates of two points, use the calulator to find the distance between the points.

Special keys: $\boxed{x^2}$ $\boxed{\sqrt{}}$ $\boxed{\text{STO}}$ $\boxed{\text{RCL}}$

Procedure: The distance formula for the distance between the points $A(a_1, a_2)$ and $B(b_1, b_2)$, and the corresponding keystroke sequence are:

distance $(A, B) = \sqrt{(a_1 - b_1)^2 + (a_2 - b_2)^2}$: $\boxed{a_1}$ $\boxed{-}$ $\boxed{b_1}$ $\boxed{=}$ $\boxed{x^2}$ $\boxed{\text{STO}}$ $\boxed{a_2}$ $\boxed{-}$ $\boxed{b_2}$ $\boxed{=}$ $\boxed{x^2}$ $\boxed{+}$ $\boxed{\text{RCL}}$ $\boxed{=}$ $\boxed{\sqrt{}}$

(This can also be done without using the $\boxed{\text{STO}}$ and $\boxed{\text{RCL}}$ keys if your calculator has parentheses keys $\boxed{(}$ and $\boxed{)}$.)

Example: Find the distance between the points $A(2, 5)$ and $B(4, 3.5)$ using your calculator.

Solution:

Distance (A, B): $\boxed{2}$ $\boxed{-}$ $\boxed{4}$ $\boxed{=}$ $\boxed{x^2}$ $\boxed{\text{STO}}$ $\boxed{5}$ $\boxed{-}$ $\boxed{3.5}$ $\boxed{=}$ $\boxed{x^2}$ $\boxed{+}$ $\boxed{\text{RCL}}$ $\boxed{=}$ $\boxed{\sqrt{}}$ $(= 2.5)$

The distance between A and B is therefore 2.5.

11. *Topic:* Coordinate geometry

Objective: Use the calculator and the distance formula keystroke sequence given in activity 10 to reinforce the coordinate geometry definition of a circle as the locus of all those points a specified distance r away from a specified center point c.

Special keys: $\boxed{x^2}$, $\boxed{\sqrt{}}$, $\boxed{\text{STO}}$, $\boxed{\text{RCL}}$

Example: Fred, Jane, and Herman are all friends who have just graduated from junior high school. They are all going to begin attending high school soon and must make plans for getting from their homes to the school. On a map of their town with miles as the unit, the school is located at coordinates (2, 2); Fred's house is at (3, 4); Jane's house is at (5, 6); and Herman's house is at (5.5, 6.7). (See Figure 6–19.) The town's school regulations state that students whose homes lie *within* a circle of radius 5 miles centered at the school must get to school on their own while students whose homes lie *on* or *outside* of this circle can use the town's school bus. Use your calculator and the distance formula keystroke sequence to calculate the distance of each house to the school, and determine which of the three friends (if any) can use the school bus.

Solution: Let the school be the center of a circle with radius $r = 5$ miles. Using the distance formula keystroke sequence with the coordinates of the three houses one at a time, we find:

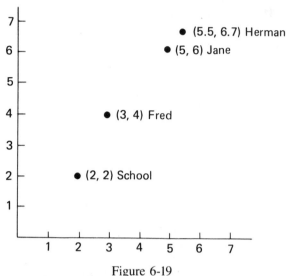

Figure 6-19

(a) The distance from Fred's house to the school is approximately 2.236067 miles. So Fred's house is *within* the circle, and he *cannot* use the school bus.
(b) The distance from Jane's house to the school is exactly 5 miles so Jane's house is *on* the circle, and she *can* use the school bus.
(c) The distance from Herman's house to the school is approximately 5.860034 miles. So Herman's house is *outside* of the circle, and he *can* use the school bus.

12. *Topic:* Solid geometry

Objective: Develop and use calculator keystroke sequences for evaluating solid geometry formulas for surface area and volume.

Special keys: Depends on the particular formulas used.

Example: The formulas for the surface area S and volume V of a sphere having radius r are:

(a) $S = 4(\text{pi})r^2$
(b) $V = \frac{4}{3}(\text{pi})r^3$

Write out a keystroke sequence for each of these formulas, and use them with your calculator to find S and V for a sphere having radius $r = 5.5$. Use the approximation 3.14 for pi.

Solution: The keystroke sequences are:
(a) $S = 4(\text{pi})r^2$: $\boxed{r}$ $\boxed{x^2}$ $\boxed{\times}$ $\boxed{\text{pi}}$ $\boxed{\times}$ $\boxed{4}$ $\boxed{=}$
(b) $V = \frac{4}{3}(\text{pi})r^3$: $\boxed{r}$ $\boxed{\times}$ $\boxed{r}$ $\boxed{\times}$ $\boxed{r}$ $\boxed{\times}$ $\boxed{\text{pi}}$ $\boxed{\times}$ $\boxed{4}$ $\boxed{\div}$ $\boxed{3}$ $\boxed{=}$
With 3.14 for pi, we obtain: $S = 379.94$, $V = 696.55666$ (approximately).

120

7

BUSINESS AND
CONSUMER
MATHEMATICS

Almost by definition, business mathematics and consumer mathematics are both based on, and dependent on, mathematical procedures and computations. There is, of course, a distinct difference between these two subjects in terms of their long-term goals for the person studying them. Business math, for example, is career-oriented, and it is intended to prepare a person for a business career or for more advanced business career courses and learning experiences. Consumer math, on the other hand, consists of mathematical understanding and techniques that every member of society should possess in order to be a more knowledgeable and discerning consumer in the marketplace.

Yet, in spite of these differences in their ultimate purposes, both business math and consumer math have many topics and techniques in common. For example, both consumers and business people need to be familiar with single discounts, with chain discounts, and with comparisons between them. Similarly, both consumers and business people need to know the differences among simple interest, compound interest, and continuously compounded interest, as well as how to compare them. Even more important than being able to compute all these values exactly, both the consumer and the business person should have an intuitive grasp of these concepts, so they can make simple comparisons quickly and easily without computation.

Due to considerable overlap between the two types of math, we will focus this chapter on how the calculator can be used in and for the teaching of topics that are common to both areas.

Single discounts and chain discounts

Single and chain discounts occur quite often in the marketplace, and it is important for both the business person and the consumer to understand what they are, how to interpret a chain discount, and how to compare them. Of course, the simplest, most direct, and most exact way to handle chain discounts, as well as to compare them with single discounts, is to find the single discount equivalent of a chain (that is, to express the chain discount in the same unit as the single discount). Although there are various ways of doing so, on many occasions a simple approximation of the single discount equivalent of a chain would suffice. So intuitive, easy-to-use estimations or bounds should be taught to the student as well.

In this section, we will endeavor to show how both these aims can be accomplished with the use of the calculator. In a suggested classroom presentation of the topic, the calculator will be used to compute single and chain discounts exactly. It will also be used to let the students themselves develop and verify chain discount relationships and estimates. Remember, however, that this way is only a suggestion. Your decision is whether to use the calculator this way, to modify it to your way of teaching, or simply not to use the calculator in this topic at all.

We will assume that you have already covered the topic of single discounts in class and that the students are able to use their calculators to perform the computations in problems of this type.

Problem 1: Mrs. Blake owns an appliance store and has a particular radio that has not been selling well at its regular price of $40. She decides to discount the price by 30 percent in order to entice customers to buy it. How much money is she reducing the sale price by, and what is the new sale price?

Solution: To obtain the dollar amount of the reduction we simply multiply the original price of $40 by the discount 30 percent (or equivalently by 0.30). Using the calculator, the discounted amount of money would be:

$$(0.30)(40): \quad \boxed{0.30} \;\boxed{\times}\; \boxed{40} \;\boxed{=}\; (= 12)$$

So the sale price is being reduced by $12. The new price would therefore be $40 − $12 = $28. An alternative procedure is to say that, since the original sale price is being reduced by 30 percent, the new price would be 70 percent of the old price or, by calculator,

$$(0.70)(40): \quad \boxed{0.70} \;\boxed{\times}\; \boxed{40} \;\boxed{=}\; (= 28)$$

Once again, the reduced sale price is found to be $28.

Once the students are reasonably proficient in doing single discount problems of this type, you can present and discuss the concept of a chain discount and give a problem to be worked out in which a simple two-discount chain is involved. For example, you might give the problem:

Problem 2: The Acme Sporting Goods Store has a pair of skis they have been trying to sell all season. The original price of the skis was $200, but after a month this price was discounted by 20 percent. After one month more, it was discounted by an additional 30 percent. Find the total dollar amount by which this chain of discounts reduces the price. Find the sale price of the skis after this chain discount. And find the single discount equivalent of this chain.

The most direct solution of this problem, of course, is to take the 20-percent discount on the original price to obtain the first discount and the corresponding first sale price. Then we take the 30-percent discount on this discounted price to obtain the second discount and the corresponding final sale price. Proceeding in this manner, and using our calculator for the computations, we find:

$$\text{First discounted amount} = (0.20)(200): \quad \boxed{0.20} \;\boxed{\times}\; \boxed{200} \;\boxed{=}\; (= 40)$$

so the first discounted price of the skis is $200 − $40 = $160.

$$\text{Second discounted amount} = (0.30)(160): \quad \boxed{0.30} \;\boxed{\times}\; \boxed{160} \;\boxed{=}\; (= 48)$$

so the final discounted price of the skis is $160 − $48 = $112. Finally, the total discounted amount is $40 + $48 = $88, and this is equivalent to a single discount of 88/200 = 0.44 = 44 percent.

An alternate procedure would be to realize that after the first discount the price of the skis would be 80 percent (or 0.80) of the original sale price, and that after the second discount the price of the skis would be 70 percent (0.70) of this amount. So the final reduced price would be the original price multiplied by 0.80 and then multiplied by 0.70. By calculator, this would give:

Final discounted price = (200)(0.80)(0.70): $\boxed{200}$ $\boxed{\times}$ $\boxed{0.80}$ $\boxed{\times}$ $\boxed{0.70}$ $\boxed{=}$
(= 112)

So the final sale price of the skis is $112, the same result that we obtained the first way. You can now reinforce these concepts and methods of solution by assigning a problem involving a three-discount chain in which the students are again asked to find the discounted amount of money, the final sale price of the object, and the single discount equivalent of the chain.

Now go back to problem 2 and ask the class to solve it again, but in the following modified form:

> *Problem 3:* In the problem 2 situation, the employee who was assigned to put the discount tags on the skis was John. Unfortunately, John got the two discount tags mixed up and instead of giving the 20-percent discount first and the 30-percent discount second, he gave the 30-percent discount first and the 20-percent discount second. Upon discovering this, John's boss reasoned that since the larger discount of 30 percent, rather than the intended smaller discount of 20 percent, was now being given on the original price of $200, the resulting total discount would be greater than the 44 percent or $88 the store intended. So the store would lose money. The boss therefore ordered John to redo problem 2 with the chain discount as 30 percent followed by 20 percent; find the amount discounted, the final sale price, and the single discount equivalent. Also pay the difference his mistake caused out of his own pocket. Do all this for John so he knows how much money he will have to pay.

Your students should be rather surprised, when they do this problem, to discover that the change in the order of the discounts has no effect on the result. The chain 30/20 percent gives the same single discount equivalent, 44 percent, as the original chain 20/30 percent. You can reinforce this observation by having them redo the subsequent problem involving a three-discount chain with the individual discounts rearranged. Once they accept this discovery, you can actually prove it to them mathematically. The proof is really fairly simple, involving the second solution procedure described in connection with problem 2. To see this, let the chain be made up of the N individual discounts $a_1, a_2, \ldots, a_N$ in this order. If the original sale price of the object is P, we obtain the successive discounted prices after each discount by multiplying by $(1 - a_1), (1 - a_2), \ldots, (1 - a_N)$ one at a time. The final sale price of the object after all the discounts in the chain have been applied would therefore be:

Final discounted sale price = $P(1 - a_1)(1 - a_2)$ b ... b $(1 - a_N)$

Yet since multiplication does not depend on the order of the factors, the terms $(1 - a_i)$ can be arranged in any other order and would still give the same result for the product. Since a rearrangement in the order of the discounts in the chain corresponds to a rearrangement of the factors $(1 - a_i)$ in the product, the result is proved. We have therefore discovered the following two rules for chain discounts:

Rule 1: In a chain discount, the order of the individual discounts in the chain does not affect the chain's single discount equivalent.

Rule 2: In a chain discount involving the individual discounts a_1, a_2, a_3, ..., a_N, the chain discount is equivalent to a single discount: $1 - (1 - a_1)(1 - a_2)$ b ... b $(1 - a_N)$.

(In rule 2, since the product of the terms in parentheses is the final reduced price of the object, we obtain the discount by subtracting this final price from 1 or 100 percent.)

With rule 2 available for use, you can now assign several additional chain discount problems for homework. In these problems the students are to use rule 2 to find the single discount equivalent of the given chain. Then they are to use their calculators to compute this single discount equivalent and the final sale price of the object involved. On a calculator with parentheses keys $\boxed{(}$ and $\boxed{)}$, the keystroke sequences would be:

Hierarchy:

$\boxed{1}$ $\boxed{-}$ $\boxed{(}$ $\boxed{1}$ $\boxed{-}$ $\boxed{a_1}$ $\boxed{)}$ $\boxed{\times}$ $\boxed{(}$ $\boxed{1}$ $\boxed{-}$ $\boxed{a_2}$ $\boxed{)}$ $\boxed{\times}$ ... $\boxed{\times}$ $\boxed{(}$ $\boxed{1}$ $\boxed{-}$ $\boxed{a_N}$ $\boxed{)}$ $\boxed{=}$

Left-to-Right:

$\boxed{(}$ $\boxed{1}$ $\boxed{-}$ $\boxed{a_1}$ $\boxed{)}$ $\boxed{\times}$ $\boxed{(}$ $\boxed{1}$ $\boxed{-}$ $\boxed{a_2}$ $\boxed{)}$ $\boxed{\times}$ ... $\boxed{\times}$ $\boxed{(}$ $\boxed{1}$ $\boxed{-}$ $\boxed{a_N}$ $\boxed{)}$ $\boxed{=}$ $\boxed{+/-}$ $\boxed{+}$ $\boxed{1}$ $\boxed{=}$

Let's illustrate the use of these keystroke sequences with the following chain discount problem:

> *Problem 4:* Last Christmas a famous, expensive Texas department store advertised "his and her" gold bicycles for $45,000 for the pair. This was 60 days before Christmas. Two weeks later they reduced the price by 10 percent. Two weeks later they reduced the price by another 20 percent. Finally, one week before Christmas, they made a final reduction of 30 percent in the price. Use rule 2 with your calculator to find (a) the single discount equivalent of this three-discount chain, (b) the amount of money discounted, and (c) the final sale price.
>
> *Solution:* Using rule 2 with $a_1 = 10$ percent $= 0.10$, $a_2 = 20$ percent $= 0.20$, and $a_3 = 30$ percent $= 0.30$, we obtain:

$1 - (1 - 0.10)(1 - 0.20)(1 - 0.30)$: $\boxed{1}$ $\boxed{-}$ $\boxed{(}$ $\boxed{1}$ $\boxed{-}$ $\boxed{0.10}$ $\boxed{)}$ $\boxed{\times}$ $\boxed{(}$ $\boxed{1}$ $\boxed{-}$ $\boxed{0.20}$ $\boxed{)}$ $\boxed{\times}$ $\boxed{(}$ $\boxed{1}$ $\boxed{-}$ $\boxed{0.30}$ $\boxed{)}$ $\boxed{=}$ ($= 0.496$)

So the single discount equivalent of this 10/20/30-percent chain is $0.496 = 49.6$ percent; the amount of the discount is:

$(0.496)(45,000)$: $\boxed{0.496}$ $\boxed{\times}$ $\boxed{45,000}$ $\boxed{=}$ ($= 22,320$)

or $22,320; and the final sale price of the objects is $45,000 - $22,320 = $22,680.

While rule 2 and the corresponding keystroke sequences allow the students to calculate the single discount equivalent of a chain exactly, rule 1 is a handy piece of information to have available for quick comparisons. For example, suppose you have a choice between chain discounts of 10/15 percent or 14/10 percent on similar items. Rule 1 tells you that the chain 10/15 percent is equivalent to the chain 15/10 percent, and this is obviously preferable to the chain 14/10 percent. Both rules are useful to know in appropriate situations.

There is one further simple rule for chain discounts that your students should be aware of and that they can be led to discover. This is a method of estimating the single discount equivalent of a chain by obtaining lower and upper bounds through inspection of the chain. Give the class a few simple numerical examples in which discount chains are presented and in which rule 2 is used with the calculator to obtain the single discount equivalent. You can do so with a chart like the one in Table 7–1.

*Table 7–1. Single discount equivalents
of chains*

Chain Discount	Single Discount Equivalent
10/12%	
17/9%	
7/10/25%	
35/15/30%	
10/15/20/25%	

When this chart is completed, ask the students to compare each chain with its single discount equivalent to see if they can discover any way to use the individual discounts in the chains to obtain lower and upper bounds on the single discount equivalent. As a hint, you might suggest that they compare the single discount equivalent with each individual discount of the chain one at a time, and with the sum of the individual discounts in the chain, respectively. They should be able to discover the following rule, which can then be formally and explicitly stated:

Rule 3: Given a chain discount comprised of the individual discounts a_1, a_2, ..., a_N. Then the single discount equivalent of this chain will be greater than any one of the individual a_i, and less than the simple sum of all the a_i.

(Of course, if the chain consists of only one discount, then this is itself the single discount equivalent.) The proof of rule 3 is simple and can be talked through as follows:

Take any individual discount a_i in the chain, and rearrange the chain by putting a_i first. Then, since in this reordered chain the discount a_i is followed by additional discounts, the chain must give a greater discount than a_i by itself. But the reordered chain is equivalent to the original chain by rule 1. So the single discount equivalent of the chain is greater than every individual a_i of the chain, and the first part of rule 3 is proved. To prove the second part of rule 3, notice that the chain will be equivalent to the simple sum of the discounts comprising it if and only if each a_i in the chain is applied to the entire original price of the object. Since only the first discount of the chain, a_1, is applied to the original price with all subsequent a_is applied to reduced prices, the chain discount must be smaller than the simple sum of the a_i.

Rule 3 can be very useful in making quick comparisons in certain appropriate situations. For example, suppose you are given the choice on a certain object between a single discount of 25 percent and a chain discount of 15/10 percent. According to rule 3, the single discount would be preferable to you as the buyer, because the single discount of 25 percent *is* the simple sum of 15 percent and 10 percent. So by rule 3 the single discount of the chain would be less than the 25-percent single discount. On the other hand, suppose the choice was between a single discount of 20 percent and a chain discount of 15/10 percent. In this case all rule 3 tells you is that the single discount equivalent of the chain is greater than 15 percent but less than 15 percent + 10 percent = 25 percent. This information is not enough for a sure choice between the two alternatives. We would have to use rule 2 to actually compute the single discount equivalent of this chain. Doing this we would obtain:

$$\text{Single discount equivalent} = 1 - (1 - 0.15)(1 - 0.10)$$
$$= 0.235 = 23.5\%$$

So the chain would be preferable to you as the buyer to the single discount of 20 percent.

Simple, compound, and continuously compounded interest

In the past, when the topic of interest and interest rates was fairly uncomplicated, the business person and consumer had relatively little trouble in interpreting the meaning of a particular interest rate or making comparisons between interest rates. Over the past few years, however, many different types of interest accounts and certificates have been developed to entice business persons or consumers to one lending or savings institution rather than to another. As a result, people must be aware of what these different types of interest are, how to interpret them, and how to compare them. A good place to start is in the classroom, and a good, basic set of interest types to use in this introduction are:

- simple interest,
- compound interest, and
- continuously compounded interest.

In Chapter 4 on trigonometry we discussed and illustrated a classroom activity in which students must use their calculators to investigate a problem and to report whatever they are able to learn. This type of investigative activity is most useful as a homework assignment after the groundwork has been laid in the classroom, since this allows the students as much time as they need to tentatively form questions, use the calculator to study them, and draw conclusions. This procedure can be employed quite nicely in the topic under discussion in this section to allow the students to discover for themselves some very interesting and useful properties of compound and continuously compounded interest.

We will assume that you have discussed simple yearly interest and given the class several simple yearly interest problems for solving with the help of their calculators. For example, you might have assigned the problem:

> *Problem 5:* You invest $1,000 in a savings account giving 12-percent simple yearly interest. At the end of the year how much interest have you earned and how much money is in your account?

The answer, of course, is that the interest earned by the end of the year is (12 percent)($1,000) = (0.12)($1,000) = $120, and the amount in the savings account is therefore $1,000 + $120 = $1,120. Now introduce the idea of simple compound interest (that is, interest compounded semiannually) and modify the problem to:

> *Problem 6:* At the same time that you invested your $1,000 at 12-percent simple yearly interest, your friend Rebecca invested $1,000 in an account that offered 12-percent interest compounded semiannually. How much interest did Rebecca earn by the end of the year? What was the simple yearly interest equivalent of her earnings? And how much did she have in her account at the end of the year?

Clearly, at the end of the first 6 months the bank gave Rebecca half of her yearly interest (12 percent/2 = 6 percent) on her $1,000. If she was given (6 percent)($1,000) = (0.06)($1,000) = $60 after 6 months, she now had $1,060 in her account. At the end of the next 6 months (the end of the year), she received the other 6-percent interest on this entire amount of $1,060, which amounted to (6 percent)($1,060) = (0.06)($1,060) = $63.60. So at the end of the year she had a total of $1,000 + $60 + $63.60 = $1,123.60 in her account; she had earned interest of $123.60; and this was equivalent to a simple yearly interest of $123.60/$1,000 = 0.1236 = 12.36 percent. In other words, the simple compounding had raised the base interest rate of 12 percent to 12.36 percent. Not a great deal, certainly, but better for Rebecca to have this extra interest than for the bank to have it. And better for you to have had it if you had been aware of the difference.

With this introduction you can now generalize the problem a bit by extending it with the same principal of $1,000 and the same base rate of 12-percent interest yearly to compoundings three times a year and four times a year, always using the calculator to help with the computations involved. Finally, you can give the class the general compound interest formula:

(7–1) $$I = (1 + \frac{i}{n})^n - 1$$

where:

- i represents the base annual interest;

- *n* represents the number of times the interest is compounded during the year; and

- *I* is the simple interest equivalent after the interest *i* is compounded *n* times.

For example, if we use formula (7–1) with the data of problem 6, we would have *i* = 12 percent = 0.12, *n* = 2, and we would find:

$$I = (1 + \frac{0.12}{2})^2 - 1 = (1.06)^2 - 1$$
$$= 1.1236 - 1 = 0.1236$$
$$= 12.36\%$$

This is the same result we obtained earlier.

If formula (7–1) looks a bit unusual, that's probably because the formula that is usually given involves the amount of money in the account at the beginning of the year *P*, as well as the amount at the end of the year *S*. That formula is:

(7–2) $$S = (1 + \frac{i}{n})^n P$$

We can easily get from formula (7–2) to formula (7–1) by taking *P* = $1 to convert the units to percentages and then subtracting off the original principal $1 to leave only the interest obtained. While formula (7–2) is more common, we want to use formula (7–1). So either start with formula (7–1) as we did or develop it from formula (7–2) if formula (7–2) is given to the class first.

The next step in this topic ordinarily would be to say something about what happens as you increase the number of compoundings *n*. Then use these comments to lead into the concept of continuous compounding and evaluating such an interest rate. Instead of doing so, however, simply announce to the class that this is all you are going to tell them about compound interest. Now it is up to them to use formula (7–1) with their calculators to discover any other interesting properties of simple and compound interest.

You might suggest that they do so by using either the 12-percent base of problem 5 and 6 or any other base interest rate they like, and then by using formula (7–1) and their calculators to find the simple yearly interest equivalent of a variety of compoundings. You can, of course, give whatever leading questions or hints that you think will help them; but the basic idea of this activity is to let students investigate and make discoveries themselves rather than simply getting the answer to an explicit question. You might, for example, suggest that they look at what happens when more and more compoundings are used or whether increasing the number of compoundings always results in an increase in the interest received. You might suggest that they look at how fast the interest rate increases with an increase in the number of compoundings. You might ask if it is always possible, with a sufficient number of compoundings, to double the base yearly interest rate, triple it, and so on. You might finally ask if there is any bound at all to how much interest you can earn on your deposit if you can just get the bank to compound often enough. The systematic way of investigating these questions, of course, is for the students to put the data they obtain in some sort of table, and you might suggest this procedure as well. The keystroke sequence for evaluating formula (7–1) on a calculator with an exponentiation key $\boxed{x^y}$ would be:

$$I = (1 + \frac{i}{n})^{n} - 1:\quad \boxed{i}\ \boxed{\div}\ \boxed{n}\ \boxed{+}\ \boxed{1}\ \boxed{=}\ \boxed{x^y}\ \boxed{n}\ \boxed{=}\ \boxed{-}\ \boxed{1}\ \boxed{=}$$

Formula (7–1) can still be evaluated without an exponentiation key, but it is a bit more difficult. Still, the calculator does simplify the computational load enormously, and this is an eminently workable task if given as part of, or as the entire, homework assignment.

As an example of what might be discovered by the students, let's suppose we decide to continue with 12 percent as our base interest rate i. Evaluate the simple interest equivalent of the compounding I for $n = 1$ compoundings through $n = 10$ compoundings inclusive, and put this data into a table. The data we would obtain is given in Table 7–2 with a column for the "change in I" included.

*Table 7–2. Simple interest equivalents I for yearly interest
of 12% compounded n times*

n	I	Change in I
1	12%	
		0.36%
2	12.36%	
		0.1264%
3	12.4864%	
		0.06448%
4	12.55088%	
		0.391%
5	12.58998%	
		0.02625%
6	12.61623%	
		0.01877%
7	12.635%	
		0.01422%
8	12.64922%	
		0.01102%
9	12.66024%	
		0.0089%
10	12.66914%	

From this table you may easily draw the following simple, tentative conclusions:

- As you increase the number of compoundings n, the interest I you receive increases as well,

- The rate of increase of I is decreasing, so you don't keep reaping the same added amount of interest for every increase in n,

- It appears from Table 7–2 that the value of I may not be unbounded and that there might be some limit to how large I can become, dependent, of course, on the initial value i, no matter how many compoundings are used.

You can now verify these observations, informing the class that there is in fact a limit value for the sequence of Is as n increases without bound, and that this limiting case is called *continuous compounding*. The formula for the limit value I^* of the sequence of Is can now be given as:

$$I^* = e^i - 1$$

Finally, you can have the students use their calculators and formula (7–3) to compute I^* for the table of I values they have been constructing. Then they can extend their table by evaluating I for a few very large values of n just to verify that, as n increases without bound, the corresponding values of I do indeed approach I^* as a limiting value.

Allow the students to discover and to verify these facts and formulas on their own, with their calculators, rather than simply giving it all to them or just having them read the textbook. They will not only remember them better, but they will also *use* them when they are so required in later courses or in life situations.

Additional calculator activities

1. *Topic:* Percentage, rate, and base

Objective: Use the calculator with the formula $P = R \times B$ to find any one of these values when the other two are given.

Example: Shirley has written a book for Endicott Publishing Company and according to her contract she is to receive 12.5 percent of all sales on this book. At the end of the first 6-month period she receives a percentage check for $5,625. How much money was taken in totally on her book and how much did the company keep?

Solution: Using the formula $P = R \times B$ with the given data $R = 12.5$ percent $= 0.125$ and $P = \$5,625$, we would find the base B by rewriting the formula as $B = P/R$ and using the calculator keystroke sequence:

$$B = P/R: \quad \boxed{P} \; \boxed{\div} \; \boxed{R} \; \boxed{=}$$

to obtain $B = \$45,000$. So the total amount of money taken in was $45,000, and the company kept $45,000 - \$5,625 = \$39,375$ of it.

2. *Topic:* Percentage of change

Objective: Use the calculator to compute the percentage of change, given the base amount and the final amount.

Example: In 1970, heating oil was selling for 32¢ per gallon in the United States, on the average. In 1980 the average selling price had risen to $1.08 per gallon. Find the percentage of change between 1970 and 1980.

Solution: With both average sale prices expressed in the same units of "cents," the prices are 32 and 108 for 1970 and 1980, respectively. If the base amount is represented by B and the final amount is represented by F, then the percentage of change PC is given by the formula $PC = (F - B)/B$, and this can be evaluated using the calculator keystroke sequence:

$$PC = (F - B)/B: \quad \boxed{F} \; \boxed{-} \; \boxed{B} \; \boxed{=} \; \boxed{\div} \; \boxed{B} \; \boxed{=}$$

Using this keystroke sequence with the given values of this example $B = 32$, $F = 108$, we find $PC = 2.375 = 237.5$ percent. In other words, the average price per gallon of heating oil has risen 237.5 percent over the specified 10-year period.

3. *Topic:* Bank accounts and reconciliation statements

   Objective: Use the calculator with a reconciliation statement to verify the final balance.

   Procedure: Give the students several reconciliation statements for both classwork and homework in which they are to use the calculator to verify the final balance. The reconciliation statement should include:
   (a) the initial balance (IB);
   (b) the individual debits (D), such as checks cashed and any service charges;
   (c) the individual credits (C), such as deposits and any interest earned; and
   (d) the final balance (FB).
   The customer should also have a list of all uncashed checks (UC). That is, checks that are listed in the checkbook but not on the reconciliation statement or on any previous statement. With this information, the student should be able to verify the final balance (FB), as well as the checkbook balance (CB), which takes into account uncashed checks. The calculator keystroke sequences to use are:

   $$FB = IB + \sum C_i - \sum D_i: \quad \boxed{IB}\ \boxed{+}\ \boxed{C_1}\ \boxed{+}\ \boxed{C_2}\ \boxed{+}\ \cdots\ \boxed{+}\ \boxed{C_n}$$
   $$\boxed{-}\ \boxed{D_1}\ \boxed{-}\ \boxed{D_2}\ \boxed{-}\ \cdots\ \boxed{-}\ \boxed{D_m}\ \boxed{=}$$

   In other words, the final balance on the reconciliation statement should be equal to the initial balance plus all the credits minus all the debits.

   And

   $$CB = FB - \sum UC_i: \quad \boxed{FB}\ \boxed{-}\ \boxed{UC_1}\ \boxed{-}\ \boxed{UC_2}\ \boxed{-}\ \cdots\ \boxed{-}\ \boxed{UC_k}\ \boxed{=}$$

   Or, the checkbook balance should be equal to the final balance on the reconciliation statement minus all the uncashed checks listed in the checkbook.

4. *Topic:* Checking accounts and interest rates

   Objective: Use the calculator to compare different types of checking accounts (such as free accounts versus minimum balance interest accounts) to see which is better and when.

   Example: Henry wants to open a checking account at his local bank and must decide between two types of accounts. The first account does not cost him any money (no service charge), but it does not give him any interest either. The second account gives him 2-percent interest each month on the minimum balance he had in his account, but also charges him a service fee of $16 if his minimum balance drops below $1,000. Use your calculator and an appropriate keystroke sequence to fill in Table 7–3 for the given minimum amounts he might have in his account and then answer the questions that follow.

Table 7–3. Checking account with interest and possible service charge

Minimum Monthly Balance (*MMB*)	Interest (*MMB*)(0.02)	Service Charge	Earnings (Interest–Charge)
$ 0		$16	
$ 200		$16	
$ 400		$16	
$ 600		$16	
$ 800		$16	
$1000		$ 0	
$1200		$ 0	
$1400		$ 0	

Question 1: Looking at the values in the last column of your table, would Henry's "Earnings (Interest–Charge)" be dependent on his monthly minimum balance in this second type of account?

Question 2: Keeping in mind that because the first type of account gives no interest but has no service charge, it always has earnings of $0. Use Table 7–3 to determine: (a) when it would be more advantageous for Henry to use the first type of account (no interest and no service charge); (b) when it would be more advantageous for Henry to use the second type of account (2-percent interest but a $16 service charge if his monthly minimum balance is below $1,000); and (c) when the earnings would be the same for both types of accounts.

Question 3: If Henry knows he can always keep a minimum monthly balance of at least $900 in his account, which type of account will give him greater earnings?

Question 4: If Henry knows that he will never be able to keep a monthly minimum balance of more than $575 in the account, which type of account will give him greater earnings?

5. *Topic:* Arithmetic averages

Objective: Use the calculator to find the one missing item in a series with a specified average.

Keystroke sequence: If a series of n items has individual values $v_1, v_2, \ldots, v_n$ and a specified arithmetic average V, then the final value v_n can be obtained from the other v_i and from V, using the following formula and keystroke sequence:

$$v_n = nV - \sum_{1}^{n-1} v_i: \boxed{n} \boxed{\times} \boxed{V} \boxed{-} \boxed{v_1} \boxed{-} \boxed{v_2} \boxed{-} \cdots$$
$$\boxed{-} \boxed{V_{n-1}} \boxed{=}$$

Example: Sharon received a bill from the Electric Company for the first 6 months of the year January through June. The average charge for the 6 months was given as $V = \$42$, and the first 5 individual monthly charges were listed as $37, $30, $53.75, $48.50, $39.27. What was the missing charge for the sixth month?

Solution: Using the given information with our keystroke sequence we find

$$v_6: \boxed{6} \boxed{\times} \boxed{42} \boxed{-} \boxed{37} \boxed{-} \boxed{30} \boxed{-} \boxed{53.75} \boxed{-}$$
$$\boxed{48.50} \boxed{-} \boxed{39.27} \boxed{=} \quad (= 43.48)$$

so the charge for the missing month must be $43.48.

6. *Topic:* Depreciation methods: straight-line and sum-of-the-years'-digits

Objective: Use the calculator to let the students discover that for the same item and for the same period of depreciation, both these methods give the same total depreciation; the sum-of-the-years'-digits method always gives a higher yearly depreciation than the straight-line method for the first few years and a lower yearly depreciation for the last few years; and the yearly difference between the two methods gets smaller and smaller as the period of depreciation increases.

Procedure: Give the class a depreciation problem in which both the original cost and the trade-in or scrap value for a specified item are given. Now divide the class up into five or six groups, and give each group a different period of depreciation for the item (2 years, 3 years, and so on). Then ask each group to use their calculators to find the yearly depreciation for the item with both the sum-of-the-years'-digits method and the straight-line method. When everyone has finished, have one person from each group put their results on the board and draw a graph representing the comparison between the two methods.

   For example, let's say the item had an original cost of $750 and a scrap value of $150. In that case, the difference is $600, and the yearly amounts of depreciation, along with their corresponding graphs for periods of 3 years and 6 years, are illustrated in Figures 7–1 and 7–2, respectively. You can now use the data and graphs of these figures to point out the comparisons mentioned in the Objective statement of this activity.

7. *Topic:* Gross pay and hourly wages

Objective: Use the calculator to compute a worker's gross weekly pay when the base hourly pay is given, the number of hours worked is given, and the worker earns time and a half after either 8 hours a day or after 40 hours a week.

Example: Fran earns a base hourly wage of $5.25 for a regular 40-hour work week, and time and a half for every hour beyond 40. If she worked 52 hours last week, what was her gross pay?

Figure 7-1 *Straight-line depreciation versus sum-of-the-years'-digits depreciation for a period of 3 years*

Year	Straight-Line	Sum-of-the Years'—Digits	Difference
1st	$200	$300	−$100
2nd	$200	$200	$0
3rd	$200	$100	$100
Sum:	$600	$600	$0

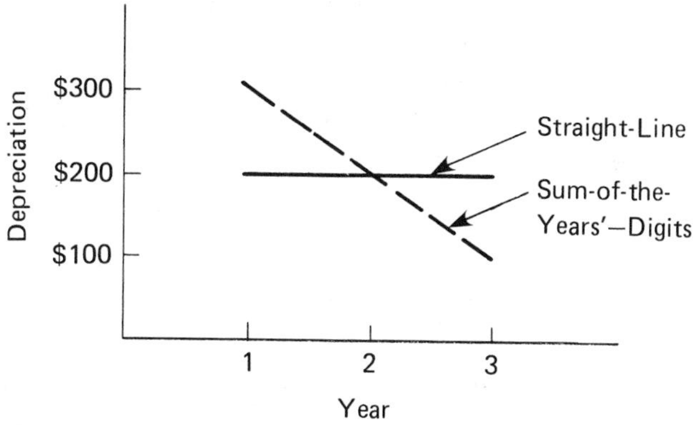

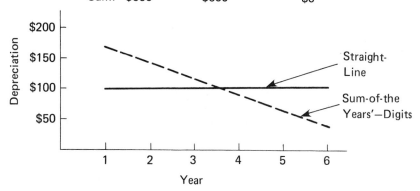

Figure 7-2 *Straight-line depreciation versus sum-of-the-years'-digits depreciation for a period of 6 years*

Year	Straight-Line	Sum-of-the Years'—Digits	Difference
1st	$100	$171.43	−$71.43
2nd	$100	$142.86	−$42.86
3rd	$100	$114.29	−$14.29
4th	$100	$85.71	$14.29
5th	$100	$57.14	$42.86
6th	$100	$28.57	$71.43
Sum:	$600	$600	$0

Solution: If B represents base hourly pay, W represents the standard number of hours in a work week, and N represents the actual number of hours worked that week, then gross pay GP is given by the following formula and corresponding keystroke sequence:

$$GP = [(N - W)1.5 + W]B:$$ $\boxed{N}$ $\boxed{-}$ $\boxed{W}$ $\boxed{=}$ $\boxed{\times}$ $\boxed{1.5}$ $\boxed{+}$ $\boxed{W}$ $\boxed{=}$ $\boxed{\times}$ $\boxed{B}$ $\boxed{=}$

Using the data of this problem ($N = 52$, $W = 40$, $B = \$5.25$) in this keystroke sequence, we obtain $GP = \$304.50$.

8. *Topic:* Straight commission versus base salary plus commission

   Objective: Use the calculator to show the students that in a comparison between a straight commission of a percent, and a base salary BS plus commission of b percent (with a percent greater than b percent):
   (a) there is a unique sales level S given by:

   $$S = BS/(a\% - b\%)$$

   for which the two methods give the same answers;
   (b) for sales below S, the base salary plus commission will be higher; and
   (c) for sales above S, the straight commission will be higher.

   Procedure: Assign a problem in which specified values of BS, a percent, and b percent are given. Then give several different sales amounts for which the students are to use their calculators to compute the salesperson's earnings under both methods. Have them display their results in a table like the one illustrated in Table 7–4. Make sure that one of the sales values you

Table 7–4. Comparison of earnings under a straight commission of $a\%$,
and under a base salary BS plus commission of $b\%$

Monthly Sales	Base Salary Plus $b\%$ Commission	Straight $a\%$ Commission

give for the table is $S = BS/(a\% - b\%)$, and that the other values include both values less than S and values greater than S. When the tables are complete, put the data on the board and represent it graphically by graphing monthly sales versus straight commission earnings, along with monthly sales versus base salary plus commission earnings on the same set of axes.

Using the data and the graphs, you can then point out the comparisons mentioned in the Objective statement of this activity.

9. *Topic:* Promissory notes

Objective: Use the calculator with the formula $M = (1 + ti)F$ (F = face value of note; i = yearly interest rate; t = term of note expressed as a part of a year; and M = maturity value of note) to find any one of the four unknowns when the other three are given.

Special key: $\boxed{(}$ and $\boxed{)}$ required only if you are trying to find F given t, i, and M.

Keystroke sequences:

$M = (1 + ti)F$: $\boxed{t}$ $\boxed{\times}$ $\boxed{i}$ $\boxed{+}$ $\boxed{1}$ $\boxed{=}$ $\boxed{\times}$ $\boxed{F}$ $\boxed{=}$

$F = \dfrac{M}{1 + ti}$: $\boxed{M}$ $\boxed{\div}$ $\boxed{(}$ $\boxed{t}$ $\boxed{\times}$ $\boxed{i}$ $\boxed{+}$ $\boxed{1}$ $\boxed{)}$ $\boxed{=}$

$t = \dfrac{\dfrac{M}{F} - 1}{i}$: $\boxed{M}$ $\boxed{\div}$ $\boxed{F}$ $\boxed{-}$ $\boxed{1}$ $\boxed{=}$ $\boxed{\div}$ $\boxed{i}$ $\boxed{=}$

$i = \dfrac{\dfrac{M}{F} - 1}{t}$: $\boxed{M}$ $\boxed{\div}$ $\boxed{F}$ $\boxed{-}$ $\boxed{1}$ $\boxed{=}$ $\boxed{\div}$ $\boxed{t}$ $\boxed{=}$

10. *Topic:* Home insurance

Objective: Use the calculator to compare premium rates when insurance is taken one year at a time, as opposed to multiple years with a discount.

Example: The Smiths want to take out a $40,000 insurance policy on their house. The company they are dealing with offers them insurance of this amount at $2.50 per $100 of insurance for one year, or 4.4 times the one year rate for five years. How much would the Smiths save over 5 years by taking the multiple-year discount rate rather than renewing the policy each year for 5 individual years?

Solution: Since $40,000 must be broken down into units of $100, we do this with the formula and keystroke sequence:

Units of $100 = $40,000/$100: $\boxed{40,000}$ $\boxed{\div}$ $\boxed{100}$ $\boxed{=}$

and obtain 400 units. At $2.50 per unit the yearly premium would be:

Yearly premium = ($2.50)(400): $\boxed{2.5}$ $\boxed{\times}$ $\boxed{400}$ $\boxed{=}$

or $1,000 per year. So if they renew the policy each year for 5 years, they will have paid a total of $5,000. If they instead take the 5-year policy at the outset, they would pay a total premium of:

5-year premium = (4.4)(Yearly premium): $\boxed{4.4}$ $\boxed{\times}$ $\boxed{1,000}$ $\boxed{=}$

or $4,400. So they would save $5,000 − $4,400 = $600 over the 5 years by taking the multiple-year policy.

11. *Topic:* Wholesale or invoice price

Objective: Use the calculator to obtain the wholesale or invoice price of an item when its list price and any trade and/or cash discounts are given.

Example: Professor Cummings wants to buy a home computer that is listed at $2,500. As a college professor he is entitled to a trade discount of 20 percent, and, since he is willing to pay cash, he is entitled to an additional discount of 15 percent. After these two discounts, what will the wholesale price of the computer be?

Solution: As we saw in the section of this chapter on single and chain discounts, the chain discount 20/15 percent is equivalent to a single discount of $1 - (1 - 0.20)(1 - 0.15)$. Using our calculator to compute this value, we obtain:

$$1 - (1 - 0.20)(1 - 0.15): \quad \boxed{(} \ \boxed{1} \ \boxed{-} \ \boxed{0.20} \ \boxed{)} \ \boxed{\times}$$
$$\boxed{(} \ \boxed{1} \ \boxed{-} \ \boxed{0.15} \ \boxed{)} \ \boxed{=} \ \boxed{+/-} \ \boxed{+} \ \boxed{1} \ \boxed{=} \quad (= 0.32)$$

So this chain is equivalent to a single discount of 32 percent. The wholesale price can now be found as:

$$\text{Discount} = (0.32)(2,500): \quad \boxed{0.32} \ \boxed{\times} \ \boxed{2,500} \ \boxed{=} \quad (= 800)$$
$$\text{Wholesale} = \text{List} - \text{Discount}: \quad \boxed{2,500} \ \boxed{-} \ \boxed{800} \ \boxed{=} \quad (= 1,700)$$

The wholesale price of the item is $1,700, a savings of $800.

12. *Topic:* Cost price, sale price, and percentage of markup

Objective: Use the calculator to find either the cost price (*CP*) or the sale price (*SP*) when the other one and the percentage of markup are given. (It must also be specified whether you are using a percentage of markup based on selling price or on cost price.)

Procedure: The formulas relating sale price (*SP*), cost price (*CP*), and percentage of markup (*i*) are:

Percentage of markup based on *SP*: $SP = CP/(1-i)$
Percentage of markup based on *CP*: $SP = CP(1+i)$

Have the students write out calculator keystroke sequences for *SP* in terms of *CP* and *i* for both these equations, and then solve percentage of markup problems using the calculator. If the *CP* is to be found, then each of these two equations must be solved for *CP* in terms of *SP* and *i* and corresponding keystroke sequences developed.

Example: Larry bought a copy of the first Superman comic book ever published two years ago for $20. He wants to sell it so as to make a percentage of markup profit of 250 percent based on his cost. What must he sell it for to make this much profit?

Solution: In this problem, $CP = \$20$, $i = 250$ percent based on cost price, and SP is the unknown. The formula and keystroke sequence to use are:

$$SP \; = \; CP(1+i): \quad \boxed{1} \; \boxed{+} \; \boxed{i} \; \boxed{=} \; \boxed{\times} \; \boxed{CP} \; \boxed{=}$$

With the data of this problem, we obtain the solution $SP = 70$. So Larry should sell his comic book for \$70.

8

PROBABILITY AND STATISTICS

Most other subject areas covered in this book have one particular level at which they are usually taught and are most appropriate: for example, secondary school for algebra one and two, trigonometry, geometry, and business and consumer math; college for elementary calculus. Probability and statistics, however, are appropriate for, and can be taught at, a variety of levels from junior high school all the way through college. In this chapter we will try to illustrate uses of the calculator in probability and statistics that might be employed—with modifications, of course—for any of these levels of presentation. In particular, we will illustrate the use of the calculator both as an aid in computation and as an aid in the development and clarification of new concepts.

Computing the arithmetic mean and the standard deviation on the calculator

Given a set of values a_1, a_2, a_3, $\ldots$, a_N, the arithmetic mean M and standard deviation S are the two most commonly used measures of the group's "central tendency" and "variability," respectively. These parameters are frequently employed in both descriptive statistics and inferential statistics, and, while the formula for evaluating M is simple and straightforward, there are many numerically equivalent formulas for evaluating S. Unfortunately, most of these formulas require the user either to put the given data into some type of tabled form or to round off and write down intermediate values, or both. On occasion, however, both during the taking of a statistics course and afterward, these statistical procedures and formulas are put into actual use, and it would be extremely convenient to be able to compute M and S quickly and accurately on the calculator, without having to do either. In other words, you could use a procedure in which the data is entered, a keystroke sequence is pressed, and the values of M and S appear in the display to be copied down. You can actually do just this if your calculator has a $\boxed{\text{SUM}}$ or $\boxed{\Sigma}$ key with which values can be added together automatically in memory. Let's look at the appropriate formulas and keystroke sequence for obtaining M and S on such a calculator. The formulas for M and S that we will make use of are:

$$(8\text{--}1) \qquad M = \frac{\Sigma a_i}{N} ; \qquad S = \sqrt{\frac{1}{N^2}\left[N\Sigma a_i^2 - (\Sigma a_i)^2\right]}$$

To employ formulas (8–1) we need to be able to accumulate both Σa_i (the sum of the a values themselves) and Σa_i^2 (the sum of the squares of the a values), as the data is entered into the calculator. On a calculator with a $\boxed{\text{SUM}}$ (or $\boxed{\Sigma}$) key, this is accomplished by using the keystroke sequence:

$$\boxed{a_i} \quad \boxed{\text{SUM}} \quad \boxed{x^2} \quad \boxed{+}$$

to enter the first $(N-1)$ a values, and the keystroke sequence:

$$\boxed{a_N} \quad \boxed{\text{SUM}} \quad \boxed{x^2} \quad \boxed{=}$$

for the final a value in the given set. With this approach, you accumulate the sum of the a_is (Σa_i) in memory, while at the same time accumulating the sum of the a_i^2s (Σa_i^2) in the display. For example, if we have the four values $a_1 = 1$, $a_2 = 2$, $a_3 = 4$, and $a_4 = 8$, the keystroke sequence for accumulating the a_is and the a_i^2s would be:

(8–2) $\boxed{a_1}\ \boxed{\text{SUM}}\ \boxed{x^2}\ \boxed{+}\ \boxed{a_2}\ \boxed{\text{SUM}}\ \boxed{x^2}\ \boxed{+}\ \boxed{a_3}\ \boxed{\text{SUM}}$
$\boxed{x^2}\ \boxed{+}\ \boxed{a_4}\ \boxed{\text{SUM}}\ \boxed{x^2}\ \boxed{=}$

The display would now show 85, the sum of the a_i^2s ($\Sigma a_i^2 = 85$). If we press the $\boxed{\text{RCL}}$ key, we obtain 15 in the display, the sum of the a_is ($\Sigma a_i = 15$).

Once keystroke sequence (8–2) has been used to accumulate Σa_i in memory and Σa_i^2 in display, it is a simple matter to make use of these values in formulas (8–1) to obtain M and S without having to write down any intermediate values. To do so, we simply:

- multiply the display value by N;

- subtract the square of the value in memory;

- divide this entire amount by N^2; and

- take the square root of the result. This will be S.

To obtain M, we then divide N into Σa_i, which we recall from memory. (Using this memory location when we evaluate S does not destroy the value; it is still in memory waiting to be recalled again when needed.) The complete calculator keystroke sequence for finding M and S for the four a values $a_1 = 1$, $a_2 = 2$, $a_3 = 4$, and $a_4 = 8$ follows. Keep in mind that all we need to do is write down the values of S and M when they appear in the display.

(8–3)

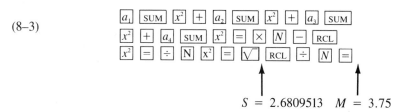

$S = 2.6809513 \quad M = 3.75$

Notice that, since all the work is performed on the calculator, intermediate computations use all the digits the calculator has available to work with, usually at least 8 or 10. So the results obtained using this procedure will in general be quite accurate to several decimal places. To show how simple this procedure is, even with decimal values of a_i, we will use it in another example.

Problem: Use the procedure described to find M and S for the following set of values:

2   3.5   6.3   7   7.9   8   8.25   9   9.15   10

Solution: Use keystroke sequence (8–3), but extend the repetitive part of it to the accumulation of the sum of all ten of our given a values and their squares. We thus obtain:

$$S = 2.4210328 \quad M = 7.11$$

This keystroke sequence might look imposing, but more than half of it is simply the repetitive accumulation of the a values and their squares. In spite of its length it is actually fairly simple to remember and enter. Although becoming familiar and proficient with this procedure requires a bit of practice, the result is very acurate, and you do not have to write down anything but the final values of M and S as they appear in the display. So learning the approach is one of the most worthwhile expenditures of effort you or your students could make for the long-run study and use of statistics. In addition, while formulas (8–1) and the corresponding keystroke sequence give M and S for use in descriptive statistics, you can easily modify both the formula for S in (8–1) and the corresponding part of the keystroke sequence to obtain by calculator the values of M and the square root of variance estimator for use in inferential statistics.

Rules for means and standard deviations

An important topic in both descriptive and inferential statistics is that of "rules for means and standard deviations." The rules themselves are actually quite simple and straightforward, and they do nothing more than describe the resultant changes in M and S when the a values in the original set are either (a) each increased or decreased by the identical amount C, or (b) each multiplied or divided by the identical amount C (with $C \neq 0$ when division is used). Yet these rules are the basis for the very useful and important standardization formulas

$$z = \frac{a - M}{S} \quad \text{and} \quad a = zS + M$$

So students should understand them. With the help of the calculator and the keystroke sequence developed in the previous section, the class can not only learn these results, they can also be led to discover them. Here's how.

First present and discuss both the mean M and standard deviation S of a set of values. Give the class practice in evaluating M and S both the regular way and with the calculator procedure. Then take a set of six or so a values, write them on the board, and ask the class to find M and S for this set. When they have done so, modify the set of values in an inconsistent fashion—add different amounts to different a_is, subtract different amounts, multiply or divide various a_is by different amounts, or make up a combination of these changes. Then ask the class to find the M and S for these changed values using their calculators. Then do all this once more.

Afterwards, ask the class whether they think there was any way they could have guessed what effect these changes in the a values would have on the M and S values other than actually computing M and S from the new a values explicitly. After a bit of discussion (and, if necessary, another example), they should be willing to accept the fact that if the original a values are changed in a haphazard and inconsistent manner, then the only way to determine what the changes in M and S are is to recompute them using the changed a_is. On the other hand, suppose all the original a values are changed in a consistent and uniform fashion and by the same amount (such as increased by 3, decreased by 7.5, multiplied by 4, or divided by 10). Then predicting the changes in M and S will be possible. Rather than telling them how to do so, however, you want them to discover it for themselves using their calculators.

At this point, distribute copies of Tables 8–1 and 8–2 to the students and ask them to simply follow the directions. With a little help from you for any student who really needs it, they should not only be able to discover the rules for means and standard deviations for themselves, but they will also get needed practice in evaluating means and standard deviations at the same time. Once the rules have been discovered and discussed, simply assign a few homework problems in which these rules must be used as a reinforcement.

Problem: Select any 6 values of a you want for the first columns of Tables 8–1 and 8–2. You can use integer values, noninteger values, positive values, negative values, or zero. Then use these values to fill in the remaining columns of the tables. When this is done, use your calculator with keystroke sequence (8–3), extended to 6 a values, to compute M and S for each column of values in each table. Place your answers below the respective columns in the spaces provided. When all this has been done, use the completed tables to answer the questions that follow.

Table 8–1. Sets of values with their M and S.

(1)	(2)	(3)	(4)	(5)
a	$a - 2$	$a - 1$	$a + 1$	$a + 2$

$M = $ __ __ __ __ __

$S = $ __ __ __ __ __

Table 8–2. Sets of values with their M and S

(1)	(2)	(3)	(4)	(5)	(6)
a	$a \div 4$	$a \div 2$	$a \cdot 2$	$a \cdot 4$	$a(-3)$

$M =$ —   —   —   —   —   —

$S =$ —   —   —   —   —   —

Question 1: Look at the values of M and S for the original set of a values in Table 8–1. Now look at the values of M and S when this original set of as has the value C added to each a for $C = -2, -1, +1,$ and $+2,$ respectively. Based on these values, can you generalize as to what happens to the M and S of a set of values when any value C is added to each original value in the set? Does the M change and, if so, by how much? Does the S change and, if so, by how much?

Question 2. Look at the values of M and S for the original set of a values in Table 8–2, and the values of M and S for the other columns. Can you generalize as to what happens to M and S when each a value is multiplied by C, or each a value is divided by $C \neq 0$. *Does M change and, if so, by how much? Does S change and, if so, by how much?*

The standard (or unit) normal curve

One of the most important and useful curves in probability, descriptive statistics, and inferential statistics is the standard (or unit) normal curve. This is the unique, normally shaped distribution curve having a mean of 0 and a standard deviation of 1 (so technically it is a "z curve"). The student of probability and statistics is usually introduced to this curve by way of binomial probabilities and the binomial probability distribution. The usual sequence of steps leading up to the standard normal curve and its use goes something like this:

- Binomial experiments are introduced and discussed, and the binomial probability formula is given and illustrated. This is the formula

$$\text{Prob}(n \text{ successes}) = \binom{n}{k}(p)^k(q)^{n-k}$$

where n represents the number of trials in the experiment; k represents the desired number of successes (and therefore $n - k$ represents the number of failures); p represents the probability of a success on any one trial; and $q = 1 - p$ represents the probability of a failure on any one trial.

- Presented and illustrated next is the idea of computing all the individual binomial probabilities in a given binomial experiment and using these values to construct a complete (theoretical) binomial probability distribution curve.

- After several illustrations of the second point, the teacher points out that, when binomial probability distribution curves are developed for experiments in which the values of both Np and Nq are reasonably "large," all the resulting curves seem to have approximately the same shape. This common shape is then given the name *normal curve*, and the mathematical family of theoretically continuous normal curves is presented and discussed.

- Finally, at some later time when either normal curves are used to approximate binomial distribution curves to answer questions about binomial experiments, or when normal curves are being studied directly for some probabilistic or statistical purpose, the class is introduced to the standard or unit normal curve. At this point, they are shown how to convert any normal curve into the standard normal curve using the z transformation, and consequently how to transform any question about any normal curve into an equivalent question about the standard normal curve, which can be answered using a table of standard normal curve areas or ordinates.

In the fourth step of this sequence, students often have difficulty. The reason for this difficulty is that, while they generally have opportunities to work on and to see numerical examples in the first three steps, they never actually get to see one or more normal curves standardized and thereby converted into one and the same curve, the standard normal curve. So this fourth step always remains conceptual rather than empirical and concrete, and students accept it because the teacher says it is so rather than because they have actually seen it happen and so really believe and understand it. Why not let the student actually transform an entire normal distribution into a standard normal distribution? The reason is that normal distributions are theoretically comprised of an infinite number of values and such a distribution cannot be worked with one value at a time. But binomial distributions are comprised of only a finite number of values, and they can be worked with one value at a time. If we make use of approximately normal binomial distribution curves, and let the students use their calculators to standardize and graph these approximately normal curves, then they can get the flavor of this step and actually see it in action. Following is a description of one way this might be done as part of the ordinary classroom presentation of binomial experiments and binomial probability distributions.

Let's assume that you have been teaching and discussing the topic of binomial experiments and the binomial probability distribution, and that you have progressed through the first three steps. As part of that night's homework assignment, divide the class into four or five groups and assign each group a particular binomial experiment to investigate. In other words, each group is given an n, p, and q with different groups getting different values of these variables. Make sure that each of the experiments assigned has np and nq large enough so that the resulting distribution bar graphs will be approximately normal in shape.

Each group takes its given values of n, p, and q and, with their calculators, evaluates all the individual binomials from $k = 0$ to $k = n$, drawing the corresponding probability bar graph. Once this is done, however, they are also to "standardize" the distribution by converting each k-value to a corresponding z-value using the transformation formula

$$z = \frac{\text{Score} - \text{Mean}}{\text{Standard deviation}} = \frac{k - np}{\sqrt{npq}}$$

Using the fact that each z-value obtained in this way has the same probability as the k-value it came from, they are to draw the corresponding "standardized" probability bar graph of z-values. Since they will have to convert a large number of k-values to z-values, and since the mean and standard deviation appearing in the transformation formula are likely to be decimal values, they should be advised to use their calculators in these transformations. The keystroke sequence would be:

$$z = \frac{k - M}{S} : \quad \boxed{k}\; \boxed{-}\; \boxed{M}\; \boxed{=}\; \boxed{\div}\; \boxed{S}\; \boxed{=}$$

On the day this assignment is due, begin by having one person from each group put their binomial probability bar graph on the board. Then point out to the class both the similarities and differences among the graphs. Clearly they will be similar in shape, since having np and nq large in each case insures that they will all be approximately normal. You can even emphasize this point by lightly drawing into each bar graph the approximating normal curve.

Yet, while they are similar in this one characteristic, it should be easy to see from the graphs that they are quite different in such other characteristics as the arithmetic mean, the standard deviation, and the range. You can even point out some more subtle ways in which they are different from each other, such as the percentage of each distribution's values that are within a specified number of points of the distribution's mean. For example, suppose you had assigned three binomial distributions for homework, and these three distributions had the following values of n, p, and q:

- $n = 15$, $p = 0.5$, $q = 0.5$
- $n = 16$, $p = 0.25$, $q = 0.75$
- $n = 20$, $p = 0.6$, $q = 0.4$.

Then their probability distributions and corresponding bar graphs would look like those illustrated in Figures 8–1, 8–2, and 8–3, respectively. As indicated, the three graphs are similar in shape but different in terms of their means, standard deviations, ranges, and percentage of values in each distribution within 1 point of the mean.

Now erase all these probability distributions and bar graphs. Ask one person from each group to come up to the board and draw the bar graph of their

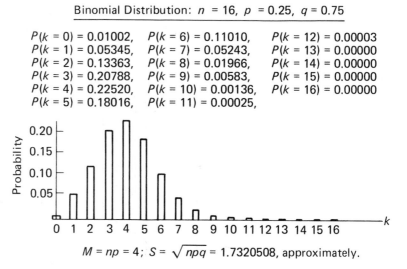

Figure 8-1

Binomial Distribution: $n = 15$, $p = 0.5$, $q = 0.5$

$P(k = 0) = 0.00003,$	$P(k = 6) = 0.15274,$	$P(k = 11) = 0.04166$
$P(k = 1) = 0.00046,$	$P(k = 7) = 0.19638,$	$P(k = 12) = 0.01389$
$P(k = 2) = 0.00320,$	$P(k = 8) = 0.19638,$	$P(k = 13) = 0.00320$
$P(k = 3) = 0.01389,$	$P(k = 9) = 0.15274,$	$P(k = 14) = 0.00046$
$P(k = 4) = 0.04166,$	$P(k = 10) = 0.09164,$	$P(k = 15) = 0.00003$
$P(k = 5) = 0.09164,$		

$M = np = 7.5;$ $S = \sqrt{npq} = 1.9364916$, approximately.

Figure 8-2

Binomial Distribution: $n = 16$, $p = 0.25$, $q = 0.75$

$P(k = 0) = 0.01002,$	$P(k = 6) = 0.11010,$	$P(k = 12) = 0.00003$
$P(k = 1) = 0.05345,$	$P(k = 7) = 0.05243,$	$P(k = 13) = 0.00000$
$P(k = 2) = 0.13363,$	$P(k = 8) = 0.01966,$	$P(k = 14) = 0.00000$
$P(k = 3) = 0.20788,$	$P(k = 9) = 0.00583,$	$P(k = 15) = 0.00000$
$P(k = 4) = 0.22520,$	$P(k = 10) = 0.00136,$	$P(k = 16) = 0.00000$
$P(k = 5) = 0.18016,$	$P(k = 11) = 0.00025,$	

$M = np = 4;$ $S = \sqrt{npq} = 1.7320508$, approximately.

distribution after they had "standardized" it by converting all the original k values to corresponding z values. The probabilities and corresponding bar graphs of the experiments illustrated in Figures 8–1, 8–2, and 8–3 after standardizing are given in Figures 8–4, 8–5, and 8–6, respectively. Point out to the class that not

149

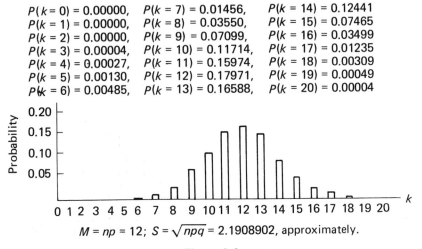

Binomial Distribution: $n = 20$, $p = 0.6$, $q = 0.4$

$P(k = 0) = 0.00000$, $P(k = 7) = 0.01456$, $P(k = 14) = 0.12441$
$P(k = 1) = 0.00000$, $P(k = 8) = 0.03550$, $P(k = 15) = 0.07465$
$P(k = 2) = 0.00000$, $P(k = 9) = 0.07099$, $P(k = 16) = 0.03499$
$P(k = 3) = 0.00004$, $P(k = 10) = 0.11714$, $P(k = 17) = 0.01235$
$P(k = 4) = 0.00027$, $P(k = 11) = 0.15974$, $P(k = 18) = 0.00309$
$P(k = 5) = 0.00130$, $P(k = 12) = 0.17971$, $P(k = 19) = 0.00049$
$P(k = 6) = 0.00485$, $P(k = 13) = 0.16588$, $P(k = 20) = 0.00004$

$M = np = 12$; $S = \sqrt{npq} = 2.1908902$, approximately.

Figure 8-3

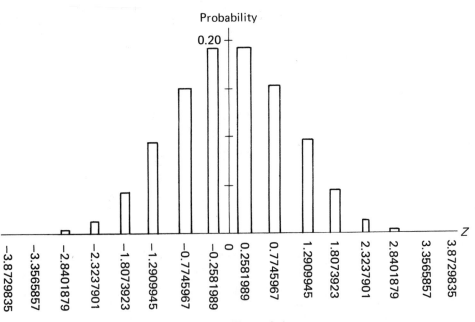

Figure 8-4

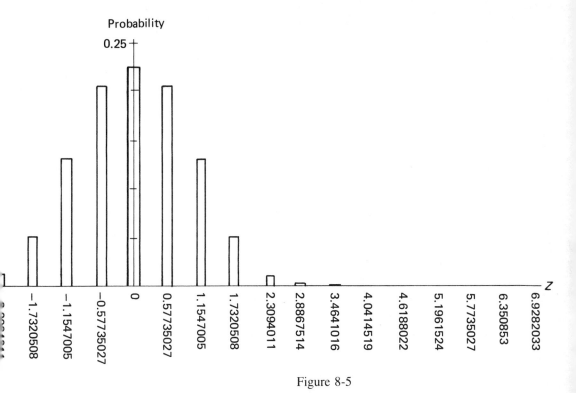

Figure 8-5

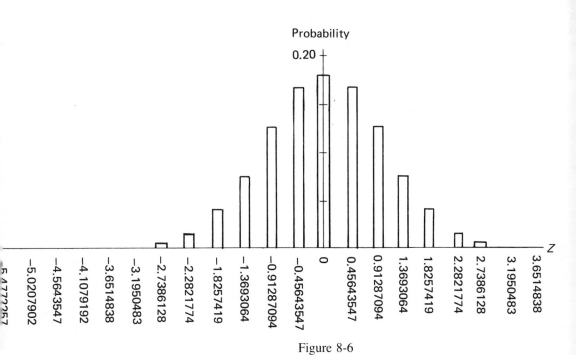

Figure 8-6

only do the three standardized curves still have the same shape as each other, just as they did before standardizing, but they now all have the same mean of 0 and the same standard deviation of 1. In fact, they are all much more similar to each other in range than they were before standardizing, even in the percentage of values of each distribution that is within 1 point of the mean. In other words, the process of standardizing the different binomial distributions and corresponding bar graphs has taken curves that were similar only in shape, and made them similar in all other aspects as well.

You can now take the final step and tell the class that if, in fact, all the original curves had been exactly normal with different means and standard deviations instead of just approximately normal binomial distribution curves, then the resulting standardized curves of *z* values would have been identical to each other. This common standardized curve with normal shape, mean of 0, and standard deviation of 1 can now be called by its proper name, the *standard (or unit) normal curve*. Its properties and corresponding tables of standard normal curve areas and ordinates may be given and discussed. The students not only see several different "normal" curves transformed into the "same" curve by standardizing them, but they also actually perform the transformations themselves. So they have a better understanding of what they are doing and why when they use this procedure in later topics.

Additional calculator activities

1. *Topic:* Mean (absolute) deviation

    Objective: To acquaint the student with another commonly used descriptive measure of the variability of a set of values, the Mean (absolute) deviation; and to use the calculator to show the students that the mean deviation is generally approximately equal to, but slightly less than, the standard deviation.

    Procedure: After the class is familiar with and able to easily compute the standard deviation *S* of a given set of values, define the mean deviation as:

    $$\text{Mean deviation} = MD = \frac{\Sigma |a_i - M|}{N}$$

    Discuss why this also gives a "measure" of the variability of a set of values. Then give several examples of sets of values and ask the class to evaluate both *S* and *MD* for each set. We have already seen how to evaluate *S* earlier in this chapter. The keystroke sequence for evaluating *MD* uses the composition of the square key and the square root key $\boxed{x^2}$ $\boxed{\sqrt{}}$ to obtain the absolute value of each deviation. (If you don't want to do this, simply tell the class to press the $\boxed{+/-}$ or $\boxed{\text{CHS}}$ key whenever a mean deviation is negative.) The sequence is:

$$MD = \frac{\Sigma |a_i - M|}{N}:$$

$$\boxed{a_1}\ \boxed{-}\ \boxed{M}\ \boxed{=}\ \boxed{x^2}\ \boxed{\sqrt{\ }}\ \boxed{\text{STO}}\ \boxed{a_2}\ \boxed{-}\ \boxed{M}$$
$$\boxed{=}\ \boxed{x^2}\ \boxed{\sqrt{\ }}\ \boxed{+}\ \boxed{\text{RCL}}\ \boxed{=}\ \boxed{\text{STO}}\ \boxed{a_3}\ \boxed{-}\ \boxed{M}$$
$$\boxed{=}\ \boxed{x^2}\ \boxed{\sqrt{\ }}\ \boxed{+}\ \ldots\ \boxed{a_N}\ \boxed{-}\ \boxed{M}\ \boxed{=}\ \boxed{x^2}$$
$$\boxed{\sqrt{\ }}\ \boxed{+}\ \boxed{\text{RCL}}\ \boxed{=}\ \boxed{\div}\ \boxed{N}\ \boxed{=}$$

Now point out to the class that, although the *MD* is generally different from the *S*, they are fairly close in most cases. So *S* can be interpreted as "approximately equal to the mean distance of each value from the group mean." Furthermore, point out that *MD* is generally slightly less than *S*. (This can be proved mathematically if you like, and it is not very difficult. But several examples in which this consistently occurs should be enough to convince the class.)

2. *Topic:* Properties of the group mean and the group median

Objective: To use the calculator to show the class that the mean *M* is closest to each value in the set it represents when error of representation is measured in square deviation; and that the median is closest to each value in the set it represents when error of representation is measured in absolute deviation. That is:

(8–4) $$\frac{\Sigma(a_i - \text{Mean})^2}{N} \leq \frac{\Sigma(a_i - B)^2}{N} \quad \text{for } B \neq mean$$

and

(8–5) $$\frac{\Sigma|a_i - \text{Median}|}{N} \leq \frac{\Sigma|a_i - B|}{N} \quad \text{for } B \neq median$$

Procedure: Ask the class for any set of 6 or 7 values, and then have them calculate the mean and median of the set. Now calculate the first expression in (8–4) with the group mean. Ask the students in the class now to each pick a value of *B* to replace the mean in this expression and to calculate the value of this average square deviation from *B*. When they have done so, ask if anyone has obtained a value smaller than yours with the mean. When it is clear that no one has, point out to the class that this is in fact a property of the mean and that there is *no* other value that is closer to all the values in a set than the mean when error of representation is measured by the average of the square deviations of the a_i values from the number representing them.

Now repeat this procedure using the median of the group and formula (8–5) to show that the median has the property of best representing a set of values when error of representation is measured by the average of the absolute deviations (rather than by the square deviations) of the values in the set from the number representing them.

3. *Topic:* Properties of a set of *z* values

Objective: Use the calculator to verify that every set of *a* values transformed by the formula:

$$z = \frac{a_i - M_a}{S_a}$$

to a corresponding set of z values does, in fact, result in a set having mean of 0 and standard deviation of 1.

Procedure: The rules for means and standard deviations discussed earlier in this chapter theoretically prove that a set of a values with mean M_a and standard deviation S_a has, after being transformed to z values using this transformation formula, a mean of 0 and a standard deviation of 1. Yet it is much more impressive and long-lasting if the students can verify this rule for themselves. So ask each student in the class to select his or her own set of a values, and then to use the calculator with the keystroke sequence given earlier in the chapter to evaluate the M_a and S_a. The students are then to use their calculators to convert their set of values to a corresponding set of z values using the keystroke sequence:

$$z = \frac{a_i - M_a}{S_a}: \quad \boxed{a_i} \; \boxed{-} \; \boxed{M_a} \; \boxed{=} \; \boxed{\div} \; \boxed{S_a} \; \boxed{=}$$

Finally, they are once again to use the keystroke sequence for M and S on their set of z values. They should be impressed to discover that each set of transformed values has mean 0 and standard deviation 1.

4. *Topic:* Transforming from one frame of reference to another

   Objective: Use the calculator to verify that the transformation formula

   $$b_i = \left(\frac{a_i - M_a}{S_a} \right) S_b + M_b$$

   transforms a set of a values with mean M_a and standard deviation S_a into a corresponding set of b values with mean M_b and standard deviation S_b.

   Procedure: After this transformation formula has been derived using the rules for means and standard deviations, ask the class to give you any set of a values and a pair of desired values for the mean and standard deviation they would like the set to have (such as a desired $M_b = 100$ and $S_b = 15$). Ask them to use their calculators to evaluate M_a and S_a for the original set of values, and then to use these values to obtain a transformation formula that should take the given a values and convert them to b values having M_b and S_b as specified by them. Finally, they should use their calculators to actually transform the a_is to b_is, and then to show that the resulting b values do indeed have the specified mean and standard deviation values.

5. *Topic:* Evaluating and interpreting simple probabilities

   Objective: Use the calculator to evaluate simple probabilities in decimal form, and then interpret these decimal values as the approximate percentages of all possible outcomes in the experiment that would have given the desired event as a result.

Example: You are going to roll a pair of dice once. Use your calculator to find, in decimal form, the probability that the two dice will give a sum of 7. Then interpret what your answer means in terms of the number of possible outcomes of the experiment.

Solution: If we represent the numbers that occur on the two dice as an ordered pair, then we can represent all the possible outcomes as the following 36 equally likely results:

$$
\begin{array}{cccccc}
1,1 & 1,2 & 1,3 & 1,4 & 1,5 & \boxed{1,6} \\
2,1 & 2,2 & 2,3 & 2,4 & \boxed{2,5} & 2,6 \\
3,1 & 3,2 & 3,3 & \boxed{3,4} & 3,5 & 3,6 \\
4,1 & 4,2 & \boxed{4,3} & 4,4 & 4,5 & 4,6 \\
5,1 & \boxed{5,2} & 5,3 & 5,4 & 5,5 & 5,6 \\
\boxed{6,1} & 6,2 & 6,3 & 6,4 & 6,5 & 6,6
\end{array}
$$

If we let the event E be defined as:

$$E = \{\text{all outcomes in which the sum is 7}\}$$

then the circled outcomes are just those that make E occur, so

$$\text{Prob}(E) = \frac{6}{36} = 0.16666666 \text{ (approximately by calculator)}$$

So approximately 17 percent of all the equally likely outcomes in this experiment would make event E occur.

6. *Topic:* Law of large numbers

Objective: Use the calculator with the law of large numbers to determine the approximate number of times a specified event can be expected to occur in a specified number of independent and identical trials.

Example: It has been estimated that there are approximately 5,000,000,000 planets in the Milky Way, and that in general the probability that any particular planet would be capable of supporting human life is only about 0.000002. Use your calculator with the law of large numbers to determine how many of these planets can be expected to be capable of supporting human life.

Solution: Let E be the event:

$$E = \{\text{the planet is capable of supporting human life}\}$$

let $N = 5,000,000,000$ be the number of planets in the Milky Way or the number of trials; and let $p = \text{Prob}(E) = 0.000002$ for any one particular planet. Then, by the law of large numbers and using the calculator for the computation:

$$Np = (5,000,000,000)(0.000002) = 10,000$$

In other words, we can expect approximately 10,000 of these planets to be capable of supporting human life. (Of course, the law of large numbers does not tell us *which* 10,000 of these 5,000,000,000 planets are the ones capable of supporting human life—just that there are approximately 10,000 of them.)

7. *Topic:* Pearson correlation coefficient *r*

    Objective: Use the calculator to show that the Pearson correlation coefficient *r* is left unchanged when either the set of *X* values, the set of *Y* values, or both sets of values are changed to an equivalent set using a linear transformation. Once this is established, the students can be shown how to transform the sets of *X* values and *Y* values so as to make the computation of *r* as simple as possible.

    Procedure: Give the class a set of pairs of *X,Y* values and ask them to use their calculators to find the correlation coefficient *r* between the given *X* and *Y* values. Now have each student select a linear transformation with which to change the given values. Specifically instruct some students to transform only the *X* values, instruct other students to transform only the *Y* values, and instruct still others to transform both the *X* and *Y* values using the same linear transformation. Finally, instruct some students to transform both the *X* and the *Y* values using different linear transformations. Now have them use their calculators to carry out the transformations and then to compute the Pearson correlation coefficient *r* for the transformed pairs of values. Once they do so, you can ask several people what they obtained, and they should all have the same *r* value as you had originally. Once they clearly understand and accept this point, discuss with the class which transformations made the computations more difficult and which made them simpler. Also discuss guidelines for how to transform the given values to make the computation of *r* as simple as possible.

8. *Topic:* Combinations

    Objective: Use the calculator, and an appropriate keystroke sequence for evaluating combinatorials, to find probabilities in combinatoric problems.

    Keystroke sequence: Thinking of the combination $_nC_k$ in the form:

    $$_nC_k = \frac{n\,b\,(n-1)\,b\ldots b\,(n-k+1)}{1\,b\,2\,b\,3\,b\ldots b\,k} = (\frac{n}{1})\,(\frac{n-1}{2})\ldots(\frac{n-k+1}{k})$$

    we can evaluate $_nC_k$ by alternately multiplying and dividing pair by pair starting with $(\frac{n}{1})$, decreasing the numerator and increasing the denominator by 1 at a time, and stopping with the pair in which the denominator is *k*. For example, to find $_5C_3$:

    $_5C_3$: $\boxed{5}$ $\boxed{\div}$ $\boxed{1}$ $\boxed{\times}$ $\boxed{4}$ $\boxed{\div}$ $\boxed{2}$ $\boxed{\times}$ $\boxed{3}$ $\boxed{\div}$ $\boxed{3}$ $\boxed{=}$ (= 10)

    Example: You own 9 cats: 3 black-and-white, 3 grey, and 3 Siamese. Late at night you go to your refrigerator to get a snack, and you hear 6 of your cats meowing for food. Since the lights are all off, you cannot see the colors of the 6 cats. Use combinatoric notation to write down an expression for the probability that the 6 meowing cats consisted of 2 black-and-whites, 2 greys, and 2 Siamese. Then use your calculator to evaluate each combinatoric and compute the probability.

Solution: Since there are 3 of each type cat totally, and you are looking for 2 of each to make up the 6 meowing cats, the number of ways this can occur is: $(_3C_2)(_3C_2)(_3C_2)$. Totally, the number of different ways you can have 6 cats meowing out of 9 cats is: $_9C_6$. Using our calculator, $_3C_2$ and $_9C_6$ are found to be:

$$_3C_2 = (\frac{3}{1})(\frac{2}{2}):\quad \boxed{3}\;\boxed{\div}\;\boxed{1}\;\boxed{\times}\;\boxed{2}\;\boxed{\div}\;\boxed{2}\;\boxed{=}$$
$$(=3)$$

$$_9C_6 = (\frac{9}{1})(\frac{8}{2})(\frac{7}{3})(\frac{6}{4})(\frac{5}{5})(\frac{4}{6}):\quad \boxed{9}\;\boxed{\div}\;\boxed{1}\;\boxed{\times}\;\boxed{8}\;\boxed{\div}\;\boxed{2}\;\boxed{\times}$$
$$\boxed{7}\;\boxed{\div}\;\boxed{3}\;\boxed{\times}\;\boxed{6}\;\boxed{\div}\;\boxed{4}\;\boxed{\times}$$
$$\boxed{5}\;\boxed{\div}\;\boxed{5}\;\boxed{\times}\;\boxed{4}\;\boxed{\div}\;\boxed{6}\;\boxed{=}$$
$$(=84)$$

Therefore the desired probability is:

$$\text{Probability} = \frac{(_3C_2)(_3C_2)(_3C_2)}{_9C_6} = \frac{(3)(3)(3)}{84}$$

$$= \frac{27}{84} = 0.32142857 \quad \text{approximately}$$

(Of course, normally we would simplify the expression for $_9C_6$ before evaluating it. But the calculator method is so fast and simple, doing so isn't really necessary. Yet knowing that $_9C_6 = _9C_3$ doesn't hurt; and as long as we know this fact, why not do the simpler one rather than the harder one?)

9. *Topic:* Combinations

Objective: Use the calculator to show the students that:

$$_nC_n = _nC_0 = 1 \qquad \text{for all } n$$

and

$$_nC_k = _nC_{n-k} \qquad \text{for all } n \text{ and } k \text{ with } k \leqslant n$$

Procedure: Introduce the general concept and formula for combinations, and have the students use their calculators to evaluate several combinations expressions. Then assign as part of the homework for that night combinations expressions of the form given in the Objective statement. When you go over the completed homework problems, explicitly point out these particular expressions and ask if the students noticed anything interesting or consistent about them. With the help of a leading question or two, they should be able to pick out these properties of the combinations expression and remember them for future use.

9

ELEMENTARY CALCULUS

To most people, calculus is the dividing line between "ordinary" mathematics and "higher" mathematics, probably because the basic mathematical training most people receive usually stops before calculus. Only those people going into scientific areas continue on to, and possibly beyond, calculus. But there is another valid reason for thinking of calculus as being "a step above" the mathematics that precedes it. The subject of calculus takes the ordinary processes we are used to in mathematics and carries them one step further, presenting the beginning calculus student with entirely new and sometimes nonintuitive concepts. For example, the simple idea of an average rate of change is extended to the new concept of instantaneous rate of change or derivative; and the simple idea of approximating the area of a curved figure with inscribed or circumscribed rectangles is extended to the new concept of the definite integral to give the exact area of the figure.

Since these concepts and procedures are so different and new, students need to have a great deal of actual computational practice in them so they can relate these new concepts to the more common and familiar ones from which they grew. In other words, the concept of an instantaneous rate of change is better understood if the student has had practice in actually calculating average rates of change with smaller and smaller increments in the independent variable and noticing that these familiar values approach the new value as a limit. Similarly, the concept of definite integral is better understood if the student has had practice in actually calculating sums of areas of inscribed and circumscribed rectangles and noticing that, as the lengths of the bases of the rectangles approach zero, these approximating areas approach the new value as a limit. The calculator lets students do actual numerical problems, to clarify the relationships between the familiar concepts of arithmetic and algebra and the new concepts of calculus. Hence the calculator is most useful in the elementary calculus course. In this chapter we will discuss and illustrate some of the ways in which the calculator can be used for this purpose.

Derived functions (derivatives) and indefinite integrals

Derived functions

After students learn and can supposedly use the basic definition of a derivative as the limit of a difference quotient, they learn many specific rules for derivatives that give the correct result in a "short-cut" manner without having to go back to the definition: for example, the product rule, the quotient rule, and the chain rule for obtaining derivatives of products of functions, quotients of functions, and compositions of functions, respectively.

But once they apply any of these rules in a particular problem to obtain the derived function, students have no simple way to "verify" whether the result obtained is correct, unless either the textbook or the teacher has supplied the answer. Often the textbook will not, and the teacher does not have the time to do so. While this problem is not serious for the advanced math student who is beyond careless errors and who is fairly conversant and skillful with the formulas, it is a problem for the novice who is just learning to use these formulas. These students would probably welcome a verification procedure, and the calculator makes such a verification procedure available. This procedure not only allows students to check the results of these problems, but it also reinforces and emphasizes the definition of the derivative.

Suppose that you have taught the class the definition of a derivative as the limit of a difference quotient, and that you have just given them the rule for the derivative of a product:

$$(9\text{--}1) \qquad \frac{d(fg)}{dx} = f\frac{dg}{dx} + g\frac{df}{dx} \quad or \quad (fg)' = fg' + gf'$$

Assign an exercise in which this rule is to be used, such as:

> *Problem 1:* Use formula (9–1) for the derivative of a product to find the derivative of the function
>
> $$h(a) = 2a^2(a + 1)^{1/2}$$
>
> with respect to *a*.

Thinking of the given function $h(a)$ as a product $h(a) = f(a)g(a)$ with $f(a) = 2a^2$ and $g(a) = (a + 1)^{1/2}$, formula (9–1) gives:

$$h'(a) = f(a)g'(a) + g(a)f'(a)$$

$$(9\text{--}2) \qquad = \frac{a^2}{(a + 1)^{1/2}} + 4a(a + 1)^{1/2}$$

How do you verify for the class that the expression given in (9–2) is in fact the correct answer, and at the same time reinforce the definition of the derivative? First, select any particular value of $a = a_0$ at which both the original function $h(a)$ and the supposed derivative expression (9–2) are defined. (Make your selections simple ones so you can do computations with them.) You might, for example, select the integer value $a_0 = 5$. Ask the class to use their calculators and the supposed expression for $h'(a)$ in (9–2) to compute $h'(5)$. Since the expression contains two terms it will probably be necessary for them either to write down the result of the first term or to store it in memory before evaluating the second term, but doing so is easy. Of course, the two terms in (9–2) could be algebraically combined into one term. But that merger introduces another opportunity for a mistake, so it is probably best to leave expression (9–2) in the form you would like to see the answer in. A keystroke sequence for evaluating expression (9–2) at any value of *a*, using the $\boxed{\text{STO}}$ and $\boxed{\text{RCL}}$ keys, is:

$\boxed{a}$ $\boxed{+}$ $\boxed{1}$ $\boxed{=}$ $\boxed{\sqrt{\ }}$ $\boxed{1/x}$ $\boxed{\times}$ $\boxed{a}$ $\boxed{x^2}$ $\boxed{=}$ $\boxed{\text{STO}}$ $\boxed{a}$ $\boxed{+}$ $\boxed{1}$ $\boxed{=}$ $\boxed{\sqrt{\ }}$ $\boxed{\times}$ $\boxed{4}$ $\boxed{\times}$
$\boxed{a}$ $\boxed{+}$ $\boxed{\text{RCL}}$ $\boxed{=}$

Using $a_0 = 5$ with this keystroke sequence, we obtain an approximate answer of $h'(5) = 59.196002$ on an 8-digit display calculator from the supposed expression (9–2) for the derivative $h'(a)$.

Now have the class write out the difference quotient for the original function $h(a)$ at $a_0 = 5$ with $\Delta a = 0.001$. This would be:

(9–3)
$$\frac{h(a_0 + \Delta a) - h(a_0)}{\Delta a} = \frac{h(5 + 0.001) - h(5)}{0.001}$$

Ask the students to use their calculators to evaluate this difference quotient—that is, expression (9–3). The result they obtain should be a fairly close approximation to the value they obtained for $h'(5)$ using expression (9–2) if, in fact, expression (9–2) was correct. In fact, on an 8-digit display calculator, expression (9–3) would give a result of 59.20455, which is quite close to the value obtained from expression (9–2), 59.196002. This difference, less than 0.01, is just the kind of difference we would expect from comparing the actual derivative of a function at a point with the approximating difference quotient at that point for a small Δa. If expression (9–2) for $h'(a)$ was incorrect, then we would have expected the two values to be very different from each other, not this close. In general, therefore, if the expression for the derivative and the difference quotient agree to within a few decimal points, the expression was probably correct. If the two values are quite different from each other, then the expression was probably incorrect. While this procedure does not guarantee your answer, it is pretty reliable.

Let's try one more verification example, this time with the chain rule.

Problem 2: Use the chain rule to find the derivative of the function: $f(a) = \ln(a^2 + 3)$. Do this by expressing the function $f(a)$ as a composition of functions and then verify your result using your calculator with $a_0 = 4$ and $\Delta a = 0.001$.

Letting $u(a) = a^2 + 3$, we can think of the function $f(a)$ as the composition $f(a) = \ln[u(a)]$. The chain rule now gives:

$$f'(a) = \frac{d \ln(u)}{du} \cdot \frac{du}{da} = \frac{1}{u} \, (2a)$$

(9–4)
$$= \frac{2a}{a^2 + 3}$$

To verify expression (9–4) using $a_0 = 4$ and $\Delta a = 0.001$, we first use our calculator to evaluate $f'(4)$ employing expression (9–4). This would give the result $f'(4) = 0.4210526$ on an 8-digit display calculator. We now compare this to the value obtained when we use the original function $f(a)$ with $a_0 = 4$ and $\Delta a = 0.001$ to form a difference quotient. This gives:

$$\frac{f(4 + 0.001) - f(4)}{0.001} = \frac{\ln(4.001^2 + 3) - \ln(4^2 + 3)}{0.001}$$

$$= \frac{2.94486 - 2.944439}{0.001}$$

$$= 0.421$$

Since this value is so close to the value obtained from expression (9–4), expression (9–4) was most probably the correct answer.

   This procedure allows students to check their results without having to call in the teacher. Quite aside from that benefit, it also constantly reminds them that the derivative is still defined as the limit of the difference quotients and that the rules for derivatives they are making use of (the product rule, quotient rule, and chain rule) are merely simplification formulas, not new definitions.

   Note: You might think that we could obtain an even better match between the value obtained from the supposed solution and the value obtained from the difference quotient by taking a smaller value of Δa than the 0.001 we have been using in our examples. Theoretically, you would be correct; but on the calculator you might not. Any calculator has only a finite number of digits available for computations, and so some round-off error is almost always involved in the calculator evaluation of a difference quotient.

   For very small values of Δa, where the difference between $f(a_0)$ and $f(a_0 + \Delta a)$ would occur not in the first few digits of each value but in the later digits, round-off could have a serious effect on the value of the difference quotient and could give an answer different from that obtained using the supposed derivative equation even if the derivative equation is correct. I have found that, in general, the increment $\Delta a = 0.001$ is small enough to give a good comparison, but large enough so that the calculator round-off does not seriously affect the result. To be on the safe side, however, you should always try out any of these problems that you intend either to use in class or to assign as homework before you use them with your students.

Indefinite integrals

The same verification procedure can be used to test the result obtained in problems involving an indefinite integral, such as:

   Problem 3: Given the function $f(a) = a(a^2 - 2)^{1/2}$. Find the indefinite integral $F(a) = \int f(a)da$, and then verify your answer using your calculator.

Using the substitution $u(a) = a^2 - 2$, $du = 2ada$, we find:

$$F(a) = \int f(a)da = \int a(a^2 - 2)^{1/2}da$$

$$= \int \frac{1}{2} u^{1/2}du = \frac{1}{3}u^{3/2} + C$$

$$= \frac{(a^2 - 2)^{3/2}}{3} + C$$

with C an arbitrary constant.

   To verify this result we choose any simple value of a for which both $f(a)$ and $F(a)$ are defined, such as $a_0 = 3$. since supposedly $F'(a) = f(a)$ if $F(a)$ is the correct indefinite integral of $f(a)$, then the difference quotient for $F(a)$ evaluated with $a_0 = 3$ and $\Delta a = 0.001$ should be approximately the same as $f(3)$. Using our calculator for all the computation, we find that $f(3) = 7.9372539$ and:

$$\frac{F(3 + 0.001) - F(3)}{0.001} = 7.940277$$

Since these two values are so similar to each other (they differ by less than 0.01), we can conclude that the expression we obtained for $F(a)$ is most likely correct.

The calculator versus mathematical theory

In Chapter 4 on trigonometry, we discussed and illustrated how the calculator could be used as the basis of a classroom contest. The same type of activity can be used in elementary calculus, since many types of problems are encountered in calculus that are essentially numerical and that could be approached either with or without a calculator. As before, the purpose of such a "contest" is twofold: Not only does it give students practice in both procedures, but it also emphasizes that, while the calculator is extremely useful in investigating a problem and finding what *appears* to be a correct answer, the only way to *prove* the answer correct is to do it mathematically as a follow-up. An alternative procedure is simply to assign these problems as part of the students' homework, and ask them to solve the problems both with and without the use of their calculators. Then, in class, discuss the two procedures and which the students prefer and why.

Contest problem 1

Given here is the first of two problems that could be used in this format in an elementary calculus course:

Problem 1: Find

$$\lim_{n \to \infty} (1 + \frac{1}{n})^n$$

for n taking on positive integer values.

The calculator approach to this problem consists of writing out a keystroke sequence for the expression $(1 + \frac{1}{n})^n$, evaluating this expression for several increasingly large values of n, and noticing if the resulting values appear to be approaching a finite limit. This approach is simplified considerably if the calculator has an exponentiation key $\boxed{x^y}$. On such a calculator the keystroke sequence would be:

$$(1 + \frac{1}{n})^n: \quad \boxed{1} \; \boxed{+} \; \boxed{n} \; \boxed{1/x} \; \boxed{=} \; \boxed{x^y} \; \boxed{n} \; \boxed{=}$$

Evaluating this expression on a calculator that does not have an exponentiation key would be a bit more cumbersome, but you could still do so fairly easily with the calculator doing the computation. Putting the data we obtain into a table, we might come up with the values shown in Table 9–1. In Table 9–1 the expression

Table 9–1. Evaluating $(1 + \frac{1}{n})^n$

n	$(1 + \frac{1}{n})^n$
1	2
10	2.5937425
100	2.7048138
1000	2.7169239
10000	2.7181459
100000	2.7182818
1000000	2.7182818

appears to approach a finite limit as n increases without bound. And, since the final two values of the expression in the table are the same, 2.7182818, this limit value to 8 digits appears to be 2.7182818.

A noncalculator approach to this problem is to let:

$$y = \lim_{n \to \infty} (1 + \frac{1}{n})^n$$

Now take the natural logarithm of both sides of the relationship and use some algebraic manipulation to obtain:

$$\ln y = \ln[\lim_{n \to \infty} (1 + \frac{1}{n})^n] = \lim_{n \to \infty} [\ln(1 + \frac{1}{n})^n]$$

$$= \lim_{n \to \infty} [n \ln(1 + \frac{1}{n})]$$

(9–5)
$$= \lim_{h \to 0} \frac{\ln(1 + h) - \ln(1)}{h}$$

with $h = 1/n$. [Notice that we can insert the term $\ln(1) = 0$ in the fractional expression without changing its value.] But the expression in (9–5) is just the difference quotient for the function $\ln x$ at the point $x_0 = 1$. So the limit *is* the derivative of the function $\ln x$ with respect to x at the point $x_0 = 1$, and this is easily found to be 1. If $\ln y = 1$, y must be the base of the natural logarithm e. Since, to 8 digits, $e = 2.7182818$, we see that this answer does agree with the answer obtained by calculator.

Note: In the last section, we used the difference quotient of a function with "small" Δa to verify the answer in problems involving derivatives. You might think that you could obtain the limit of the given expression immediately just by substituting a large enough value of n, such as $n = 100,000$. This approach is theoretically correct in the sense that, for a sufficiently large value of n, the expression should agree with the actual limit value in the first 8 digits, and, in contest problem 1, it would actually give the correct answer.

But, it will not always work. The reason is that, since a calculator has to round off decimals that exceed its capacity, it is possible that, as *n* gets larger, the corresponding values of the expression obtained from the calculator start to approach the true limit but then veer away from this limit when *n* gets too large. Just by picking a large value of *n* and evaluating the expression, you cannot tell if the calculator value is still approaching the true limit or not. By using a table with larger and larger values of *n*, however, you can see if the values for the expression are consistently approaching some finite value and, if they are, that value is most likely the limit. If, on the other hand, they seem to be approaching some finite value as *n* gets larger but at some point suddenly become irregular, you can go back to where the irregularity began and use the last consistent value as your approximate answer. Furthermore, using a table like that illustrated in Table 9–1 emphasizes the distinction between the evaluation of a "limit," and simply "plugging in" a particular value for *n* in the expression.

Contest problem 2

Here is one involving a trigonometric function:

Problem 2: Suppose you know that

$$\lim_{\theta \to 0} \frac{\sin \theta}{\theta} = 1$$

when θ is measured in radian measure. Use this to find the limit of this same ratio when θ is in degree measure.

The straightforward calculator approach is, as in contest problem 1, to simply evaluate the ratio in degree mode for a set of decreasing values of θ, put the obtained values in a table, and see what finite number (if any) the values of the ratio appear to be approaching as a limit. The keystroke sequence for doing all this would be:

$$\frac{\sin \theta}{\theta}: \quad \boxed{\theta} \ \boxed{\text{SIN}} \ \boxed{\div} \ \boxed{\theta} \ \boxed{=}$$

One such set of values that might be obtained is shown in Table 9–2. Based on this table, the first 8 decimal places of the limit value would appear to be 0.01745329.

Here's one way of solving this problem without a calculator. The only time it makes a difference as to whether θ is in radian or degree measure is when θ is the angle of a trigonometric function. When θ stands by itself, it is just a number, and whether it is in radians or degrees has no bearing on its use in computations. So in the given ratio, only the numerator is affected by switching θ from being measured in radians to being measured in degrees. What we do now is to make a

$$\text{Table 9–2. Evaluating } \frac{\sin \theta}{\theta} \text{ in degree mode}$$

θ	$\dfrac{\sin \theta}{\theta}$
10	0.01736482
1	0.01745241
0.1	0.01745329
0.01	0.0174533
0.001	0.01745329
0.0001	0.01745329

transformation in the numerator from θ to its equivalent radian measure, and then make a compensting change in the denominator. This procedure is:

$$\lim_{\theta \to 0} \frac{\sin(\theta \text{ degrees})}{\theta} = \lim_{\theta \to 0} \frac{\sin(\text{pi b } \theta/180 \text{ radians})}{\theta}$$

$$= \frac{\text{pi}}{180} \lim_{\theta \to 0} \frac{\sin(\text{pi b } \theta/180 \text{ radians})}{\text{pi b } \theta/180}$$

$$= \frac{\text{pi}}{180} \lim_{a \to 0} \frac{\sin(a \text{ radians})}{a}$$

$$= \frac{\text{pi}}{180} \text{ b } 1$$

$$= \frac{\text{pi}}{180}$$

where $a = \text{pi b } \theta/180$. Since pi/180 = 0.01745329 to its first 8 decimal places, we see that this answer agrees with the calculator answer obtained earlier.

The epsilon-delta method of proving a function is continuous at a point

In the previous two sections of this chapter we have shown how the calculator can be used to reinforce and to make clearer the meaning of three of the four most fundamental and important concepts of the calculus: the derivative, the indefinite integral, and the limit. In this section we will discuss and illustrate the use of the calculator with the fourth fundamental concept: continuity of a given function at a specified point in its domain.

The usual approach to teaching about the continuity of a function is to begin with an intuitive, global definition such as:

The function f is continuous on a certain domain if you can draw its graph for the values in this domain in one continuous motion without taking your pen or pencil off the paper.

This is usually followed by an intuitive definition of what it means for $f(a)$ to be continuous at a particular point $a = a_0$ in its domain:

The function $f(a)$ is continuous at the point $a = a_0$ if $f(a_0)$ is defined and, for *any* sequence of points $\{a_i\}$ in the domain that approaches a_0, the corresponding sequence of function values $\{f(a_i)\}$ approach $f(a_0)$.

The difficulty with intuitive definitions such as these is that, while they are clear and understandable, they are difficult to use in actually proving that a given nontrivial function is indeed continuous. What is needed is a rigorous mathematical definition that can actually be employed with a given function. The usual definition is the epsilon-delta definition:

The function $f(a)$ is continuous at the point $a = a_0$ if $f(a_0)$ is defined and, for every ϵ greater than 0, there exists a corresponding δ greater than 0, such that whenever $|a - a_0| < \delta$, it must be true that $|f(a) - f(a_0)| < \epsilon$.

Unfortunately, most students never really understand that this more formal definition of continuity is saying exactly the same thing as the informal, intuitive definition of continuity at a point. So most teachers simply give the epsilon-delta definition, do one or two problems with it, and then never bother with it again. With the aid of a calculator, however, the student can be given a better understanding of what the epsilon-delta definition means and how to use it.

Here's one way of doing so: Let's assume you have already spent some time with the class on the intuitive definitions of continuity and have just given the more formal epsilon-delta definition. Tell the class you will use this definition to solve the following problem:

Problem 4: Use the epsilon-delta definition of continuity to prove that the function $f(a) = 5a + 4$ is continuous at $a_0 = 7$.

The usual mathematical proof would be as follows:

$$|f(a) - f(7)| = |5a + 4 - 39| = |5a - 35|$$
$$= 5|a - 7|$$

This last expression will be less than ϵ if $|a - 7|$ is less than $\epsilon/5$. So if we take $\delta = \epsilon/5$, then whenever $|a - 7| < \delta$, we must also have $|f(a) - f(7)| < \epsilon$ and the condition for $f(a)$ to be continuous at $a_0 = 7$ is satisfied. With this result, $\delta = \epsilon/5$, the problem would be completed and the teacher would ordinarily progress to another example or to another topic. Instead, however, put Table 9–3 on the board and ask the class to look it over.

Ask the students to fill in the third column with any 5 values of a such that each a is within that row's δ value of 7, and so that the values of a get closer and closer to 7 as you go down this column. When this is done, ask them to use their calculators with the given expression for $f(a)$ and the values of a that they have selected to fill in the rest of the table. Now show them the following things from the completed tables:

Table 9–3. Verifying the continuity of the function f(a) = 5a + 4 at a_0 = 7
using the epsilon-delta definition

(1)	(2)	(3) *a* within	(4)	(5)	(6)
ϵ	$\delta = \epsilon/5$	δ of 7	$f(a)$	$\|a - 7\|$	$\|f(a) - 39\|$
10	2				
5	1				
1	0.2				
.1	0.02				
.01	0.002				
0	0	7	39	0	0

- From the third and fourth columns of Table 9–3, you see that as the selected set of *a*s approach a_0 = 7 going down the third column, the corresponding set of function values $f(a)$ approach $f(a_0) = f(7)$ = 39 as you go down the fourth column. But this observation is just the intuitive definition of the continuity of a function at a point. So the epsilon-delta definition of continuity is essentially the same as the intuitive definition, only in a more mathematical and rigorous form.

- From the fifth and sixth columns of Table 9–3, we can see that, whenever the selected value of *a* is within the given δ value of a_0 = 7, the corresponding function value of $f(a)$ is within the corresponding ϵ value of $f(7)$ = 39. Hence the expression we found for δ in terms of ϵ, $\delta = \epsilon/5$, really does "work" and satisfy the conditions of the epsilon-delta definition.

- Finally, the fifth and sixth columns of Table 9–3 let us actually see the relative speeds with which the values of *a* approach a_0 and the values of $f(a)$ approach $f(a_0)$. It would appear that while the $f(a)$s are always further from $f(a_0)$ than the *a*s are from a_0, they approach their limit value five times as fast. But we can tell this directly from the relationship $\delta = \epsilon/5$ or, equivalently, $\epsilon = 5\delta$. Since ϵ measures the distance from the $f(a)$s to $f(a_0)$, and δ measures the distance from the *a*s to a_0, $\epsilon = 5\delta$ indicates that a change of 1 unit in the distance from an *a* to a_0 results in a change of 5 units in the corresponding distance from $f(a)$ to $f(a_0)$. So, although the epsilon-delta definition is really no different from the earlier intuitive definition, it does have the advantage that from the expression for δ in terms of ϵ, we can get some idea as to the relative speeds with which these two sequences are approaching their limits.

While the example we used involved a linear function $f(a)$, the same procedure can be employed with nonlinear functions as well. First use the epsilon-delta definition to obtain an expression for δ in terms of ϵ. Next, give the students a table with a decreasing set of values of ϵ and the corresponding values of δ to be filled in with the aid of their calculators. Then make the same three observations for the new table that you made for Table 9–3. This approach

169

includes a discussion of the relative speeds with which the as approach a_0 and the $f(a)$s approach $f(a_0)$, as well as how this information can be obtained directly from the expression for δ in terms of ϵ. If this format is used when epsilon-delta continuity problems are presented and discussed, the students will gain a better understanding of the use of the epsilon-delta method of proof, and what it really means.

Additional calculator activities

1. *Topic:* Limit of a function

    Objective: Use the calculator to reinforce the meaning of the limit of a function.

    Procedure: Give the class a simple function $f(a)$ and a specified point a_0 in the domain of $f(a)$. Ask the students to each select a sequence of several values of a that approach a_0, and then to use their calculators to compute the corresponding function values $f(a)$ at these values of a. They are then to put these values into a table and, based on their tables, to guess the limit value of the function as a approaches a_0. Ask several students what they think the limit value is, and then point out to the class that, even though everyone used different sets of a values, they all obtained the same limit value. This emphasizes the fact that, if the limit of $f(a)$ exists as a approaches a_0 and is a finite value, you obtain the same limit value for every sequence of a values approaching a_0.

2. *Topic:* Limit of a function at a point of discontinuity

    Objective: Use the calculator to show that in some situations a function can have a finite limit at a point, but you cannot find this limit value just by substituting the limit value of the as, a_0, into the expression for $f(a)$. This is a good way to introduce *continuity* of $f(a)$ at a_0 as the situation in which you *can* obtain the limit of $f(a)$ as a approaches a_0 just by substituting a_0 into the expression for $f(a)$.

    Example: Try to find the limit of the function $f(a) = (a^2 - 9)/(a - 3)$ as a approaches $a_0 = 3$ simply by substituting the value $a_0 = 3$ into the expression. Then evaluate the limit by selecting 10 values of a that approach $a_0 = 3$, evaluating $f(a)$ for each of these values and using these function values to guess the limit.

    Solution: A keystroke sequence for evaluating $f(a)$ is:

    $$f(a) = \frac{a^2 - 9}{a - 3}: \quad \boxed{a}\ \boxed{-}\ \boxed{3}\ \boxed{=}\ \boxed{\text{STO}}\ \boxed{a}\ \boxed{x^2}\ \boxed{-}\ \boxed{9}\ \boxed{=}\ \boxed{\div}\ \boxed{\text{RCL}}\ \boxed{=}$$

    When $a_0 = 3$ is used in this keystroke sequence, the calculator will indicate an error due to the expression being of the form 0/0. So we cannot evaluate the limit by direct substitution of $a_0 = 3$ into the expression. If we now select the 10 values $a = 10, 6, 5, 4, 3.5, 3.1, 3.01, 3.001, 3.0001$, and 3.00001, and use the keystroke sequence to compute $f(a)$ for each of these a values, we obtain the data in Table 9–4. This table shows that, as the values of a approach 3, the corresponding function values appear to approach the limit value 6.

Now would be a good time to make the observation that the property of being able to simply substitute the value of a_0 into the formula for $f(a)$ and obtain the limit is a special property. When this *can* be done, we say that $f(a)$

Table 9–4. Investigating the limit of
$$f(a) = \frac{(a^2 - 9)}{(a - 3)}$$
as a approaches $a_0 = 3$

a	$f(a)$
10	13
6	9
5	8
4	7
3.5	6.5
3.1	6.1
3.01	6.01
3.001	6.001
3.0001	6.0001
3.00001	6.00001

is continuous at a_0; when this *cannot* be done, we say that *$f(a)$ is not continuous at a_0*. In this example, we would therefore say that $f(a) = (a^2 - 9)/(a - 3)$ is *not* continuous at $a_0 = 3$.

3. *Topic:* Definite integral

Objective: Use the calculator to verify the answer to a definite integral problem and to reinforce the definition of the definite integral in terms of upper and lower Riemann sums.

Procedure: Given a fairly simple problem in which a definite integral is to be found. After the problem is solved mathematically by finding an antiderivative and evaluating the antiderivative at the endpoints of the given interval, have the students use their calculators to compute a lower Riemann sum s, and an upper Riemann sum S, for the given interval partitioned into ten or so subintervals. (The lower and upper Riemann sums are simply sums of areas of inscribed and circumscribed rectangles, respectively.) If the mathematical result is correct, it should fall between the values of s and S obtained in this way. If the mathematical result does not fall between the values of s and S, then it is most likely incorrect.

4. *Topic:* Properties of limits of functions

Objective: Use the calculator either to reinforce or to let the students discover the limit properties of products of functions and quotients of functions. Given functions $f(a)$ and $g(a)$ with both functions having finite limits as a approaches a_0. Then (a) the limit of the product of $f(a)$ and $g(a)$, as a approaches a_0, is equal to the product of the individual limits; and (b) if the limit of $g(a)$ is not 0, then the limit of the quotient $f(a)$ divided by $g(a)$, as a approaches a_0, is equal to the quotient of the individual limits.

Procedure: Assign problems in which the limit of a product of two functions and the limit of a quotient of two functions must be found. Have the students use their calculators to compute the function values of the functions individually, as well as the product and the quotient for the set of values of a selected by them that approach the limiting value a_0. Using their completed tables, they are now to guess the limits of $f(a)$, $g(a)$, $f(a)g(a)$, and $f(a)/g(a)$ as a approaches a_0. Finally, you can point out to them that they could just as well have obtained the limit of the product function by taking the product of the individual limits, and that they could just as well have obtained the limit of the quotient function by taking the quotient of the individual limits. You can now state the general rules for the limit of a product of functions and for the limit of a quotient of two functions, with this example as an illustration.

5. *Topic:* Maxima and minima

Objective: Use the calculator to verify the answer in a maxima or minima problem.

Procedure: Suppose, in a maxima or minima problem, the use of first and second derivatives shows that the function $f(a)$ attains either a maximum or a minimum at the point a_0. To verify this result we use the calculator to obtain the function values at the points a_0, $a_0 - 0.001$, and $a_0 + 0.001$. If a_0 gives a maximum function value, then both $f(a_0 - 0.001)$ and $f(a_0 + 0.001)$ should be less than but very close to $f(a_0)$. On the other hand, if a_0 gives a minimum function value, then both $f(a_0 - 0.001)$ and $f(a_0 + 0.001)$ should be greater than but very close to $f(a_0)$. Of course, since the maximum or minimum at a_0 could be only a relative extrema rather than an absolute extrema, it's possible that the increment 0.001 is "too far away" from a_0 to accurately represent whether a_0 is an extremum point. But this situation would be very unusual, and so this verification procedure should work most of the time.

Example: Find the point a_0 at which the function $f(a) = 2a^2 - 5a + 3.5$ attains its minimum value. Compute this minimum value with your calculator, and then verify your result with your calculator.

Solution: Taking the first and second derivatives of this function with respect to a, we obtain: $f'(a) = 4a - 5$ and $f''(a) = 4$. The first derivative is equal to 0 at $a_0 = 5/4 = 1.25$, and, since the second derivative at this point (and everywhere else, since $f''(a)$ is a constant) is positive, $a_0 = 1.25$ must give a minimum for the function. The keystroke sequence for evaluating $f(a)$ is:

$2a^2 - 5a + 3.5$:

Hierarchy:

$\boxed{2}\ \boxed{\times}\ \boxed{a}\ \boxed{x^2}\ \boxed{-}\ \boxed{5}\ \boxed{\times}\ \boxed{a}\ \boxed{+}\ \boxed{3.5}\ \boxed{=}$

Left-to-Right [write $f(a)$ as $(2a - 5)a + 3.5$]:

$\boxed{2}\ \boxed{\times}\ \boxed{a}\ \boxed{-}\ \boxed{5}\ \boxed{\times}\ \boxed{a}\ \boxed{+}\ \boxed{3.5}\ \boxed{=}$

Using this keystroke sequence with $a_0 = 1.25$, we obtain $f(1.25) = 0.375$ as the minimum value of $f(a)$. To verify this result, we use the preceding keystroke sequence to evaluate $f(a_0 - 0.001)$ and $f(a_0 + 0.001)$, and thus to find:

$$f(a_0 - 0.001) = f(1.249) = 0.375002$$

$$f(a_0 + 0.001) = f(1.251) = 0.375002$$

Since both these values are close to, but slightly greater than, $f(1.25) = 0.375$, $a_0 = 1.25$ is most likely a minimum point for the given function. This situation, as well as what our function values show, is illustrated in Figure 9–1.

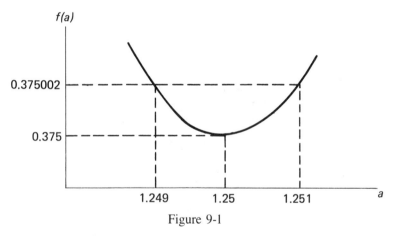

Figure 9-1

6. *Topic:* Mean value theorem

Objective: Use the calculator to verify the answer in problems involving the mean value theorem.

Procedure: Suppose, in a problem involving the mean value theorem, that the point c has been found that satisfies the condition: $f'(c) = [f(b) - f(a)]/(b - a)$ where a and b are the endpoints of the interval under consideration, $a < b$, and f is the function. To verify that c is the correct point, simply use the calculator to evaluate $f(c - 0.001)$ and $f(c + 0.001)$, and use these to obtain the ratio $[f(c + 0.001) - f(c - 0.001)]/0.002$. This ratio is the slope of the secant connecting the point $[c - 0.001, f(c - 0.001)]$ to the point $[c + 0.001, f(c + 0.001)]$, and it will be approximately equal to the slope of the tangent to the curve at $[c, f(c)]$. If c is the correct point, then we should have

$$(9\text{--}6) \quad \frac{f(c +0.001) - f(c -0.001)}{0.002} \approx f'(c) = \frac{f(b) - f(a)}{b - a}$$

So if the first and last expressions in (9–6) give approximately the same result, then c is most likely the correct value for the mean value theorem. If the first and last expressions in (9–6) do not give approximately the same result, then c is most likely not the correct value for the mean value theorem.

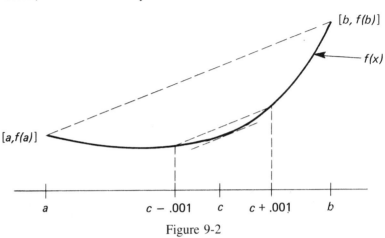

Figure 9-2

Example: Given the function $f(a) = a^3 + 2a + 6$ on the interval $[1, 5]$. Find the value c for which the mean value theorem holds, and then verify this value of c with your calculator.

Solution: The keystroke sequence for evaluating the function $f(a)$ is:

$f(a) = a^3 + 2a + 6$:
    Hierarchy:
        $\boxed{a}\;\boxed{\times}\;\boxed{a}\;\boxed{\times}\;\boxed{a}\;\boxed{+}\;\boxed{2}\;\boxed{\times}\;\boxed{a}\;\boxed{+}\;\boxed{6}\;\boxed{=}$
    Left-to-Right [write f(a) as (a² + 2)a + 6]:
        $\boxed{a}\;\boxed{\times}\;\boxed{a}\;\boxed{+}\;\boxed{2}\;\boxed{\times}\;\boxed{a}\;\boxed{+}\;\boxed{6}\;\boxed{=}$

Using this keystroke sequence we find $f(1) = 9, f(5) = 141$, and so from the statement of the mean value theorem:

$$f'(c) = 3c^2 + 2 = \frac{f(5) - f(1)}{5 - 1} = \frac{132}{4} = 33$$

Using the square root key on our calculator, c is found to be approximately $c = \sqrt{10.333333} \approx 3.2145503$. To verify this value of c, we use the preceding keystroke sequence to evaluate $f(c -0.001)$ and $f(c +0.001)$ and to compute:

$$\frac{f(c +0.001) - f(c - 0.001)}{0.002} = \frac{45.679128 - 45.613129}{0.002}$$
$$= 32.9995$$

Since this "slope of the secant around c" is so close to the value 33 that we found earlier for the slope of the secant joining the initial and terminal points of the curve segment, the value of c that we found is most likely correct.

7. *Topic:* Product and quotient rules for derivatives

Objective: Use the calculator to show the students that, in general, the derivative of a product is *not* the same as the product of the individual derivatives, and that the derivative of a quotient is *not* the same as the quotient of the individual derivatives.

Procedure: Suppose you have already given the rules for the derivative of a sum or difference of two functions: The derivative of a sum is the sum of the derivatives, and the derivative of a difference is the difference of the derivatives. Before giving the rules for products and quotients, select two polynomial functions $f(a)$ and $g(a)$ for which the product and quotient functions $(fg)(a) = f(a)$ b $g(a)$ and

$$\left(\frac{f}{g}\right)(a) = \frac{f(a)}{g(a)}$$

can be obtained explicitly in simple form. For example, you could use:

$$f(a) = 2a^2 + 4a - 30 \quad \text{and} \quad g(a) = a + 5$$

so that:

$$(fg)(a) = 2a^3 + 14a^2 - 10a - 150$$

and

$$\left(\frac{f}{g}\right)(a) = 2a - 6$$

Now have the students find the derivatives for these four functions: $f'(a)$, $g'(a)$, $(fg)'(a)$, and $\left(\frac{f}{g}\right)'(a)$. Finally, let them use these expressions for the derivatives to fill in the following table according to the accompanying instructions and then answer the questions that follow:

(1)	(2)	(3)	(4)	(5)	(6)	(7)
a	$f'(a)$	$g'(a)$	$f'(a)$ b $g'(a)$	$(fg)'(a)$	$\dfrac{f'(a)}{g'(a)}$	$\left(\dfrac{f}{g}\right)'(a)$

Are these the same?   Are these the same?

Select any 4 values of *a* and place these values in the first column labeled *a*. Then use your calculator with the values of *a* that you have selected to complete the rest of the table. When you have done so, answer the questions that follow.

Question 1: Judging from the fourth and fifth columns of your table, would you say that $f'(a)$ b $g'(a)$ and $(fg)'(a)$ are the same for the functions $f(a)$ and $g(a)$ we have used?

Question 2: From the last two columns of your table, are $\dfrac{f'(a)}{g'(a)}$ and $(\dfrac{f}{g})'(a)$ the same for the functions $f(a)$ and $g(a)$ we have used?

Question 3: Recall that when we studied sums of functions and differences between functions, we could obtain the derivative of a sum or a difference just by taking the sum or difference, respectively, of the individual derivatives:

$$(f + g)'(a) = f'(a) + g'(a);$$
$$(f - g)'(a) = f'(a) - g'(a).$$

Based on your table and your answers to questions 1 and 2, do you think, in general, that the derivative of a product is equal to the product of the derivatives and that the derivative of a quotient is equal to the quotient of the derivatives as well? In other words, do you think the following rules are true?

$$(fg)'(a) \overset{?}{=} f'(a) \text{ b } g'(a);$$

$$(\frac{f}{g})'(a) \overset{?}{=} \frac{f'(a)}{g'(a)}$$

10

PROGRAMMABLE CALCULATORS

If you have read through the previous nine chapters of this book, and if you have tried out the calculator activities and keystroke sequences on your own calculator, you should now be quite knowledgeable about what a calculator can do. You should also be proficient in developing and using appropriate calculator keystroke sequences. With this background and practice, you should have no trouble in learning how to extend this capability to the programmable calculator as well.

What is a programmable calculator? It is nothing more than an ordinary calculator that is able to "remember" certain keystroke sequences so that we may use them over and over again without having to press the sequence into the calculator by hand each time we need it. On a programmable calculator, you can tell the machine to "remember" any keystroke sequence you can enter by hand, as long as the machine has enough program step capability for the length of the sequence you are giving it. Most programmable calculators can remember keystroke sequences of at least fifty steps, and this memory is usually more than enough for our purposes. Telling a programmable calculator to remember a particular keystroke sequence is called *programming* the calculator, and our intention in this chapter is therefore to learn how to program a programmable calculator.

Like nonprogrammable calculators, the vast majority of programmable calculators use one of the three basic types of logic: Reverse Polish Logic, Left-to-Right Algebraic Logic, and Hierarchy Algebraic Logic. As before, we will restrict our discussion and examples to the latter two types of Algebraic logic. Furthermore, since there are a wide range of different programmable calculators, even within the same manufacturer's product line, we will focus our discussion and illustrations in this chapter on one inexpensive, simple to use, yet extremely typical machine: the Texas Instruments TI–57 programmable calculator. The price for this calculator in 1981 was between $35 and $50, and it will probably go down in the near future. The programs we develop for it can be used on most other common programmable calculators, either as is or with only slight modifications. This particular machine would therefore seem to be a suitable choice for illustrative purposes.

Why is a chapter on programmable calculators included in this book at all? Most likely, you will never find yourself in a position where all the students in your class have programmable calculators, or where you can ask them all to buy them for your class. Why, then, should we take up a chapter on programmable calculators in a book dealing with the teaching of mathematics? There are two basic reasons. First, even if you never have an entire class with programmable calculators, you might very well have one or several students who do have them. These students are often curious enough and inquisitive enough to want to know how they can use their calculators' special programming capability to work out some of the calculator problems you do in class or assign for homework. So it would be a shame not to encourage them by showing them how and pointing them in the right direction. This chapter will give you the basic understanding of, and practice in, programming a programmable calculator, to enable you to help and guide students like these. Second, when you yourself are preparing calculator examples and assignments for your class, you might have to try out a large number of values in a particular expression or formula to make sure the calculator works the way you want it to. Or you might have to try out a lot of values in a trigonometric identity. While the class will be asked to do this by hand on a nonprogrammable calculator, you can save yourself a great deal of time and effort if you can program the expression or the identity into your programmable calculator and let the machine do most of the work for you. This chapter will show you how to do so.

In this chapter we will learn how to program a programmable calculator (in particular, the TI–57), and how to use this programming capability in actual classroom and homework activities. We will select several of the activities already presented and discussed in earlier chapters for nonprogrammable calculators, and adapt these activities to the programmable calculator. Having already developed the basic keystroke sequences for these activities for the nonprogrammable calculator, your learning of programming will be simplified, and you will have ready-made examples to which you can apply our new calculator capability. Let's begin by discussing some of the fundamentals of programming.

Fundamentals of programming

Programmable calculators have two modes of operation: *programming mode* and *run mode*. When the calculator is in programming mode, it is ready to accept a keystroke sequence that it will remember until it is either cleared of its program memory or turned off (although calculators with "continuous" memories retain programs even when they are turned off). In run mode, either we can do ordinary computations on the calculator, or we can recall and use keystroke sequences that were programmed earlier in programming mode. Since calculators are automatically in run mode when they are first turned on, a special key or switch is needed to put them into, and to take them out of, programming mode. In the TI–57 that key is the LEARN key ⌊LRN⌋. Because this key is called LEARN we will refer to programming mode for the TI–57 as *learn mode*.

The two basic programming keys on the TI–57 are the RUN/STOP key ⌊R/S⌋ and the RESET key ⌊RST⌋. The ⌊R/S⌋ key has two uses. First, in run mode, pressing the ⌊R/S⌋ key tells the calculator to start executing the program that has been previously entered. It says to the calculator: "Take the keystroke sequence I told you to remember before, and do it now!" On the other hand, when the ⌊R/S⌋ keystroke is used as part of a program, it commands the calculator to stop and wait when that step in the keystroke sequence is reached. The keystroke sequence will not be continued until you again press the ⌊R/S⌋ key to tell the program to commence running again. This use of the ⌊R/S⌋ keystroke within a program allows us to develop programs in which values must be inserted in the middle of the keystroke sequence. We will see how this is done shortly. The RESET key ⌊RST⌋ can also be used either in run mode or as part of a program. To understand what this key does, you must understand that, when you program a keystroke sequence into the calculator, each keystroke in the sequence is automatically assigned a step number by the calculator. In the TI–57 these step numbers have two digits each and begin with the step number 00 for the first keystroke. The RST key simply tells the calculator to immediately go to step 00. The use of this key will also be illustrated. In fact, since the best way to learn about programming is actually to program, let's turn to our first activity, "Evaluating Algebraic Expressions."

Activities for the programmable calculator

Evaluating algebraic expressions

One of the most useful applications of the calculator is the evaluation of algebraic expressions for different values of the independent variable (Chapter 3). For example, suppose we have the function:

$$f(t) = \frac{t - 5}{2}$$

Suppose further that we want to be able to evaluate $f(t)$ for a variety of values of t so that we can sketch the graph of the function. The keystroke sequence for $f(t)$ would be:

$$f(t) = \frac{t - 5}{2}: \quad \boxed{t} \ \boxed{-} \ \boxed{5} \ \boxed{=} \ \boxed{\div} \ \boxed{2} \ \boxed{=}$$

We could use this keystroke sequence to evaluate $f(t)$ for each t we want to use. Yet we can save ourselves the trouble of repeating this keystroke sequence over and over simply by programming our calculator to do so for us automatically whenever, and as often as, we need it. Specifically, what we would want is to be able to enter any particular value of t into the display, press the R/S key to set the program going, and see the resulting function value $f(t)$ in display; then enter another value of t into the display, again press the R/S key, and again get the resulting function value $f(t)$ in the display; and so on. The program for doing so follows, along with the step number listed for each keystroke in the program keystroke sequence, starting with step 00.

Step Number	Keystroke
00	−
01	5
02	=
03	÷
04	2
05	=
06	r/s
07	rst

Keeping in mind that we will enter the value of t by hand, steps 00 to 05 simply evaluate $f(t)$, which is, at the end of step 05, calculated and in the display. Step 06, the RUN/STOP key R/S, tells the calculator to stop with $f(t)$ in display.

The calculator will stay at step 06, displaying the value of $f(t)$ for you to see and write down if you like, until you once again press the $\boxed{\text{R/S}}$ key to tell it to go ahead again. If, prior to pressing the $\boxed{\text{R/S}}$ key to get it going again, we have entered a new value of t, then the calculator will proceed to step 07, $\boxed{\text{RST}}$ or RESET, which will just send it back to step 00 with the new value of t to compute $f(t)$ again.

Let's now actually "program" our calculator with this simple program. Turn on the calculator, and press the $\boxed{\text{LRN}}$ key to get the calculator into learn or program mode. Press the eight keystrokes listed (steps 00 to 07), then press $\boxed{\text{LRN}}$ again to switch the calculator from learn mode to run mode, and press the $\boxed{\text{RST}}$ key to initialize the calculator at step 00. (Once you start to use the program, the $\boxed{\text{RST}}$ key at step 07 will initialize the program automatically. But the first time you have to do it yourself in run mode to get it ready.) Now enter any value of t, say $t = 1$, and press the $\boxed{\text{R/S}}$ key to tell the calculator to start the program. You should see some changes in the display as the calculator runs through the programmed sequence of steps with $t = 1$, and then the value -2 will appear in display. The calculator has computed $f(1) = -2$ in steps 00 to 05, and then in step 06 it reached the command to stop. So it stops.

Now put in any other value of t, such as $t = 11.25$, and again press the $\boxed{\text{R/S}}$ key to set the program in motion. Once again you will see the display flashing a little as calculations are performed, and then the machine will stop with the number 3.125 in display to show that $f(11.25) = 3.125$. By pressing the $\boxed{\text{R/S}}$ key you told the calculator, which had stopped at step 06, to start again. So it advanced to step 07, which sent it back to step 00 with the number 11.25 you had entered in display, and it proceeded to calculate the new function value and stop again at step 06. You can keep entering new values of t, pressing $\boxed{\text{R/S}}$, and obtaining the function value $f(t)$ in display for as many values of t as you want. When you are finished with this program, simply turn the calculator off and on, and the program will have been erased.

By the way, after running the program for $t = 11.25$, press the $\boxed{\text{LRN}}$ key to switch to learn mode and look at the display. You should see the following:

07   71

The first 2 digits, 07, give the step number the machine is ready to perform when you press the $\boxed{\text{R/S}}$ key to make it go again. The second 2-digit number, 71, tells you in matrix notation form what the keystroke for step 07 actually is. The number 71 tells you to look at the rectangular array of keys on your calculator and locate the key at row 7 and column 1 (like locating a position in a matrix). This key at row 7 and column 1 is just the $\boxed{\text{RST}}$ key, and that is exactly what we put into the program at step 07. Now press the $\boxed{\text{LRN}}$ key again to switch back to run mode. As you can see, the programmable calculator can save you an enormous amount of work in evaluating expressions for different values of the variable.

The discriminant of a quadratic equation

Another use of the calculator in elementary algebra is in identifying the nature of the roots of a quadratic equation by computing the discriminant of the equation:

Discriminant of $ax^2 + bx + c = b^2 - 4ac$

If the discriminant is positive, the equation has two distinct real roots; if the discriminant is zero, the equation has one double real root; and if the discriminant is negative, the equation has no real roots (both roots are imaginary, and they are conjugates of each other). On a nonprogrammable calculator we can easily evaluate the discriminant with the following keystroke sequences:

$$b^2 - 4ac:$$

Hierarchy:

| b | | x^2 | | − | | 4 | | × | | a | | × | | c | | = |

Left-to-Right:

| 4 | | × | | a | | × | | c | | +/− | | + | | b | | x^2 | | = |

What we would like to do is write out a program for evaluating the discriminant so that all we have to do is enter the values of the coefficients a, b, and c for a particular quadratic equation and the calculator automatically computes the discriminant and displays it for us. In particular, it would be helpful if we could write the program so the coefficients could be entered in the natural order a, followed by b, followed by c.

To do so, we use some of the TI–57's seven different memory or storage locations. To put a displayed value in storage location i, we press the keystroke [STO i] while to recall a value from storage location i and have it displayed, we press the keystroke [RCL i]. Our discriminant evaluation program will do the following:

- It will take the first value we enter into display, the coefficient a, put it into storage location 1, and then stop to let us enter the value of b.

- It will take the value of the coefficient b and put it into storage location 2, and then stop to let us enter the value of c.

- It will use the value of the coefficient c in display, along with the values of a and b it has in storage, to calculate the discriminant and to stop with this value in display.

- It will reset itself to evaluate a new discriminant with new values of a, b, and c when we tell it to.

A program that does all this is:

Step Number	Keystroke
00	STO 1
01	R/S
02	STO 2
03	R/S
04	×
05	RCL 1
06	×
07	4

Step Number	*Keystroke*
08	$+/-$
09	$+$
10	RCL 2
11	x^2
12	$=$
13	R/S
14	RST

To put this program into the calculator, turn the calculator off and then on to clear any previous programs or values in storage. Then press the ⎡LRN⎤ key to put it into learn mode. Now enter the keystrokes in the program as they are written from step 00 to step 14. Then press the ⎡LRN⎤ key again to switch the calculator to run mode, and press the ⎡RST⎤ key to initialize the calculator at step 00. We are now ready to use the program. As an example of its use, let us take the quadratic equation:

$$2x^2 + 7x + 5$$

This quadratic equation has $a = 2$, $b = 7$, and $c = 5$. Enter the value of a, 2, and press the ⎡R/S⎤ key to begin the program. The calculator will progress through steps 00 to 01 and stop at step 01 when it comes to the RUN/STOP instruction after having put the value $a = 2$ in storage location 1. Now enter the value of b, 7, and press the ⎡R/S⎤ key again to tell the calculator to continue. The calculator will now progress through steps 02 to 03 and stop at step 03 when it comes to the next RUN/STOP instruction after having put the value $b = 7$ in storage location 2. Finally, enter the value of c, 5, and once again press the ⎡R/S⎤ key to tell the calculator to continue. This time the calculator will progress through steps 04 to 13 and stop after having calculated the discriminant. The value in display should now be the discriminant of the equation, 9. Since this is a positive value we know that the given quadratic equation has two distinct real roots.

Let's say we now want to immediately evaluate the discriminant of a second quadratic equation $18x^2 + 10x + 7$, with $a = 18$, $b = 10$, and $c = 7$. Simply enter 18 (the value of a) and press ⎡R/S⎤; enter 10 (the value of b) and press ⎡R/S⎤; and enter 7 (the value of c) and press ⎡R/S⎤. The display will flash for a few seconds and then stop with the discriminant of this second quadratic equation, -404, in display. Since this discriminant is negative, the quadratic equation $18x^2 + 10x + 7$ has no real roots (both its roots are imaginary). The first time we pressed ⎡R/S⎤ for this second equation the calculator, which had stopped at step 13, proceeded to step 14 where it was told to RESET itself at step 00 and repeat the program. We can now keep using this program over and over again to evaluate the discriminants of as many quadratic equations as we like. When we are finished using it, we simply turn the calculator off to clear the program.

Of course, this is not the only program that will allow us to enter the coefficients of a quadratic equation and evaluate the discriminant. Many other programs are just as good and just as correct, and some are possibly even shorter in length than this program of 15 steps (steps 00 through 14, inclusive). But the program given here is direct, it is reasonably short, and it does allow us to enter the coefficients a, b, and c in this easy-to-remember natural order. Finally, and most important, it works!

Graphing trigonometric functions

In Chapter 4 we illustrated the use of the calculator in graphing trigonometric functions. One of the functions to which we applied this method was:

$$f(\theta) = (\sin \theta)(\cos \theta) \qquad 0° \leq \theta \leq 360°$$

and the keystroke sequence used was:

$$f(\theta) = (\sin \theta)(\cos \theta): \quad \boxed{\theta} \ \boxed{\text{SIN}} \ \boxed{\times} \ \boxed{\theta} \ \boxed{\text{COS}} \ \boxed{=}$$

This evaluation can be accomplished much more easily with our programmable calculator since it is essentially a repetitive procedure. We want to program the calculator to evaluate $f(\theta)$ for $\theta = 0°$, then automatically increment the angle θ by, say, 10°, and evaluate $f(\theta)$ again, and keep repeating this until θ reaches 360°. A program that does just this is:

Step Number	Keystroke
00	STO 1
01	R/S
02	SIN
03	×
04	RCL 1
05	COS
06	=
07	R/S
08	RCL 1
09	+
10	1
11	0
12	=
13	RST

Turn your calculator off and on again to clear any previous program and any values in storage; then press the $\boxed{\text{LRN}}$ key to put the calculator into learn mode so we can enter the program. Now enter this program one keystroke at a time from step 00 through step 13. Then press $\boxed{\text{LRN}}$ again to return the calculator to run mode so that we can run the program, and press the $\boxed{\text{RST}}$ key to initialize the program at step 00. To begin the program, enter the first value of θ we want to use, 0, and press $\boxed{\text{R/S}}$. The display will flash and then show this value, $\theta = 0°$. If we press $\boxed{\text{R/S}}$ again, the display will show the corresponding function value $f(0°)$ = 0. When we press $\boxed{\text{R/S}}$ again, the program will increment θ by 10 and display the new value of θ, 10°; and still another pressing of the $\boxed{\text{R/S}}$ key will display the corresponding function value, $f(10°)$. As we continue pressing the $\boxed{\text{R/S}}$ key, the calculator will alternately display 20°, $f(20°)$, 30°, $f(30°)$, and so on. In other words, it gives us the values of θ and then $f(\theta)$ with each new angle incremented $10°$ from the previous angle. We can simply copy down the pairs $[\theta, f(\theta)]$ as they are displayed until we reach $\theta = 360°$. When we are finished, we have a table of values of the given function from which we can draw our graph and investigate any properties of the function we are interested in. When we have all the function values we need, we simply turn the calculator off to clear the program. Of course we could have arranged the program to increment the values of θ by any amount, not just $10°$. All we would have to do is replace the value 10 in steps 10 and 11 by the digits of the increment we want to use, and that is what the program would use.

Relationships among the lengths of the sides of a triangle

In Chapter 5 we showed how to use the calculator to determine whether three given positive numbers a, b, and c could serve as the side lengths of a nontrivial triangle. For a nontrivial triangle with sides of length a, b, and c to exist, it is necessary and sufficient for the three expressions $a + b - c$, $a + c - b$, and $b + c - a$ to be positive. Using the calculator, you can evaluate these three expressions for the given numbers and make a decision as to whether the condition is satisfied.

We can simplify this testing procedure by writing a program for the programmable calculator in which the three values a, b, and c are entered. The program automatically evaluates the three expressions and displays their values. We can then tell simply by inspecting the three displayed values, whether the condition is satisfied. A program that does this is:

Step Number	Keystroke
00	STO 1
01	R/S
02	STO 2
03	R/S
04	STO 3
05	+
06	RCL 2
07	−
08	RCL 1
09	=
10	PAUSE
11	RCL 1
12	+
13	RCL 2
14	−
15	RCL 3
16	=
17	PAUSE
18	RCL 1
19	+
20	RCL 3

Step Number	Keystroke
21	—
22	RCL 2
23	=
24	R/S
25	RST

In steps 00 through 04 we enter the values of a, b, and c one at a time, and the program stores these values in storage locations 1, 2, and 3, respectively. In steps 05 through 09, the expression $b + c - a$ is evaluated and displayed. In steps 11 through 16, the expression $a + b - c$ is evaluated and displayed. And in steps 18 through 23, the expression $a + c - b$ is evaluated and displayed. Notice the use of a new key, PAUSE , at steps 10 and 17 of this program. While the R/S keystroke in a program causes the program to stop at that point (so we can see the value in display), its use requires that we press the R/S key again to start the program running again. The PAUSE key does not stop the program, but it does make the program pause for three-quarters of a second. This is long enough for us to clearly see the value in display. If you need a longer pause, you can press the keystroke PAUSE twice in a row in the program, and you will get a pause of ¾ + ¾ = 1½ seconds. After this amount of time, the program automatically begins running again. In this program, the pause at step 10 comes right after the evaluation of $b + c - a$ and gives us time to observe this value being displayed before the program continues. The pause at step 17 comes right after the evaluation of $a + b - c$ and gives us time to observe this value before the program continues. And the R/S at step 24 comes right after $a + c - b$, and it stops the program to show us this value being displayed, since this is the last of the three values to be computed. Let's see this program in action.

Turn your calculator off and then on again to clear any previous program and any values in storage. Now press the LRN key and enter the given program one keystroke at a time from step 00 through step 25. Then press the LRN key again to return the calculator to run mode, and press the RST key to initialize the program at step 00. We will test the program with the three values $a = 5$, $b = 12$, and $c = 13$. Enter 5 and press R/S . When the display stops flashing, enter the next value 12 and press R/S again. When the display stops flashing, enter the final value 13 and press R/S again. You will now see the display flash for a few seconds and then pause to display the value 20 for the expression $b + c - a$. It will again flash for a few seconds and then pause to display the value 4 for the expression $a + b - c$. Finally it will flash for a few seconds and stop to display the value 6 for the expression $a + c - b$. Since all three of these values 20, 4, and 6 are positive, we know that a nontrivial triangle does exist with sides of length 5, 12, and 13. (In fact, this is the well-known "5-12-13 right triangle.")

Let's immediately test the values $a = 15$, $b = 6$, and $c = 8$. Enter 15 and press R/S . When the display stops flashing, enter 6 and press R/S , and when the display stops flashing, enter the third value 8 and press R/S . The display will flash and then pause to display -1, flash again and pause to display 13, and then flash and stop to display 17. Since one of these numbers is negative ($b + c - a = -1$), a nontrivial triangle cannot exist with these values 15, 6, and 8 as the lengths of its sides. You can proceed to test as many triples a, b, c as you like this way, and when you are finished, simply turn the calculator off to clear the program.

Compound and continuously compounded interest

In Chapter 7 we described a discovery activity in which the students are given the formula:

$$I = (1 + \frac{i}{n})^n - 1$$

This formula relates the following:

- an initial base yearly interest rate i,

- the number of times the interest is compounded during the year n, and

- the resulting yearly interest for the year I.

In this activity the students are asked to use their calculators with this formula to discover any properties of compound interest they can. It was suggested that the base interest be taken as $i = 0.12$ and that the students put the data they obtain into a table so that interesting properties could more easily be observed.

This activity is ready made for a programmable calculator. We want to write a program in which we enter a first value of n, say $n = 1$, and then the calculator automatically:

- computes the corresponding value of I,

- increases n by a specified amount and computes the new corresponding value of I, and

- continues this for as long as we want.

We also have a choice here of whether to use the $\boxed{\text{R/S}}$ key or the $\boxed{\text{PAUSE}}$ key after each evaluation. Since the values of n will be simple integers and easy to write down quickly, we will employ a pause keystroke after the computation of each new value of n. But since the values of I will be decimal interest rates and difficult to see, to remember, and to write down in a pause of only three-quarters of a second, we will employ a RUN/STOP keystroke after the computation of each new value of I. This will enable us to compute each new pair n, I and write them down in our table. Then we simply press the $\boxed{\text{R/S}}$ key to set the program into motion again to compute the next pair n, I. We will use an increment for n of 10. A program that does this for us is:

Step Number	Keystroke
00	STO 1
01	PAUSE
02	.
03	1
04	2

Step Number	Keystroke
05	÷
06	RCL 1
07	+
08	1
09	=
10	x^y
11	RCL 1
12	=
13	−
14	1
15	=
16	R/S
17	RCL 1
18	+
19	1
20	0
21	=
22	RST

Turn your calculator on, press ⎡LRN⎤, enter this program, press ⎡LRN⎤ again to return to run mode, and press ⎡RST⎤ to initialize the program at step 00. We are now ready to use the program. Begin by entering the first value of n we want to use, 1, and pressing the ⎡R/S⎤ key to set the program into motion. The display will flash, then pause to show the value 1 for n, then flash again as it continues on until it stops with the value 0.12 for the corresponding value of I showing. Press the key ⎡R/S⎤ again, and the display will flash, pause to show the new value 11 for n ($n = 1$ incremented by 10), then flash again and stop with the value 0.1267644 showing. This is the value of I corresponding to $n = 11$. If we press ⎡R/S⎤ again, we will see in display the value 21 for n followed by its corresponding value of I, and so on for as many newly incremented values of n as we want for our table.

Suppose now that, in the middle of constructing our table, we decide an increment of 10 each time is too slow, and that we would like instead to change the increment to 25. Remember that we have just had the calculator compute and display to us the value $n = 21$ and its corresponding I. If we look at the program we wrote, we notice that the increment occurs at steps 19 and 20. If we could somehow get "inside" the program and change the digit 1 at step 19 to a 2, and the digit 0 at step 20 to a 5, we will have modified the program to have the desired increment of 25 without having to reprogram the calculator. We make this change in the following way. Press the ⎡LRN⎤ key on your calculator and look at the display. You should see

17   33   1

The first 2 digits, 17, tell us that the calculator is now at step 17 in the program. Press the key ⎡SST⎤ and you will find that you have advanced one step in the program to step 18. Press ⎡SST⎤ one more time, and you will find yourself at step 19 in the program, with the display showing:

19   01

The first 2 digits, 19, are the step number, while the next 2 digits, 01, show that the digit 1 was entered here. Recall that all we want to do is replace this digit 1 by the digit 2. To do so, simply press 2, and step 19 is changed. You should now find yourself at step 20, and to change this from the digit 0 to the digit 5, just press 5. The two changes have now been made, and you are at step 21 with the display reading:

21   85

Since we came into the program at step 17, we must get back to step 17 before we can return to run mode and continue the program. To get there, simply use the $\boxed{\text{BST}}$ key. This BACK STEP key takes you one step back in the program when it is pressed. By pressing it four times, we will go back to steps 20, 19, 18, and finally 17. Now press $\boxed{\text{LRN}}$ to return to run mode. Since the last *n* displayed was 21, and since we have switched the increment from 10 to 25 the next value of *n* should be 21 + 25 = 46. To verify this, simply press the $\boxed{\text{R/S}}$ key and watch the display. The display will flash, pause to show the new value of *n*, 46; then flash and stop to show the corresponding value of *I, I* = 0.1273207.

Computing a running average

In Chapter 8 we used the calculator and its storage locations to obtain the sum of a set of given values and the sum of their squares, and from these to obtain the arithmetic mean ("average") and the standard deviation of these values. Computing another "type" of average is very useful, and it is perfectly suited to programmable calculator evaluation: This is the *running average* of a given ordered set of values.

Suppose, for example, that Table 10-1 shows your monthly electric bills for last year. Suppose you wanted to know, one month at a time, what your average

Table 10–1. Monthly electric bills

Month	Electric Bill
January	$58.50
February	$64.82
March	$56.00
April	$45.76
May	$34.90
June	$25.46
July	$22.00
August	$23.68
September	$30.00
October	$36.74
November	$42.80
December	$50.62

electric bill was "up to that month." That is, you wanted to be able to compute:

- the average monthly bill just for January; then

- your monthly bill just for January plus February; then

- your monthly bill just for January plus February plus March;

- and so on . . . until finally your monthly bill for January through December all together.

This would be called a running average because you would like to get the intermediate averages as each new monthly bill is added on. This type of average can let you see a "trend" in your average bill over the course of the year. For such problems, it would be helpful to have a program that showed you the number of items in the set at that point and the average up to that point, every time you added a new value from the set. A program to do so is:

Step Number	Keystroke
00	+
01	RCL 1
02	=
03	STO 1
04	RCL 2
05	+
06	1
07	=
08	STO 2
09	PAUSE
10	RCL 1
11	÷
12	RCL 2
13	=
14	R/S
15	RST

In this program, storage location 1 is used to keep a running sum of the values entered, while storage location 2 is used to keep track of how many values have been entered. Both storage locations 1 and 2 start with 0 in them. When a value is entered into display and the [R/S] key is pressed:

- Steps 00 through 03 recall the previous sum from location 1 and add the new value, then put this new sum back into location 1.

- Steps 04 through 08 recall the previous number of items from location 2, add 1 to it to indicate another value has been added in, and then put this new number of values back into location 2.

- Step 09 then pauses to display this number of values.

- Steps 10 through 13 compute the average by dividing the sum of values (storage location 1) by the number of values (storage location 2).

- Step 14 stops the program to display the average to us.

• The ⌐RST⌐ keystroke in step 15 sends the program back to step 00, after we have entered the next value and pressed the ⌐R/S⌐ key so the next average can be computed and displayed.

To enter this program into the calculator, turn the calculator off and then on again to clear any previous program and values in storage. Now press the ⌐LRN⌐ key to put the calculator into learn mode, and enter the program one step at a time. Then press ⌐LRN⌐ again, to return the calculator to run mode, and press the ⌐RST⌐ key to initialize the program at step 00. We are now ready to begin. Enter the first value in Table 10–1, 58.50, and press ⌐R/S⌐. The display will flash, pause to show the number of values 1, then flash and stop with the average 58.50 in display. Now enter the second value from Table 10–1, 64.82, and press ⌐R/S⌐. The display will flash, pause to show the number of values 2, then flash and stop with the average of these two values, 61.66, in display. Each time you enter a new value from Table 10–1 and press ⌐R/S⌐, the display will flash, pause to show the number of values, then flash and stop with the average in display.

When you have obtained and copied down all the 12 running averages for the set of data in Table 10–1, you can either turn the calculator off to clear the program or use the program again on another set of data. Before using it on the second set of data, however, you must first return storage locations 1 and 2 to their initial values of 0. To do so, simply enter 0 and press ⌐STO 1⌐, ⌐STO 2⌐. In so doing, you replace whatever was in storage locations 1 and 2 with the starting values 0. You can now enter the new values one at a time, press ⌐R/S⌐, and obtain the correct running averages of this new set.

INDEX

Absolute deviation, 152–53
Absolute value, 85–86
Acute triangles, 113
Algebra
  advanced, 72–93
    absolute value, 85–86
    arithmetic operations with radical
      expressions, 87–88
    evaluation of polynomials, 72–75
    expressions with zero and negative integer
      exponents, 82–85
    filling and emptying problems, 80–82
    geometric series, 91
    parabolic equation, 89–90
    polar representation of complex numbers,
      91
    properties of logarithm function, 92–93
    quadratic equations, 88–89
    radical or irrational equations, 88
    rules of logarithms, 92–93
    scientific notation, 90
    simplifying radical expressions, 86–87
    synthetic division, 75–77
    work problems, 78–82
  elementary, 20–44
    algebraic expressions, 20–23
    formulas, 42–44
    functions, 23–31
    investment problems, 33–36
    linear equations, 37, 39–40
    linear inequalities, 37–38
    mixture problems, 31–36
    open sentences, 36
    ordering of signed numbers, 36–37
    properties of exponents, 40–41
    Pythagorean theorem, 44
    quadratic equations, 38–39
    radicals, 41–42
    truth sets, 36
  with programmable calculator, 180–84
Algebraic Logic, 7–10
  in programmable calculators, 178
Amplitude, demonstration of, 67
Angles
  classifying triangles according to, 113
  complementary, 112–13
  principles for polygons, 115–16
  supplementary, 112–13

Angular mode, 46–47
Arc cosine, 68
  illegal operations with, 15
Arc sine, 68
  illegal operations with, 15
Arc tangent, 68
Area
  of circle, 117–19
  of parallelogram, 70
  of polygons, estimating pi using, 101–3
  of trapezoid, 117
  of triangle, 70
Arithmetic averages, 133–34
Arithmetic mean
  computing, 142–44
  rules for, 144–46
Arithmetic operations with radical expressions,
    87–88
Averages
  arithmetic, 133–34
  running, 189–91

Bank accounts, 132
Base, rate, and percentage, 131
Binomial distribution, 149, 150
Business and consumer mathematics, 122–39
  arithmetic averages, 133–34
  bank accounts and reconciliation statements,
    132
  checking accounts and interest rates, 132–33
  cost price, sale price, and percentage of
    markup, 138–39
  depreciation methods, 134, 135
  gross pay and hourly wages, 134, 136
  home insurance, 137–38
  interest, 127–31
  percentage, rate, and base, 131
  percentage of change, 131–32
  with programmable calculator, 187–89
  promissory notes, 137
  single discounts and chain discounts, 122–27
  straight commission versus base salary plus
    commission, 136–37
  wholesale or invoice price, 138

Calculus, 160–76
  calculator versus mathematical theory,
    164–67
  definite integral, 171
  derived functions, 160–63
  epsilon-delta method, 167–70
  indefinite integrals, 163–64
  limit of function, 170
    at point of discontinuity, 170–71
    properties of, 172
  maxima and minima, 172–73
  mean value theorem, 173–75
  product and quotient rules for derivatives,
    175–76
Chain discounts, 122–27
Change, percentage of, 131–32
Change Sign key, 13–14

Checking accounts, 132–33
Circle
  area of, 117–19
  in coordinate geometry, 119–20
Circular functions, 63–64
Combinations, 156–57
Commissions, 136–37
Complementary angles, 112–13
Complex numbers, polar representation of, 91
Composition of functions, 28–30
Compound interest, 127–31
  on programmable calculator, 187–89
Conditional trigonometric equations, 52–54
Consumer mathematics, *see* Business and
    consumer mathematics
Continuity of function, 167–70
Continuously compounded interest, 127–31
  on programmable calculator, 187–89
Coordinate geometry, 119–20
Cosine key, 46
Cosines, law of, 21, 68–70
Cost price, 138–39
Curve, normal, 146–52

Definite integral, 171
Degree measure, relationship between radian
    and, 64–66
Degrees, 46–47
Depreciation, 134, 135
Derivatives, 160–63
  product and quotient rules for, 175–76
Deviation
  mean (absolute), 152–53
  standard, 142–46
Differences, trigonometric functions of, 66–67
Discontinuity, limit of function at point of,
    170–71
Discounts, 122–27
Discriminant of quadratic equation, 181–84
Display, 10–13
Division, synthetic, 75–77
Domain of function, verification of, 27–28

Epsilon-delta method, 167–70
Equations
  conditional, 52–54
  irrational, 88
  linear, 37, 39–40
  parabolic, 89–90
  of polynomials, 72–77
  quadratic, 38–39
    discriminant of, 181–84
    systems of equations with, 88–89
  radical, 88
Error messages, 14–15
Exponentiation key, 16
Exponents
  negative integer, 82–85
  properties of, 40–41

Factorials, illegal operations with, 15
Filling and emptying problems, 80–82

Formulas, 42–44
Frame of reference, transforming from one to
    another, 154
Functions, 23–31
  composition of, 28–30
  continuity of, 167–70
  derived, 160–63
  "function machine" approach to, 23–24
  graphing, 24–27, 184–85
  inverse, 28–30, 68
  limit of, 170
    at point of discontinuity, 170–71
    properties of, 172
  logarithm, 93
  of sums and differences, 66–67
  trigonometric, 47–52, 184–85
  verifying domain and range of, 27–28

Geiselmann, Harrison A., 32
Geometric series, 91
Geometry, 96–120
  area of circle, 117–19
  area of trapezoid, 117
  complementary and supplementary angles,
    112–13
  coordinate, 119–20
  "evaluation" of pi, 95–105
  point and line number patterns, 105–12
  polygon angle principles, 115–16
  with programmable calculator, 185–87
  solid, 120
  triangles
    classification according to angles, 113
    relationships among lengths of sides, 114
    similar, 114–15
Gradients, 46
Graphs of functions, 24–27, 184–85
Gross pay, 134, 136
Group mean and group median, 153
Guess-and-correct procedure, 32–36

Hierarchy Algebraic Logic, 7–10
  in programmable calculators, 178
Home insurance, 137–38
Hourly wages, 134, 136

Identities, trigonometric, 54–57
Illegal operations, 14–15
  in algebra, 21–22
Indefinite integrals, 163–64
Inequalities
  linear, 37–38
  systems of, with one or more quadratics, 89
Insurance, 137–38
Integrals
  definite, 171
  indefinite, 163–64
Interest, 127–31
  checking accounts and, 132–33
  on programmable calculator, 187–89
  promissory notes, 137

Inverse functions, 28–30
  trigonometric, 68
Investment problems, 33–36
Invoice price, 138
Irrational equations, 88

Large numbers, law of, 155–56
Law of cosines, 21, 68–70
Law of large numbers, 155–56
Law of sines, 21, 68–69
Left-to-Right Algebraic Logic, 7–10
  in programmable calculators, 178
Limit of function, 170
  at point of discontinuity, 170–71
  properties of, 172
Line pattern, geometric, 105–12
Linear equations, 37, 39–40
Linear inequalities, 37–38
Logarithms
  illegal operations, 15
  properties of function, 93
  rules of, 92–93
Logic, types of, 7–10
  in programmable calculators, 178

Markup, percentage of, 138–39
Mathematical theory, calculator versus
  in calculus, 164–67
  in trigonometry, 58–63
Maxima, 172–73
Mean deviation, 152–53
Mean value theorem, 173–75
Means
  computing, 142–44
  group, 153
  rules for, 144–46
Median, group, 153
Minima, 172–73
Mixture problems, 31–36

Negative integer exponents, 82–85
Negative numbers, 13–14
  illegal operations with, 15, 21–22
Nonrechargeable calculators, 10
Normal curve, 146–52
Number patterns, geometric, 105–12

Obtuse triangles, 113
Open sentences, 36
Ordering of signed numbers, 36–37

Parabolic equation, 89–90
Parallelogram, area formulas for, 70
Pearson correlation coefficient r, 156
Percentage
  of change, 131–32
  of markup, 138–39
  rate and base and, 131
Perimeters of polygons, estimating pi using,
  98–101
Pi, 96–105
  defined, 96

Pi *(Cont'd.)*
"discovering," 97–98
estimating, 98–103
Plus/Minus key, 13–14
Point pattern, geometric, 109–12
Polar representation of complex numbers, 91
Polygons
angle principles, 115–16
areas of, 101–3
perimeters of, 98–101
Polynomials, evaluation of, 72–77
Positive-integral value, 16–18
Price
cost or sale, 138–39
wholesale or invoice, 138
Probability and statistics, 142–57
arithmetic mean and standard deviation,
142–46
combinations, 156–57
evaluating and interpreting simple
probabilities, 154–55
law of large numbers, 155–56
mean (absolute) deviation, 152–53
Pearson correlation coefficient r, 156
with programmable calculator, 189–91
properties of group mean and group median,
153
properties of set of z values, 153–54
standard (or unit) normal curve, 146–52
transforming from one frame of reference to
another, 154
Product rules for derivatives, 175–76
Programmable calculators, 178–91
discriminant of quadratic equation, 181–84
evaluating algebraic expressions, 180–81
fundamentals of programming, 179–80
graphing trigonometric functions, 184–85
interest, 187–89
relationships among lengths of sides of
triangle, 185–87
running average, 189–91
Promissory notes, 137
Pythagorean theorem, 44, 55

Quadratic equations, 38–39
discriminant of, 181–84
systems of equations with, 88–89
Quotient rules for derivatives, 175–76

Radians, 46–47
relationship between degree measure and,
64–66
Radical equations, 88
Radical expressions
arithmetic operations with, 87–88
simplification of, 86–87
Radicals, rules with, 41–42
Range of function, verification of, 27–28
Rate, base, and percentage, 131
Recall key, 21
Rechargeable calculators, 10
Reciprocal key, 46

Reconciliation statements, 132
Reverse Polish Logic (RPL), 7–8
in programmable calculators, 178
Riemann sums, 171
Right triangle, 113
definitions, 47
proof, 55
"Rounding-off," 12–13
Running average, 189–91

Salary plus commission, 136–37
Scientific notation, 90
display capability for, 11–12
Sets, solution or truth, 36
Signed numbers, ordering of, 36–37
Simple interest, 127–31
Simple probabilities, 154–55
Simpson's rule, 21
Sine key, 46
Sines, law of, 21, 68–69
Single discounts, 122–27
Solid geometry, 120
Solution sets, 36
Square root key, illegal operations with, 15, 22
Standard deviation
computing, 142–44
rules for, 144–46
Standard normal curve, 146–52
Statistics, *see* Probability and statistics
Storage key, 21
Straight-line depreciation method, 134, 135
Sum-of-the-years'-digits depreciation method,
134, 135
Sums, trigonometric functions of, 66–67
Supplementary angles, 112–13
Synthetic division, 75–77

Tangent key, 46
Trapezoid, area of, 117
Triangle
area formulas for, 70
classified according to angles, 113
relationship among lengths of sides of, 114,
185–87
similar, 114–15
Trigonometry, 46–70
angular measurement, 46–47
area formulas for triangle and parallelogram,
70
classroom contest for, 58–63
conditional equations, 52–54
demonstration of amplitude, 67
functions, 47–52
circular, 63–64
inverse, 68
of sums and differences, 66–67
wrapping function $P(t)$, 63–64
identities, 54–57
law of cosines, 68–70
law of sines, 68–69
on programmable calculator, 184

Trigonometry *(Cont'd.)*
  relationship between radian and degree
    measure, 64–66
  trigonometric function calculators, 46
Truth sets, 36

Unit circle proof, 56
Unit normal curve, 146–52

Value, absolute, 85–86

Wages, hourly, 134, 136
Wholesale price, 138
Work problems, 78–82
Wrapping function *P(t),* 63–64
  definitions, 47

Zero, expressions with, 82–85

PUSHBUTTON MATHEMATICS

This practical handbook explains how anyone can solve math problems more effectively and efficiently by using a hand-held calculator.

PUSHBUTTON MATHEMATICS gives you numerous examples, problems, and activities that can help you use calculators to easily solve your day-to-day math problems, whether you're involved in teaching a class, running a business, or managing a household.

From figuring out your grocery bill and balancing your checkbook to computing your odds in the stock market and calculating your interest rates, PUSHBUTTON MATHEMATICS is the one book that will help you get the most out of your hand-held calculator. It includes information on:

- special keys and features that any calculator user should be aware of
- important differences between calculators and what to look for when buying one
- applications for high school and college level math subjects as well as consumer and business mathematics
- how to solve any math problem from simple algebra and geometry to more advanced problems in trigonometry, probability, statistics, and calculus
- a special chapter on how to use a programmable calculator
- and much more.

In addition, each chapter covers a specific subject and includes easy-to-follow instructions on how to do each problem, what buttons to push and when, and solutions for the suggested exercises.

ABOUT THE AUTHOR: Kenneth P. Goldberg has taught math, math education, and educational statistics since 1969. He teaches courses at New York University on the use of hand-held calculators and on microcomputers, has given numerous lectures and workshops, and has written a basic statistics textbook and a number of articles on math-related topics, five of which appear in the 1982 edition of *Encyclopaedia Britannica*.

PRENTICE-HALL, Inc.
Englewood Cliffs, New Jersey 07632

ISBN 0-13-743300